Issues in World Politi

Issues in World Politics

**Brian White, Richard Little
and Michael Smith**

Editors

St. Martin's Press
New York

ISSUES IN WORLD POLITICS

St. Martin's Press, Scholarly and Reference Division,
175 Fifth Avenue, New York, N.Y. 10010

First published in the United States of America in 1997

This book is printed on paper suitable for recycling and
made from fully managed and sustained forest sources.

Printed in Great Britain

ISBN 0–312–17547–7 (cloth)
ISBN 0–312–17548–5 (paper)

Library of Congress Cataloging-in-Publication Data
Issues in world politics / edited by Brian White, Richard Little, and
Michael Smith.
p.   cm.
Includes bibliographical references and index.
ISBN 0–312–17547–7 (cloth). — ISBN 0–312–17548–5 (paper)
1. World politics—1989–   I. White, Brian.   II. Little, Richard.
III. Smith, Michael, 1947–   .
D860.I87 1997
909.82'4—dc21   97–9650
                                                          CIP

Contents

Preface

One of the exciting and challenging effects of the 'modularization' of undergraduate programmes is the growing number of students sampling areas of study outside their main field(s), particularly in the first year of study. In common with many other academics, the challenge for university teachers of International Relations/World Politics is to devise and write introductory textbooks that will not only serve the interests of specialist students but will also appeal to a wider range of undergraduates fascinated by particular aspects of the contemporary world but who may not want to pursue the subject further.

This book attempts to meet that challenge by adopting as its focus the range of issues that are at the heart of the agenda of contemporary world politics. The working assumption here is that issues which are often the subject of topical debate and media coverage provide an important point of access to world politics for a large number of students. The book therefore seeks to build upon some knowledge and an existing interest not only by providing relevant information and a context for making sense of particular issues but also by explicitly addressing the question of what these issues collectively tell us about the nature of world politics at the end of the twentieth century.

What began as an idea and a challenge could only develop to a successful conclusion with the cooperation of a number of people. Steven Kennedy, our publishing editor, gave the project enthusiastic support and encouragement from start to finish. Brian White succeeded in tempting Richard Little and Michael Smith to share editorial duties while undertaking to manage the project. The editors in turn were delighted to receive the support of experts on particular issues who rose to the challenge of writing for non-specialist as well as specialist students and managed to stick to the common format and a very tight set of deadlines. Edited volumes can be a difficult experience for editors but in this case it was a pleasure – for which many thanks to the contributors. Grateful thanks are also due to Sheila Berrisford, Jean Edwards and Barbra Georgellis who all provided crucial help and support at various stages of the project.

BRIAN WHITE
RICHARD LITTLE
MICHAEL SMITH

Notes on the Contributors

Sita Bali is a Senior Lecturer in International Relations at Staffordshire University. Her doctoral research explored the international political implications of migration through an examination of the British Sikh community, and she is the author of a forthcoming book on the politics of the Sikh diaspora titled *Sikhs: The Search for Statehood.* She has also written articles on Indian politics.

Anoushiravan Ehteshami is Reader in International Relations and Director of Postgraduate Studies at the Centre for Middle East and Islamic Studies, University of Durham. His recent publications include (as co-editor) *Islamic Fundamentalism* (1996); *After Khomeini: The Iranian Second Republic* (1995); and (as editor) *From the Gulf to Central Asia: Players in the New Great Game* (1994). His latest book (with Professor Hinnebusch) is *Syria and Iran: Middle Powers in a Penetrated Regional System* (1997)

Richard Little is Professor of International Politics at the University of Bristol. He has also taught at the Open University and Lancaster University and was the editor of the *Review of International Studies* from 1990 to 1994. He has written extensively in the area of international relations theory and his publications include (with Robert McKinlay) *Global Politics and World Order* (1986) and (with Barry Buzan and Charles Jones) *The Logic of Anarchy* (1993).

Michael Pugh is a Senior Lecturer in the Department of Politics at the University of Plymouth. He is the editor of the journal *International Peacekeeping* and has written or edited works on maritime security issues and humanitarianism and peacekeeping, including *Maritime Security and Peacekeeping* (1995); 'Humanitarianism and Peacekeeping', *Global Society* (10:3, 1996); and *The UN, Peace and Force* (1997).

Melvyn Reader is currently completing a Ph.D. in the Department of Politics at the University of Southampton. His doctoral thesis is on 'The Rise of Protestant "Fundamentalism" in World Politics: A Case Study of Brazil', which examines the relationship between the impact of globalization on development and the growth of religious fundamentalism in the 'South'.

Alan Russell is a Senior Lecturer in International Relations at Staffordshire University. He is the author of *The Biotechnology Revolution: An International Perspective* (1988). His recent publications include 'Merging Technological Paradigms and the Knowledge Structure in the International Political Economy' in *Science and Public Policy* (22:2, 1995), and 'Technology as Knowledge: Generic Technology and Change in the Global Political Economy', in Talalay *et al.* (eds), *Technology, Culture and Competitiveness and the Global Political Economy* (1996).

Stephen Ryan is a Senior Lecturer in the School of History, Philosophy and Politics at the University of Ulster. He is the author of *Ethnic Conflict and International Relations* (2nd edn, 1995) and has written several chapters and articles on the themes of ethnic conflict, conflict resolution and international relations.

Michael Smith is Professor of European Politics and Jean Monnet Chair holder in the Department of European Studies at Loughborough University. He was previously Professor of International Studies and Dean of the School of International Studies and Law at Coventry University. His publications include (edited with Richard Little) *Perspectives on World Politics* (2nd edn, 1991); (with Stephen Woolcock) *The United States and the European Community in a Transformed World* (1993); and (with Brian Hocking) *World Politics: An Introduction to International Relations* (2nd edn, 1995).

Joanna Spear is a lecturer in the Department of War Studies at King's College, London. She recently returned from two years as a research fellow at the Center for Science and International Affairs, Harvard University. Her most recent publications are *Carter and Arms Sales: Implementing the Carter Administration's Arms Transfer Restraint Policy* (1995), and 'The Role of Arms

Limitations and Confidence and Security Building Measures', in Brown (ed.), *The International Dimensions of Internal Conflict* (1996).

Caroline Thomas is Reader in Politics at the University of Southampton and her primary research interest is in the 'South' in international relations. Her recent publications include (with Peter Wilkin as co-editor) *Globalization and the South* (1996); (as editor) *Rio: Unravelling the Consequences* (1994); and *The Environment in International Relations* (1992).

John Vogler is Professor of International Relations at Liverpool John Moores University. Since 1990 he has been the Convener of the BISA Environment Group and a member of the Economic and Social Research Council Global Environmental Change Programme Committee. His recent publications include *The Global Commons: A Regime Analysis* (1995) and (with Mark Imber as co-editor) *The Environment and International Relations* (1996)

Mark Webber is a lecturer in the Department of European Studies at Loughborough University. His recent publications include *The International Politics of Russia and the Successor States* (1996); 'Coping with Anarchy: Ethnic Conflict and International Organizations in the Former Soviet Union', *International Relations* (13:1, 1996); and 'The Soviet Union, Russia and 1945: One Step Forward, Two Steps Back', *Journal of Area Studies* (7, 1995).

Brian White is Professor of International Relations and Head of International Relations and Politics at Staffordshire University. His publications include *Britain, Detente and Changing East–West Relations* (1992); (with Michael Clarke as co-editor) *Understanding Foreign Policy: A Foreign Policy Systems Approach* (1989); and (with Michael Smith and Steve Smith as co-editors) *British Foreign Policy: Tradition, Change and Transformation* (1988).

List of Abbreviations

AIDS	Acquired Immune Deficiency Syndrome
AMRAAMs	Advanced, Medium-Range, Air-to-Air Missiles
AOSIS	Association of Small Island States
APEC	Asia-Pacific Economic Cooperation
ASEAN	Association of South-east Asian Nations
BAe	British Aerospace
BMD	Ballistic Missile Defence
BWC	Biological and Toxin Weapons Convention
CAAT	Campaign Against the Arms Trade
CAFOD	Catholic Fund for Overseas Development
CBW	Chemical and Biological Weapons
CCW	Convention on Conventional Weapons
CFCs	Chlorofluorocarbons
CITES	Convention on Trade in Endangered Species
CMEA	Council for Mutual Economic Assistance
CoCom	Coordinating Committee on Multilateral Export Controls
CSD	Commission for Sustainable Development (of the UN)
CTBT	Comprehensive Test Ban Treaty
CWC	Chemical Weapons Convention
DHA	Department of Humanitarian Affairs (of the UN)
ECO	Economic Cooperation Organization
ECOWAS	Economic Community of West African States
ERM	Exchange Rate Mechanism
ETA	*Euskadi ta Askatasuna*
EU	European Union
FAO	Food and Agriculture Organization (of the UN)
FCCC	Framework Convention on Climate Change
FDI	Foreign Direct Investment
G-7	Group of Seven
GATT	General Agreement on Tariffs and Trade
GDO	Grassroots Development Organization
GDR	German Democratic Republic
GEC	Global Environmental Change

GNP	Gross National Product
HCFC	Hydrochloroflourocarbon
ICES	International Council for the Exploration of the Seas
ICO	Islamic Conference Organization
ICPF	International Commission on Peace and Food
ICRC	International Committee of the Red Cross
ICTY	International Criminal Tribunal for the former Yugoslavia
IFOR	Implementation Force (of NATO)
IFRC	International Federation of the Red Cross and Red Crescent Societies
IGO	Intergovernmental Organization
IMF	International Monetary Fund
IMO	International Maritime Organization
INGO	International Non-Governmental Organization
IPCC	Intergovernmental Panel on Climate Change
IPE	International Political Economy
IRA	Irish Republican Army
IUCN	International Union for the Conservation of Nature
LDC	Less Developed Country
MARPOL	Convention for the Prevention of Pollution from Ships
MENA	Middle East and North Africa
MERCOSUR	Mercado Comun del Cono Sur (Southern Common Market)
MNC	Multinational Corporation
MPLA	Movimento Popular de Libertação de Angola
MTCR	Missile Technology Control Regime
NAFTA	North American Free Trade Agreement
NATO	North Atlantic Treaty Organization
NGO	Non-Governmental Organization
NIC	Newly-Industrializing Country
NPT	Nuclear Non-Proliferation Treaty
NSG	Nuclear Suppliers Group
OAS	Organization of American States
OAU	Organization of African Unity
OECD	Organization for Economic Cooperation and Development

OSCE	Organization for Security and Cooperation in Europe
P5	Permanent Five Members of the UN Security Council
PLO	Palestine Liberation Organization
RPF	Rwandan Patriotic Front
SALT	Strategic Arms Limitation Talks
SAP	Structural Adjustment Programme
SIPRI	Stockholm International Peace Research Institute
TNB	Transnational bank
UAE	United Arab Emirates
UN	United Nations
UNCED	United Nations Conference on Environment and Development
UNCTAD	United Nations Conference on Trade and Development
UNDP	United Nations Development Programme
UNEP	United Nations Environment Programme
UNGA	United Nations General Assembly
UNHCR	United Nations High Commission for Refugees
UNICEF	United Nations International Children's Emergency Fund
UNIDO	United Nations Industrial Development Organization
UNITA	União Nacional para a Independencia de Angola
UNPROFOR	United Nations Protection Force
UK	United Kingdom
US	United States
USSR	Union of Soviet Socialist Republics
VAT	Value-Added Tax
WCED	World Commission on Environment and Development
WEU	Western European Union
WMD	Weapons of Mass Destruction
WMO	World Meteorological Organization
WTO	World Trade Organization

1

Issues in World Politics

BRIAN WHITE, RICHARD LITTLE AND MICHAEL SMITH

The dramatic television pictures of the dismantling of the Berlin Wall, that powerful symbol of the Cold War, may already have faded from memory, but the hopes and expectations generated by the set of events between 1989 and 1991 known collectively as the end of the Cold War, have not. Accounts of world politics written in the 1990s have all highlighted the idea that we are living in an exciting new world in which political leaders struggle to come to terms with distinctively new problems. But, commentators also suggest, this new world holds out the promise at least of solving other problems hitherto regarded as intractable. This book introduces the reader to world politics by providing an understanding of issues that are at the heart of the agenda of contemporary world politics. Our assumption is that the identity of those issues, the general problems that they represent, and the reasons for their location on the international agenda will tell us much about the nature of world politics at the end of the twentieth century.

There are, of course, other ways of writing an introductory textbook on world politics. We might, for example, have focused on the ways in which political activities at the global level have (or have not) changed in recent years, looked at as a whole – as an interacting system of activity as it is often called – or, to use a different analogy, we might have concentrated on the foreign policy behaviour of the principal 'players' who participate in a game of world politics. Alternatively, we might have reviewed the main theories by which students of world politics try to make sense of the global political world in which we live. These are conventional approaches and there are several good examples of textbooks that employ one or a combination of these approaches.

1

The approach adopted here is rather different, not in terms of the objective – to understand contemporary world politics – but in terms of the way we seek to achieve that objective. Without suggesting that our approach is superior, we would claim that an introductory textbook that focuses on global issues has the advantage of building upon a general interest in and knowledge of world politics that the reader may already have from exposure to the media – press and television coverage of world politics in particular. Of its nature, media coverage of world politics tends to focus on immediate, easily identifiable, often dramatic issues that will attract and hold the attention of its audience, rather than on longer-term trends or explanatory theories that are deemed to be less 'newsworthy' by producers/editors who are preoccupied with sales or ratings. By using issues as our principal focus, we also hope to attract a more general reader who is intrigued by particular aspects of world politics, as well as the more specialized student of world politics. This book can be used as a main text where introductory courses/modules are issue-based or where second-level courses/modules are focused on key issues or themes. Alternatively, this book can be used alongside more theoretical or system-orientated texts at both levels.

The purpose of this first chapter is two-fold: to put issues discussed in later chapters into both an historical and an analytical context and, more importantly, to establish a common framework for the discussion of those issues. Put in a more direct way, we are seeking here a preliminary answer to two deceptively simple questions: what are the most significant issues in contemporary world politics? and why ?

The End of the Cold War and a New Global Agenda?

It should be stated clearly at the outset that there is no attempt here to cover *all* the major issues in contemporary world politics, if only because of limitations of space. But, choosing to discuss certain issues rather than others does require making the criteria for selection explicit. An obvious starting point is to look critically at the idea outlined at the beginning of this chapter, namely that the world today is distinctively different from, say, the world of the 1970s or 1980s – because of the end of the Cold War.

This suggests not only that the operating structures have changed – with world politics no longer defined essentially by an ideological-military struggle between two dominant centres of power controlled respectively by two 'superpowers', the United States and the Soviet Union – but also that the agenda of world politics has been transformed. The 'agenda' in this context may be defined as the cluster of issues around which political activity takes place. No longer is world politics dominated by issues arising from East–West relations – the threat of nuclear war, the ideological struggle between liberal democracy and Marxism-Leninism, crisis diplomacy, and so on. The international community is now preoccupied with other issues such as the search for a 'New World Order', the disparities in wealth between developed and less developed countries (LDCs), and environmental/ecological issues.

The most cursory look at the world today, however, suggests that an analysis that focuses exclusively on dramatic change, on the emergence of 'new' issues replacing 'old', understates important elements of continuity in world politics and lacks a sense of historical perspective. The period 1989–91 – from the dismantling of the Berlin Wall, through the removal from office of several Communist governments in Eastern Europe, to the demise of the Soviet Union-may well mark a watershed that will be compared by future historians to other key 'turning points' in history such as 1789–94, 1917–18, and 1945–7. But as the distinguished international historian, John Lewis Gaddis has commented with respect to the end of the cold war, 'precisely what has "turned" . . . is much less certain' (Hogan, 1992, p. 22).

The short-lived euphoria of 1990–1, when a multinational military force legitimized by United Nations resolutions defeated Saddam Hussein's Iraq and gave some substance to Western triumphalism, has given way to the painful realization that a 'New World Order', however defined, is still a long way from achievement. For all the immediate gains of post-Cold War world politics, and these must include the dissolution of apartheid in South Africa and a revived peace process in the Middle East and Northern Ireland, we must also note the eruption of bloody armed conflict in such places as Bosnia, Angola, Rwanda and Zaire which the international community, far from being strengthened in its resolve or ability to solve problems, seems incapable of stopping. Some at least of these problems appear to be either a product of the end of the Cold War or to have been exacerbated by these changes.

If we consider one of the so-called 'new' issues that has emerged in the wake of the Cold War, we may discover the limits of the 'everything has changed' argument. A major issue that confronts the international community, already alluded to, is the military conflict between ethnic groups within, for example, the states that succeeded the former Yugoslavia and the former Soviet Union – Croat versus Muslim versus Serb; Azeri versus Armenian, and so on. Clearly, the demise of the Soviet Union was directly or indirectly the catalyst for the emergence of open conflict in these areas. The sources of these and other conflicts, however, lie in a more complex struggle for national self-determination that has both a much longer historical explanation over time and a much wider spread geographically. Inter-ethnic conflict has emerged at different times and places and in different forms and posed different sorts of problems for the international community.

Whether an issue is 'old' or 'new' then appears to be less important than the factors that determine the form in which an issue appears on the international agenda. What we can suggest at this stage is that the prevailing international context provides one set of factors that determines the shape or form in which an issue appears. A different set of issues is likely to emerge at different times and (probably) in different forms – in part determined by the international context or situation. But there are other factors involved in determining why an issue emerges, when and in what form and these need to be investigated.

Issues and Problems

An issue in world politics attracts the attention of those who engage in that activity and requires the expenditure of resources in some form, if only the expenditure of diplomatic resources. Similarly, issues engage the attention of those who wish to understand world politics. But understanding an issue goes beyond knowing the facts and figures associated with it, however important that might be. It is necessary to put the issue into context. Part of that context has already been established – the international situation as it is at any point in history. The end of the Cold War has played a part in presenting issues in a particular form in contemporary world politics. Another, equally important context from an analytical perspective is to establish the problem area within which the issue resides and which gives meaning to that issue. The debt crisis, for example, was an issue that attracted considerable attention from the international community in the 1980s. The fear was that many LDCs who were in considerable debt would default on their loans and create chaos in international economic relations.

The debt issue had a specific international context from which it emerged. It was a product essentially of two developments. First, many LDCs borrowed heavily from abroad encouraged by the example of the oil-rich states who appeared to be successfully using 'commodity power' to change the terms of trade between developed and less developed states. But the recession that followed the dramatic rise in oil prices in the late 1970s/early 1980s ironically and equally dramatically eroded the ability of LDCs to repay the debts incurred. By the late 1980s, the issue began to attract less attention as various strategies designed to alleviate the crisis were put in place, to some effect.

The point being made here by reference to this illustration is not only that issues rise and fall on the international agenda for specific reasons but, more importantly, that they usually represent one 'face' of a more persistent problem or set of problems that confront world politics. In this case, the debt crisis was a particular manifestation of a problem that is usually known in a shorthand form as the 'Rich/Poor' or the 'North–South' problem. In general terms, this refers to the post-colonial situation in which a large number of new states (the 'South') find themselves forced to operate at a significant disadvantage in an international economic system controlled by and run for the benefit of a much smaller group of wealthy, developed states (the 'North'). This international context compounds the problems that less developed states face from a host of domestic political, economic and social problems. From this inherently structural set of problems flow a number of interrelated issues that challenge the international community.

Issues, Agendas and Agenda-Setting

If problems spawn issues in various forms, there is also an even more overtly political context that may determine whether or not an issue emerges on the international agenda and certainly helps to determine the form in which the issue appears. It can be assumed that the contents of the agenda of world politics at any point in time are not random. Those who participate in world politics (representatives of governments, various types of governmental and non-governmental organizations, and so on) are essentially political actors which means that they have interests to advance and defend. The resolution of these competing interests at the global level provides a simple definition of what world politics is all about. This is often presented rather snappily as 'who gets what, when and how'. There is a structure of power and interests in world politics and we should not be surprised to see this reflected on the agenda, the range and type of issues located on that agenda, and the form in which those issues appear.

This political context can be illustrated by reference to another issue which has attracted much attention and debate, particularly since the end of the Cold War – the rise of what is called 'Islamic fundamentalism'. This issue can be described briefly as the resurgence of the Islamic world in religious and political terms, following a new confidence in indigenous social, cultural and political structures. Islam is clearly a global force of some significance, if only because some 20 per cent of the world population is Muslim, and Muslims constitute at least 50 per cent of the population in more than thirty countries. In terms of heightening awareness of the resurgence of Islam, an event of major significance for both the Muslim and the non-Muslim world was the Islamic revolution in Iran in 1979 which brought to power the Ayatollah Khomeini.

The wider problem from which this issue has emerged also has a post-colonial context, though historians of Islam remind us that there have been several resurgences of Islam on almost a cyclical basis. After independence from colonial rule had been achieved, many leaders of Islamic countries took the view that the requirements of development necessitated the downgrading of traditional Islamic values and the enthusiastic embrace of what was variously called modernization, secularization and Westernization – adopting, in short, the liberal democratic social and political values of the

West. For a number of reasons, however – including frustrated post-independence aspirations, rapid urbanization, population explosions, increasingly evident disparities in wealth – a popular disillusionment with Western values and materialism in particular began to set in. The result evident since the 1970s within and beyond muslim states has been a continuing tension at best between very different sets of religious, cultural and political values.

Going beyond this simple description of an issue and a problem, however, we have to take note here of the political context which helps to present the issue in a particular form. The clue comes from the use in the West of the term 'fundamentalism' – rather than 'rise' or 'resurgence' – which has been commonly associated with Islam since the Iranian revolution. While the term 'Islamic fundamentalism' can refer to the growth of Islam as a religious force and a political ideology and, most accurately perhaps, to the desire to reinstate the Islamic legal code, the Sharia law, it has come to have rather different connotations in popular usage.

For many in the West, 'Islamic fundamentalism' is synonymous with a form of religious bigotry and violence that poses not only a religious but also a political threat to Western values and institutions. Some even talk of an inevitable confrontation between Islam and the West (see, for example, Huntington, 1993). In the mid-1990s, media speculation in the West focused upon the possible 'fall' of Turkey to Islamic fundamentalism following the 'fall' of Iran and Algeria. To seasoned observers of world politics, this sort of language is reminiscent of similar fears expressed in the West when the perceived threat came from Marxism-Leninism rather than Islam. The 'falling domino' analogy, coined by US President Eisenhower in the mid-1950s, was intended to heighten Western fears of the Soviet Union and its allies.

Clearly, the presentation of any issue in world politics in a particular form is likely to serve political interests. It is intended to evoke a particular sort of reaction from other players in the global political game. The student of world politics, whose prime concern is to understand what is going on, should take this political context into account. One way of doing this is to look critically at the assumptions that underpin the presentation of an issue and review the evidence that supports it. With reference to the resurgence of Islam, it might simply be asked whether or not Islam constitutes a cohesive group that is united in its determination to overthrow Western institutions. The answers may well cast doubt on the more lurid connotations associated with Islamic fundamentalism.

Issues and the Media

Almost all of the information we receive about what is happening in the world around us, locally, nationally, and internationally, is supplied by the media. Occasionally, we may receive an account of a dramatic event experienced at first hand by a friend or an acquaintance. Even more rarely, we ourselves may get caught up in a newsworthy event. But generally we experience the outside world through the television screen, the radio, or the pages of the newspaper.

At first sight, it might appear that with the revolution in modern communications, we are now in a much better position to be informed about the outside world than our forbears. At the beginning of the twentieth century, there were still large areas of the world that remained remote and inaccessible. It could take weeks or even months before information about events in these areas would seep out to the outside world. Now, not only is updated information available twenty-four hours in the day, but we can observe instantaneously what is happening anywhere around the globe. The media is playing a vital part in the complex process known as globalization which is eliminating the effects of time and space. The technology is available that allows us to observe in our own sitting rooms what is happening on the other side of the globe. We were able to watch the massacre in Tiananmen Square in Beijing as it was taking place. Even President Bush is reported to have watched CNN to find out what was happening in the Gulf Conflict.

One of the consequences of globalization is that the media itself not only plays a role in reporting world news, but these reports can on occasion feed back and have a direct effect on subsequent events. This development was very apparent during the period when communism collapsed in Eastern Europe and the Soviet Union. Authoritarian governments have always been aware of the impact of information and, with the growing importance of the media, they have made strenuous efforts to regulate the information given to their citizens. The media is always tightly controlled by the state in authoritarian systems and attempts are invariably made to prevent access to alternative sources of information.

Throughout the Cold War, the United States and the other West European countries beamed radio programmes into the Soviet Union and Eastern Europe. Some of the Hungarians who rebelled in 1956 believed, for example, that the West would come to their assistance because of the broadcasts they had heard on Radio Free Europe. The Soviet Union and the communist regimes in Eastern Europe regularly jammed these broadcasts in an attempt to insulate the population from this 'Western propaganda'. But in 1989, when the seeds of dissent were sown in Eastern Europe, events took a very different turn from the previous attempts to promote rebellion. On 7 October 1989, Gorbachev attended the 40th anniversary of the German Democratic Republic (GDR). Dissenters in the crowd began to call out his name and, in full view of the world's television cameras, the police began to club the dissenters in an effort to quell the rebellion. On this occasion, the East Germans were able to see the news programmes being shown in West Germany. The level of opposition was apparent and the rebellion spread.

More often than not, the pictures we see on our television screens have little or no impact. It is sometimes argued that we are now so used to seeing the most graphic details of events around the world that we have become desensitized to even the most shocking of these images. Yet, every so often, these images do have an impact. We have been stirred by pictures of people starving in Ethiopia and governments have been pressed to take action. Decision-makers are now acutely conscious that there is a constant although generally only a latent potential for these images from other parts of the globe to galvanize public opinion. Frequent reference is made to the fact that the Vietnam War in the 1960s was the first TV war and that the images of the war being fought in Vietnam, on the one hand, and the protest movement in the United States, on the other, had a significant impact on the outcome of the war. Ever since then, American Presidents have been anxious to ensure that they avoid what came to be known as the 'Vietnam Syndrome' by which is meant the uncontrollable growth of domestic opposition to American action abroad. During the Falklands War in 1982, the release of information was very tightly regulated by the British government and the Americans followed the British example during the Gulf War.

There is little doubt, therefore, that the media is coming to play an increasingly important role in world politics. As a consequence, there is growing interest in the nature of this role. Does the media simply act as a kind of giant mirror, making it possible for events around the globe to be made instantly accessible to a world audience? No one could seriously believe this to be the case. There are innumerable events taking place around the world and only a tiny fraction of these events can get reported by the world media. So, in the first instance, decisions are constantly being made by media moguls about what kind of news is to be presented. The earthquake in Kobe, a major Japanese city, which killed over 5,000 people at the beginning of 1995, hit the headlines across the world. But there have been many other earthquakes, equally devastating, which have received much less attention. There is a simple explanation which can be put forward to account for this fact.

News editors, it is said, put out news which they think their audiences will find interesting. There is good evidence to substantiate this argument. An event that provides the first story of the day gets shuffled on subsequent days to the end of the newscast, and is then dropped altogether. This is because it is assumed we get bored quickly and need news of fresh events to maintain our interest. But there is more to it than that. The world does move on. New events do occur and these events also deserve to be reported. So it is inevitable that the focus of the media is constantly shifting. This may give the impression of the media and its audience – which, of course, is us – being fickle. And this may often be the case. But even when interest is retained, the pressure of events inevitably pushes the media into new locations. But if we use the media to try to track what is happening in the world, it is hard to avoid the impression that we are being confronted by a constantly moving target. Nothing is permanent or stable. There are no issues which are always on the agenda. One of the aims of this book is to counteract this impression.

There are critics of the media, however, who believe that its influence is more actively malevolent and complicit than the picture we have so far presented would suggest. It has been indicated that although the media is selective, it is nevertheless trying to give an accurate picture of what is happening around the world and that, on occasions, the media can be seen to be engaged in a struggle with governments wishing to muzzle the press. Critics like Noam Chomsky, a very distinguished American academic who has become better known as a political activist, argue that this assessment of the media is erroneous. It ignores the fact that the world's media is carefully controlled and regulated by the people who own the media. The world's media is, in practice, owned by a handful of people and these people have a vested interest in seeing a particular view of the world presented. The constant flux of events portrayed by the media masks a hidden agenda, according to these critics, which is evident with every encounter with the world's media – once this hidden agenda has been exposed.

From the perspective of Chomsky, the media plays a vital role in maintaining the interests of a corporate elite. Events are selected and interpreted in a way which is designed to reinforce these interests. Chomsky deliberately uses polemical language to break through what he sees as the barrage of propaganda to which we are subjected on a daily basis from the world's media. He argues, for example, that the media distinguishes between nefarious and constructive blood baths. Nefarious blood baths are occupied by the enemies of corporate interests and are widely publicized in the media. He is thinking of the atrocities committed by men like Idi Amin in Uganda and Pol Pot in Cambodia. Constructive blood baths are occupied by allies of corporate interests and their actions are condoned or, more often, ignored. Here, Chomsky would make reference, for example, to the genocide committed by the Indonesian military in East Timor which, he insists, has been largely ignored by the world's media.

There is little doubt that Chomsky has amassed a formidable body of information to substantiate his claims. But his arguments have failed to win widespread support because few people accept that corporate interests possess the level of control over the media necessary to render Chomsky's thesis plausible. Nevertheless, it is unquestionably the case that the images we receive via the media have been heavily filtered and that governments, in particular, have enormous influence over our image of the outside world. It is essential to be aware of this fact and to evaluate all information critically. Again it is the intention of this book to provide you with some of the tools which can help to pierce through the fog which the media can generate.

Types of Issues

History has been said to consist of 'one damned thing after another'. And the same thing could be said of world politics. Certainly the media encourages this view of reality. One of our tasks, however, is to help you to move away from such an assessment. There is nothing wrong with thinking of world politics as a continuous stream of events, but it becomes very difficult to analyze issues if they are always thought of in this way. Social scientists argue that it is necessary to classify issues so as to facilitate the task of comparing and contrasting them. The importance of this approach is now often taken for granted by social scientists because so many areas of the natural sciences seem to have reaped such enormous benefits from following this approach. Branches of the biological sciences, in particular, seem to have derived their initial impetus from analysts who displayed an interest in establishing typologies and taxonomies of living things.

It is dangerous, however, to draw too close a parallel between the natural and social sciences. The typologies established by natural scientists map on to an external reality which is left unaffected by the process of classification. In the social sciences, however, typologies can actually form part of the reality which is being analyzed. Because the typologies used by social scientists can be implicated in social reality, they can actually change the nature of social reality. Think, for example, of the various ways in which individuals get classified by the state, according to age, gender, class, race, religion, and so on. The labels used in classifications can become very politically sensitive because on closer inspection it can be observed how the labels can become linked very directly to a political agenda. In former Yugoslavia, for example, it was the state that began to classify people according to religion. This was of no great consequence in Croatia, where the people were Catholic, or in Serbia, where the people were Orthodox Christians. But it did make a difference in Bosnia which had for centuries been a multi-cultural community made up of people who identified themselves first and foremost as Bosnian. Once the religious differences began to be accentuated, however, whereas the Muslims in the region continued to identify themselves as Bosnian, the Catholics in the area began to identify themselves more clearly as Croatian and the Orthodox Christian as Serbian. When tensions rose following the break-up of

Yugoslavia, this development was to contribute to the tragic consequences.

Ethnic identification is an issue that has risen rapidly up the world politics agenda in recent years. But for much of the Cold War, it was not a prominent issue. It is of interest, therefore, to look back on the classificatory schemes which prevailed during that period, not only because they illustrate that such schemes are a product of their time, but also because they help to reveal the origins of contemporary classification schemes. There were two dominant and interrelated typologies which prevailed in the early Cold War period. In retrospect, what is most apparent is how simplistic these typologies now appear. In the first instance, there appeared to be a neat and tidy as well as relatively uncontroversial distinction to be drawn between *domestic* and *international* issues. Because states were considered sovereign and autonomous entities, they were habitually identified, metaphorically, as billiard balls or chess pieces, moving within the arena of world politics. Issues arising *within* these impermeable entities were identified as domestic, while issues arising *between* them were considered to be international. On the basis of this initial distinction, international issues were then further distinguished in terms of *high* and *low* politics. The nature of this distinction, however, is not at all obvious and requires some elaboration.

It would be tempting, but only superficially accurate, to suggest that 'high politics' concerns important issues and 'low politics' concerns unimportant issues. But it would be closer to the truth to suggest that high politics involves issues that determine the nature of the environment within which low politics can take place. High politics, therefore, was seen to be concerned with the maintenance of state security and the management of the diplomatic environment within which states interact. High politics were conducted by officials from the foreign office and the defence department. By ensuring the security of the state and the stability of the international diplomatic environment, it was possible for officials concerned with low politics to undertake their tasks. They could negotiate the rules governing trade between states, establish rules that ensured that communications between states could take place, formulate rules that prevented pollution from entering the environment, and all the other rules that enable states to interact freely and fruitfully. From this perspective, then, the Korean War, the Suez

Crisis, the Test Ban Treaty and the Strategic Arms Limitations Talks (SALT) all involved high politics, whereas the negotiations over the General Agreement on Trade and Tariffs (GATT), the establishment of the Law of the Seas, and the implementation of the Antarctic Treaty all involved low politics.

There are two important implications that can be seen to follow from this typology. The first is that high politics takes precedence over low politics. This is not to say that high politics is necessarily more important than low politics, although there is a very strong temptation for those involved in high politics to think in this way. But there is a presumption that low politics cannot take place in the absence of the framework established by the participants in high politics. The second implication is that academics studying world politics should focus on issues that emerge in the realm of high politics at the expense of issues identified in low politics. It then follows, if this typology is accepted, that the study of world politics must concentrate on security and diplomatic issues. And there is little doubt that in the early Cold War days, there would be some truth to the claim that it was issues in these areas that provided the main focus in most textbooks on world politics.

Both of these classificatory schemes, however, have been challenged. In the first place, it is argued that the distinction drawn between domestic and international issues reflects a false distinction. A wide array of issues has been identified which cannot be neatly classified as either international or domestic. The distinction presupposes that states really are hermetically sealed units. But the reality is that they are not. Frequently issues can be seen to have their origins within the state and their consequences beyond the boundary of the state. Problems related to the environment obviously fit into this category. But so, too, do a whole range of other issues, from refugees to terrorism. A glance at the list of issues being dealt with in this book reveals that few of them can be neatly classified as international. They form a type that has been somewhat inelegantly labelled 'intermestic' suggesting that they cannot be neatly located in either the international or the domestic category. These issues are essentially *trans*national rather than *inter*national in character and are regularly used to illustrate that it is simply not helpful to think of sovereign states possessing impermeable boundaries.

Once it is accepted that the distinction between domestic and international issues is inadequate, then it can come as no surprise that the distinction between high and low politics has also come under attack. Critics insist that it is simply not helpful to suggest that issues associated with military and diplomatic affairs fall into a distinctive category. The refugees who flooded out of Rwanda and Burundi into Zaire in 1994 posed just as much of a threat to this state as if they had been an invading military force. By 1996, this threat was already becoming a reality. And, by the same token, the radiation that escaped following the accident at the nuclear plant at Chernobyl in 1986, had environmental consequences that would have been no different from the explosion of a nuclear bomb. In contemporary world politics, economic collapse or ethnic conflict are far more likely to bring about the demise of a state than an external war. So the distinction between high and low politics starts to appear increasingly dated.

There was, however, a very powerful logic that underpinned the distinction between high and low politics. There is no alternative typology that possesses the same level of coherence. In practice what has happened is that an *ad hoc* typology of issues has grown up, which gets added to, as new types of issue come on to the agenda. This may not seem to be an entirely satisfactory state of affairs. On the other hand, it does represent an accurate reflection of the increasingly complex and diverse range of issues that are emerging in world politics. It is no longer possible, indeed it never was, to think of world politics being defined in military and diplomatic terms. The distinction between high and low politics was always an artificial one. There is no alternative but to take account of the increasing number of issues that spill across the boundaries of states and have profound and long-lasting effects on the nature of world politics.

The Significance of Issues in World Politics

It is clear from what has already been said that issues in world politics will inevitably vary in their salience or significance, and that this is related in quite complex ways to the interests of various groups and institutions operating in the world arena. What makes an issue 'significant' or 'insignificant' at any given time or for any given group? One straightforward definition would be that 'significance' is another word for drama or impact: the most significant issues are those which capture the attention of political leaders or the media at any particular time. But we have already noted that this can be a rather artificial way of defining what matters: the whims of news editors or the ability of groups to capture the headlines may give only a very misleading impression of significance.

It is therefore necessary to add to drama or impact an awareness of the attention paid or priority given to an issue by 'those who matter' – the political leaders or institutions that can make a difference through the kinds of decisions or action they take. This helps us to ask the question 'significant for whom?' which is important in framing an analysis of political action and interaction. A third way of refining our notion of significance is to ask about the long-term implications of an issue: whatever the short-term drama or salience of a particular issue, there needs to be some interpretation of the ways in which it contributes to broader processes of international change and development.

This gives us a set of three initial questions to ask about any issue. First, what is its short-term impact and salience? Second, what is its importance to 'those who matter'? Third, what are its longer-term implications? Seen in the light of these questions, an issue such as global environmental change can be seen to have varied on all three dimensions. In the first place, there have been periodic and often rather dramatic 'eruptions' of the issue – for example, when holes in the ozone layer are identified or their growth noted. At such points, speculation about future developments and 'doomsday scenarios' can proliferate, often fuelled by the media or by interest groups. But it is not apparent that such short-term attention translates into long-term salience for the issue. Such extended attention is likely to be given by the scientific community in particular, but increasingly also it is ensured by the fact that governments and other institutions have 'taken the issue on board' and have developed structures to monitor and analyze it. Thus, the existence of departments for environmental affairs and the associated growth of the environmental policy community ensures a more consistent evaluation – if not more consistent policy outcomes – in such areas as 'global warming'. In turn, this begins to build some awareness of the longer-term significance of the issue, exposing both the dangers of environmental degradation and the ways in which it can be handled through national or international policy-making. In this way, it could be argued that the 'environmental dimension' gets built into the world arena and cemented into the agendas of particular actors.

So far, the question of 'significance' has been assessed in a rather 'political' manner, with the emphasis on the ways in which issues enter the political arena and are noticed. There is a further set of more specific questions that can be asked about a given issue which help to establish more clearly its location in the world arena. Often, these questions are asked more or less explicitly by political actors in framing their strategies and their responses to calls for action. Four such questions can be identified and used to classify issues:

1. What is the *extent or scope* of an issue? Does it affect large parts of the global arena, or can it be confined and contained? This, for example, is the kind of question often asked about civil wars and other limited conflicts. How far are they likely to spill over into the broader arena, and thus become of concern to a wide variety of actors?

2. What is the *urgency or intensity* of a particular issue? This, of course, is a rather subjective question, since it relates to the general question 'significant to whom?' To go back to the issue of global environmental change, it is quite clear that such an issue has different levels of urgency for different political actors, who will as a result give it different degrees of priority, attention and resources.

3. What is the *salience or visibility* of a given issue? This question relates to a number of questions already raised in this chapter, and to the roles of the media or other groupings who confer urgency or intensity. It also relates to the ways in which a 'head of steam' can build up behind an issue to make it a fit subject for national or international action, whatever its objective impact.

4. What is the *centrality or location* of an issue? This is partly an objective issue of geography, implying that the closer an issue is to important actors the greater the attention and significance it will acquire. Perhaps the most famous or notorious expression of this quality is that of Neville Chamberlain when he described Czechoslovakia in 1938 as 'a faraway country of which we

know little'. But this example also reveals the other dimension of centrality and location: they are expressions of sensitivity to the issue, and of its links to vital interests. Where these links are powerful, the constraints of geography are of little importance, and such links are enhanced by the developments in the media and international communication outlined earlier.

The Management of Issues in World Politics

Very often, when international issues are identified and given 'air-time', there is an implication that 'something must be done'. Sometimes this is expressed in terms of national action, or action by specific private groupings such as companies or pressure groups. But with many issues, there is also the feeling that national or private action is insufficient: the 'world community' should act, and establish some kind of management processes to deal with the issue. The question of management is clearly inseparable from the analysis of many issues in world politics, but it is often unclear how the 'world community' or those acting in the world arena can get past the crude call for action and the feeling that if nothing is done things might get out of hand. The question of management is thus partly a matter of the mechanisms through which things can be handled and the interests of different groupings reconciled. At the same time, though, there are inescapable normative questions: about whether management itself is a desirable activity, and about what might be the most effective forms of management. Given that world issues are subject to conflicting assessments of significance and that they are often politically sensitive, these normative issues are likely to be among the most difficult to address and resolve.

A first question to ask about an issue is 'why should it be managed?' After all, the term 'management' itself has some overtones of conservatism and the desire to contain problems rather than to let them play themselves out. There is clearly a spectrum of ways in which the question can be answered. At its crudest, the answer may be 'because if it is not managed we shall all be worse off', and this has often been applied to the issue of global environmental change. But there may well be those who feel that such an answer is just a way of suppressing legitimate demands for change. Who is to say that LDCs, who may need to pollute in order to achieve economic growth, should 'manage' the environment by standards set in the industrial world? The same often applies to international or internal conflicts: if they are not 'managed', they may get out of hand and have damaging effects on world order, but the same loss of control might enable specific groups to achieve their objectives. The question 'why manage' is thus not an open-and-shut one, and it is linked with some highly sensitive political issues.

Secondly, we can ask 'how can or should an issue be managed?' Again, the answer to this question is likely to be conditioned by differences of political values, aims and strategies. Perhaps the most obvious way in which this question expresses itself is through the tension between national action and action through international organizations. One of the most fundamental problems in world politics is the contradiction between national action and collective action, and this is made even more complex by the intrusion of non-state groupings calling for their own versions of management. Two dimensions of the problem stand out. First, there is the dimension of *scale and participation*. Should issues be managed unilaterally, bilaterally or multilaterally? This is a crucial question, for example, in the management of the world political economy: such matters as trade conflicts can be managed through unilateral measures such as trade protection, through bilateral agreements between concerned actors or through the development of international rules and agreements such as the GATT, which is now contained within the World Trade Organization (WTO). Very often, issues are managed through a rather uneasy combination of actions at different levels: the national, the regional and the global, and by a combination of different groups and organizations: governments, international organizations and a wide range of private commercial bodies.

The 'how to manage' issue has a second dimension: that of *mechanisms*. To stay with the example of world trade, it can be shown that an immense variety of mechanisms come into play in the attempt to manage. Some of these are linked to international institutions and the rules they set down for the conduct of international dealings. Others, though, are the reflection of a huge variety of national, international and transnational interactions. These can set up wide-ranging and complex mechanisms of conflict and cooperation, and they lead to a process of continuous and wide-ranging negotiation in the international trade system. Thus the

GATT embodies a powerful set of legal mechanisms and procedures, but these can be put under pressure or even rendered redundant by negotiation at the regional level or in the context of large international corporations producing in many national jurisdictions. Alongside these international processes can go those of national economic and commercial management, which may in turn be at odds with the global or regional processes. Thus, members of the European Union find themselves dealing with and attempting to reconcile all levels of the world trading system whilst at the same time dealing with their own specifically national problems.

A final aspect of the 'management' problem is that of *results and outcomes*. In many ways, this links back to the 'why manage?' question, since it is apparent that the attempt to manage world political issues can create winners and losers as well as the more efficient handling of particular problems. At one level, it could be argued that the management of issues in world politics is for the common good: it could equally be argued that this is a 'winner's argument', reflecting the position of those who are satisfied with the current situation or management mechanisms. For the 'losers', the effective management of world issues may simply be another dimension of their subordination and the perpetuation of their loser's status. The result can sometimes be the rejection of management at the international level and the resort to unilateral action outside both the institutions and the rules of the 'world community'. Take, for example, the issue of nuclear weapons and their spread. There has emerged a powerful set of agreements sometimes known as the 'non-proliferation regime' and centred on the Non-Proliferation Treaty, which was renegotiated and extended in 1995. But for a number of states on the verge of acquiring nuclear weapons, and particularly those facing what they see as threats to their national existence, this regime appears far from natural or legitimate: the result *for them* is not an expression of neutral 'management', but it is rather a reflection of their containment and oppression. In the same way, although the GATT has operated to increase world trade and the flows of goods and services, there is a widespread feeling in the developing world that it operates to widen the gap between them and the industrial countries. A final example can be found in the negotiation of peace agreements: these are an explicit case of 'management', it seems, but they can also be seen as a reflection of the underlying power balance and as a means of suppressing change. In other words, as in the cases of nuclear weapons and trade, we need to ask not only what the results are in tangible terms, but also what they tell us about the winners and losers in both tangible and intangible terms.

Selection of Issues and Key Questions

Before moving on to begin our investigation of particular issues, the final part of this chapter provides a justification for the issues selected and describes the way in which each chapter will be organized in terms of key questions to be asked. It is worth repeating that there is no attempt here to offer a comprehensive set of issues that can be taken to encapsulate all the main features of contemporary world politics. What can be claimed, however, is that the selection here comprises an interesting and a representative sample that addresses some of the important analytical issues introduced in this chapter.

To merit inclusion in this book, an issue needed to meet certain criteria. First, the issue must be representative of the range of issues on the contemporary international agenda. Interestingly, some of the issues selected would not automatically have been included on the list if this book had been written, say, ten years ago – migration and refugees is an obvious example. Several of these issues are unlikely to have been included if this book had been written twenty or thirty years ago: to migration and refugees can be added environment and natural resources, Islamic fundamentalism and political Islam, and possibly regions and regionalism. By the same token, certain issues – those relating to arms and the international economy, for example – would almost certainly have been included, though not necessarily in the form that they are presented here.

While covering a selection of 'old' and 'new' issues, we were also concerned to provide a range of issues that, in terms of traditional typologies, were illustrative of 'low' as well as 'high' policy areas and that some, at least, were issues that crossed the boundary between domestic politics and international relations/world politics. In the event it would be difficult to argue that any of the issues analyzed here are simply 'international' issues. They form part of a set of issues that help to define the current state of world politics but, at the same time, they are also issues that contribute to the shaping of domestic political, economic and social agendas. Most if not all the issues covered here can be described as genuinely 'intermestic' in character.

More important criteria perhaps relate to the end of the Cold War. We have tried to select issues that appear to have been affected by the end of the Cold War, at least in the form in which they are presented on the international agenda. Among the questions we posed for planning purposes were: Did a new period of world politics begin in the 1990s which could be characterized by a new agenda of issues? Or do 'new' issues simply represent 'old' problems presented in a new guise? Is contemporary world politics marked by change or continuity, or more radically, by a total transformation? In the wake of the end of the Cold War, has the international community devised new techniques or strategies for solving problems? Another criteria for selection was whether a particular issue promises to show novel forms of 'management' and control in terms of resolving problems or, at least, does a particular issue illustrate the continuing dilemmas in trying to resolve problems at a global level in a post Cold War era.

Clearly, in an important sense, the appropriateness or otherwise of the issues selected can only be judged after the individual chapters have been presented. Therefore, the concluding chapter of this book critically reviews the issues selected and attempts to describe the picture of contemporary world politics that emerges from them. Meanwhile, to help the reader not only to understand the particular issues chosen but also to develop a more general understanding of world politics, all the contributors were asked to address a common set of questions. Though contributors could interpret these questions in ways that were consistent with their subject matter, it was felt to be necessary to establish as far as possible a common structure. The key questions posed that provided that structure were as follows:

1. What is the nature of the issue or set of issues to be discussed?
2. What type of issue or set of issues is it and how significant is it?
3. What general problems does the issue represent?
4. Who or what is responsible for the location of the issue on the international agenda?

5. How has the end of the Cold War affected the form in which the issue is presented?
6. What institutional or other mechanisms have emerged to manage the issue at the international level?
7. What does the issue tell us about the nature and concerns of contemporary world politics?

2

States and Statehood

MARK WEBBER

The post-war period has witnessed a remarkable growth in the number of states, from around fifty in 1945 to more than 180 in 1996. These range from the tiny city states of Monaco and the Holy See all the way up to the Russian Federation and China, respectively the world's largest and most populous states. During the twentieth century, there have been several great waves of 'state creation': in the period after the First World War, again after the Second World War, and then in the 1960s. Most recently, the collapse of the Soviet Union in the early 1990s led to claims of statehood on the part of a large number of formerly subject peoples such as those of Central Asia, whilst other states such as those in the Baltic which had been suppressed by their absorption into the USSR re-emerged on to the international scene. Statehood, to put it simply, is more popular and sought-after than it has ever been, but this raises important questions about the changing nature both of states and of statehood more generally.

Three central questions can be asked, all of which have evoked considerable disagreement. First, how is the state to be defined in terms of its constitutive features? Second, what are the purposes of the state, or, in other words, what is it for? Third, how important is the state in relation to other actors in world politics?

The first of these questions has in the study of world politics a rather straightforward answer. The accepted orthodoxy asserts that a state has common characteristics, of which a territory, a sovereign government and a subject population are the most important. These constitute the 'organization' of statehood and will be considered in greater detail in the next section. Suffice to say here that this rather legalistic definition is a far from satisfactory one. As we shall discover, most states do not and perhaps have never sustained these characteristics in full. Furthermore, some would argue that the definition is incomplete without mention of other allegedly requisite features of statehood from, depending on the persuasion of the author, a list that includes the existence of a common culture and sense of national identity (or, in its more xenophobic formulation, the possession of an exclusive ethnicity), a minimum level of political stability and order, and a modicum of social and economic welfare (Jackson and James, 1993, p. 18; Del Rosso Jr., 1995, p. 178).

As for our second question, here opinion is particularly divided. In a far from exhaustive list, Mervyn Frost has identified four separate schools of thought. States can be conceived of as being motivated by either: (i) the promotion of international order; (ii) their own survival, with a consequent emphasis on security; (iii) the protection of a particular form of political rule, democratic or otherwise; or (iv) the defence of dominant class interests and thus the regulation of a dominant economic form – capitalism. Yet as Frost points out, despite their differences, these four approaches share a crucial common assumption: the state is important. It is conceived of as a piece of machinery geared to the achievement of certain ends. It is rational, powerful and pre-eminent (Frost, 1991, pp. 186–7).

As a cursory glance at any quality newspaper will confirm, this is a popular image. Headlines that focus on state action and pro-nouncement in the form of phrases such as 'the United States issues a warning to Cuba' or 'Russian–Chinese relations are improving' certainly suggest that the state is paramount in world politics. Yet a more careful examination of our chosen newspaper can also reveal a slightly different image. References to the actions of say the European Union (EU) (with regard to British beef exports) and of the International Monetary Fund (IMF) (in relation to the terms and conditions of loans made to Russia) reflect the fact that the state is by no means alone in world politics. It is accompanied by a host of other actors that include: international inter-governmental organizations (IGOs) of which the United Nations (UN) and the EU are familiar examples; international non-governmental organi-zations (INGOs) such as Greenpeace and Amnesty International; and multinational companies (MNCs) such as General Motors and British Petroleum. It is the existence of these so-called 'non-state actors' that provides the context to our third question: how important is the state in relation to other actors in world politics?

To this, there is no simple answer. Few, however, would argue that the state enjoys an untrammelled supremacy. It interacts with other actors in myriad relationships. On certain issues this may affirm state dominance, but on others the role of the state is far less assured. To illustrate this take the two examples cited above. The power of the EU to ban British beef exports is at odds with the desire of the British state to maximize its sales. Similarly, the ability of the IMF to link the provision of loans to the monthly performance of the Russian economy reflects a presumption of authority on the part of this financial body that detracts from that of Russia.

The variety of answers to the three questions posed above indicates that the state is a contested concept (Navari, 1991). Its very meaning and purpose are the subjects of dispute and little approximating a consensus of views is apparent. This renders exploration of the nature of statehood especially problematic. In order to alleviate this problem some narrowing of the focus of enquiry will be necessary. We make a start in this direction in the following section by examining further the orthodox definition of statehood noted above.

The Nature of Statehood: Organization and Practice

For all their great diversity, states, if they are to qualify for the title, must possess the three common characteristics noted above: a territory, a sovereign government and a subject population. All three are important, yet it is the second that is crucial. The possession of sovereignty – commonly understood to mean the absence of any higher authority above the state both in domestic and external affairs – confers upon states a privileged position as the principal actor in international life. In numerous ways, it is a 'source of vitality' for the state, providing guarantees of formal equality and political independence, access to resources and connections, and an international identity or capacity that is unmatched (Miller, 1986). Sovereignty, however, requires practical organization; this is provided by governments. It is the personnel of government that represent the state and, by means of foreign policies, claim to act in defence of its interests.

To outline the three features of statehood is not, however, to suggest that states enjoy a placid or unchallenged life. Since the very inception of the international system of states (usually dated from the Treaty of Westphalia in 1648), these features have been the subject of regular violation and infringement.

Take first the quality of territoriality, the assumption that a delimited geographic area is the responsibility of a single state only. The obvious point to be made here is that historically speaking, territory has been the source of fierce dispute, precisely because it has been claimed by more than one state. This may result in legal dispute conducted at a diplomatic level, state-sponsored subversion and, in certain cases, inter-state war. Both the First World War and the Second World War were precipitated at least partly by unresolved claims for territory on the part of major powers. The latter route to acquisition, it is true, has become something of a rarity, not least because of the expansion of legal restrictions on the use of force since 1945 and because the costs of war often outweigh any presumed benefits. This has, however, only changed the methods by which claims might be pursued, not the abundancy and potency of the claims themselves.

Even when the territorial integrity of a state is unchallenged (and this is a luxury that European states, at least, have come to expect and enjoy since the end of the Second World War), territoriality can nonetheless be infringed in other ways. Stephen Krasner has highlighted the importance of 'authority structures that are not coterminous with geographic borders'. Examples include condominiums (for instance, that of Andorra, a co-principality of Spain and France); supranational organizations, notably the EU, which involve member states' submission to the binding decisions of extraterritorial bodies; and international regimes such as the Exclusive Economic Zone, which limits the jurisdiction of states over commercial shipping even within their own territorial waters (Krasner, 1995–6, p. 116).

Encroachments upon territoriality also entail a violation of sovereignty, the second core feature of statehood. In fact, sovereignty can be compromised in a number of different ways: through processes of domination, imposition, delegation, and intrusion.

The first of these arises from imbalances of power between states. Here the legal equality embodied in the principle of sovereignty is not reflected in the possession of state capabilities (military structures, economic prowess, resource endowments and so on). Such an uneven distribution results in relationships between states that are far from equal and, in certain cases, the imposition by one state of limits upon another's freedom of action. Soviet influence over Eastern Europe during the period of communist rule and American oversight of much of the Caribbean and Central America are clear examples of such a pattern.

The second, imposition, involves situations where a coalition of states forces conditions upon a third party as a result either of the latter's defeat in war, or its transgression of accepted norms of behaviour. The peace treaties that Germany and Japan were forced to accept in 1945 are examples of the former, and economic sanctions directed against pariah states (for instance, apartheid South Africa) of the latter. In both cases, actions are taken from outside that either have a direct and obvious effect upon sovereignty (for instance, the supervision of Berlin by the Allied powers) or influence the domestic political developments of a state to such a degree that sovereignty is severely dented (as in the impact of sanctions on the removal of white-minority rule in South Africa).

Delegation is a less coercive form of infringement upon sovereignty. It is, however, no less important for that. Delegation has two dimensions. It can involve, first, states transferring sovereignty 'upward' to supranational organizations (as in the case of the EU noted above). This is a rare occurrence, but has, in Western Europe at least, progressed to a point where the sovereign status of the EU's member states has been questioned and the impression created that they are being absorbed into a larger, 'multi-level polity', an entity which itself has some of the features of a state (Caporaso, 1996). Second, delegation occurs 'downward', to regions within the state by means of granting them degrees of autonomy. In its more familiar guise this process is known as federalism and is the practice of states as diverse as the US, Switzerland and Brazil. While the scope for action open to the component parts of federal states is constitutionally delimited, their powers are nonetheless often fairly extensive. Moreover, federalism itself often presents real problems for state cohesion in that the internal administrative borders of a federated state can provide the basis of powerful claims of secession. As we shall note below, in the cases of the communist federations such claims have ultimately proven fatal to state survival.

As for intrusion, this entails challenges to sovereignty that arise from 'issues and . . . (and) relationships . . . that dissolve the national-international divide' (Camilleri and Falk, 1992, p. 39). Take, for instance, economic issues. Here the ability of the sovereign state to pursue policies of its choosing has been fundamentally challenged in recent decades by the 'globalization' of trade, production and finance (see also Chapter 3). The subjection of national economies has occurred in several ways. The deepening of global markets results in borders that are more porous to unregulated economic activity, multinational companies that are increasingly free of state control, and economically-oriented international organizations (for instance, the IMF, the World Bank and the World Trade Organization [WTO]) that are capable of an awesome influence (Camilleri and Falk, 1992, pp. 69–77).

Turning to the third feature of statehood, that of a subject population, here too qualification is necessary. This is not to say, of course, that states are without peoples over whom they rule; rather, that some populations have often felt compelled to escape the state in which they are contained. This is a problem that is at its most profound in states that are multi-ethnic and which simultaneously display a poor sense of overarching national identity. In these cases, an ethnic minority views its usually subordinate position as demeaning and the only proper course of action that of self-determination – the construction of its own statehood. Such a situation is commonplace in the Third World. Here, decolonization created a large number of states whose borders, based on former lines of colonial administration, failed to conform to the patterns of population distributed both within and among them. This mismatch has not led to the creation of a large number of new states (Bangladesh and Eritrea being rare cases in point). It has, however, resulted in battles for self-determination pursued with a force sufficient to render whole areas effectively beyond state jurisdiction. This is a condition especially marked in Africa, where large swathes of Angola, Sudan and Zaire have been lost to central rule for much of the last two decades. Moving away from the Third World, the problem of self-determination has been no less acute. It has reared its head in Western Europe in the violence perpetrated by the Irish Republican Army (IRA) in Northern Ireland and by *Euskadi ta Askatasuna* (ETA) in the Basque region of Spain. More destructively, it has been apparent in the inability of non-democratic

communist federations to offer sufficient voice to captured minorities, resulting as in the cases of the Soviet Union and Yugoslavia
in dissolution and the proliferation of a raft of new successor states.

Statehood as a Problem in World Politics

In reality, challenges, both domestic and external, are by now the
familiar experience of all states. In some instances, however, this
need not be perceived as detrimental. Sovereignty may be willingly
surrendered if some lasting benefit can be obtained. Hence, to
return to an example cited above, Russia's readiness to submit to
the strictures of the IMF has been motivated by the realization that
the huge finances offered by that organization are a price worth
paying for a partial loss of domestic economic jurisdiction. Moreover, there are many functions that the state can best achieve
through collective action and this too requires a relinquishing of
sovereignty. While the act of surrender is never stated in so many
words – for purely political reasons the governments of most states
will rarely admit to presiding over a loss of sovereignty – in practice
there is often no alternative. Few states, for instance, are capable of
guaranteeing their own military defence and many consequently
enter into alliances. Such an arrangement may involve a state
binding itself to commitments that infringe upon its foreign policy
and, in certain instances (the case of the North Atlantic Treaty
Organization [NATO]) the subordination of its armed forces to a
higher command structure. The resulting limitations to freedom of
action are seen as tolerable if, through the acquisition of allies and
arms, it offers a greater guarantee of the state's security. A similar
logic can also apply in other areas, be this trade, transportation,
communication or environmental protection, all of which have led
states to recognize that constraint on individual action is a necessary cost of pursuing an otherwise unobtainable objective.

Many states, then, will tolerate under certain circumstances some
constraints on their own particular statehood. They are, however,
extremely cautious when it comes to any revision of the concept of
statehood in general and the norms of international behaviour
which follow from it. States that for instance indulge in wilful acts
of conquest are not just guilty of a resort to force but, equally
important, of violating the territorial dimension of statehood. As

such they are the subject of condemnation and often find themselves up against a powerful coalition of states keen to restore the international order. Such was the fate of Nazi Germany and, more recently, Saddam Hussein's Iraq. Of a slightly lesser order of gravity, there is a general predisposition against the notion of spheres of influence, owing to the gross undermining of the principle of sovereignty that it entails. Even those states that endeavour to dominate in such an arrangement have consequently felt the need to excuse their actions in some way. The Soviet-led military interventions in Hungary (1956) and in Czechoslovakia (1968), for example, were justified by reference to dubiously-based 'invitations' issued by the government of the violated state. More generally, despite Moscow's obvious oversight of the east European states at this time, it was still considered necessary to place inter-state relations within treaties of 'Friendship and Cooperation' that made ritualistic reference to mutual respect for sovereignty. The sham of this claim was, however, abundantly clear, such that when the Soviet Union under its last leader Mikhail Gorbachev reversed the policies of his predecessors this was trumpeted as amounting, in effect, to a welcome restoration of sovereignty for the subject states.

The bias of the international system toward respect for statehood can have perverse effects. True, respect for a principle may sometimes be the stimulus for action that is at once heroic and decisive (as in the case of the reaction to Nazism noted above), but it can also be a recipe for inertia and prevarication, and, at worse, a passive acceptance of the intolerable. Take for instance the case of what Robert Jackson refers to as 'quasi-states'. These enjoy the attributes of formal 'juridical' statehood (most importantly, external recognition) but lack its 'empirical' qualities; their governments are 'deficient in . . . political will, institutional authority, and organised power'. Such states would seem unviable entities. They were created as a consequence of the recognized right of self-determination of ex-colonial territories. They have endured because of, first, the reluctance of established states to modify this recognition (fearful of an unmanageable proliferation of new states) and, second, the existence of various forms of development assistance directed at improving their capacity for self-government. As a result, quasi-states that are often blighted by economic under-development, political instability and even civil war have enjoyed a charmed existence, surviving when in a previous age the absence of a credible basis for statehood would have denied them membership of international society (R. H. Jackson, 1990, pp. 21, 31, 42).

In some cases respect for statehood takes a far more ambiguous form. It is widely accepted that sovereignty precludes outside interference in a state's domestic affairs (this is spelled out notably in Article II of the UN Charter). Even so, it has been argued that there are grounds on which the norm of non-intervention may be overridden (Berridge, 1992, pp. 164–5). These are:

- *Self-defence*. This can take two forms: the launch of a preemptive strike by one state upon another to forestall an attack, and a retaliatory strike against a state charged with aggression. An example of the former is the Israeli assault on the Arab states in 1967 (an operation welcomed in the West, but criticized by the Soviet bloc and many Third World states). An example of the latter is the American bombing of the Libyan capital Tripoli in 1986 (an event fully supported only by Britain and Israel).
- *Humanitarian intervention*. This may involve actions to rescue one's own nationals in a foreign country, as in the case of Israel's operation at Entebbe airport (Uganda) in 1976, and intercession to end human rights abuses. Examples of the latter include Tanzania's 1979 overthrow of Idi Amin in Uganda and, more controversially, Vietnam's invasion of Kampuchea in 1978–9. While the intervening state in both cases claimed a humanitarian motive, its actions were nonetheless seen by many as illegal encroachments upon the domestic affairs of others. Furthermore, as well as infringing upon sovereignty, the cause of humanitarian intervention has proven controversial because of inconsistent application. Intervention has not been forthcoming in cases of sustained human rights abuses if the offending state is powerful enough to resist or precious enough to be treated with sympathy by the international community. (Witness in this regard the absence of decisive action to correct Chinese abuses in Tibet or Indonesian abuses in East Timor.)
- *Civil war*. In this case intervention is considered justified if it is a response to a previous intervention by another state. Thus, the US felt justified in arming anti-Marxist insurgents in Afghanistan, Nicaragua and Angola in the 1980s in opposition to what they saw as the seizure of power by Soviet-supported revolutionaries.

These examples nothwithstanding, there is still no generally agreed *right* of intervention. Indeed, controversy arises precisely because the norm of non-intervention survives. To understand why this is so, simply consider what would happen if the norm did not exist at all. 'If it were regarded as normal that states *should* meddle in each other's domestic affairs the points of friction (already ample enough) would multiply hugely, all trust would dissolve, and civilised international relations would become impossible' (Berridge, 1992, p. 163).

The politics of statehood

As well as generating controversy at the level of general principles, issues pertaining to statehood can also stimulate debates of a more expressly political nature. The existence of a perceived threat to statehood is a common charge in politics. Republicans in the US complain of the threats posed by unregulated immigration from Mexico; Conservatives in Britain warn of the dilution of sovereign powers that flow from encroachments by the EU; while the parliament in the Soviet successor state of Belarus deplores the potential loss of statehood that would result from a possible merger with neighbouring Russia. Such protests are not just the outcome of cynical political calculations. The outlook of politicians, and indeed the world's public, is rooted in a traditional perception of the qualities of statehood and consequently of the primacy of the state in international affairs (Miller, 1994, p. 61). In the conduct of foreign affairs, this results in an unwillingness on the part of national leaders to be seen to be pursuing anything other than the interests of the state that they serve. It is a rare politician who justifies a foreign policy in anything other than the 'national (meaning state) interest'. And even in those exceptional cases – for instance, the Soviet Union's pursuit of the apparently altruistic cause of 'proletarian internationalism' – a more selfish interest is never far behind.

Not surprisingly a preoccupation with the national interest has great political consequence, both domestically and internationally. Two illustrative examples show to just what degree.

Consider first the case of British membership of the EU. Since the 1960s this has proven to be one of the more divisive issues in British political life. Successive Prime Ministers from Harold Macmillan to

John Major have been forced to juggle dual demands. On the one hand, they have tried to keep sweet a British public and sections of their own parties appreciative of the unique features of the British system, while, on the other, they have been sensitive to the imperative of integrating Britain carefully into a continental structure, absence from which is seen as economically and politically untenable. Managing this delicate balance has not been easy. The Conservative Party, the party of government during the 1980s and much of the 1990s, found itself at times paralyzed over the issue of Europe, split between a leadership resigned to the inevitability of European involvement and a 'Euro-sceptic' wing, implacable in its opposition to the integrationist tendencies of the EU. The foreign policy consequences of this stance are also considerable. The championing of a specifically British interest has resulted in isolation within the EU on issues ranging from monetary union to social protection.

The second example is provided by Russia. Unlike the British case, where debates are conducted within a fairly stable political framework, here they occur against a far more painful backdrop, that of state collapse. The fall of the Soviet Union in 1991 and the consequent emergence of an independent Russia, was at first the cause for some considerable jubilation, not only because it meant a restoration of an explicitly Russian (as opposed to a Soviet) state identity, but also because it was part and parcel of a parallel process of removing unpopular communist rule. Russia's subsequent political development, however, has been adversely affected by the legacy of this profound transition. As economic collapse and a loss of superpower status attended the Soviet Union's dissolution, the new Russian state has been viewed by many as a poor cousin of its Soviet, and indeed even its Tsarist, predecessor. This has resulted in the poisoning of political debate as virtually all major issues have tended to be overwhelmed by the question 'who was to blame?' It has also led communist and nationalist parties to join forces in calling for the territorial enlargement of the modern Russian state to include those lands historically occupied by the Russian nation. In foreign policy the debates have been no less vitriolic. The attenuated power of post-Soviet Russia meant its first President, Boris Yeltsin, was forced to give priority initially to improved relations with the West. This course, however, elicited from his political opponents repeated charges of weakness and of wilful neglect of Russia's state interests. These proved so powerful as to result, from the end of 1992, in a major turnaround in favour of a foreign policy which, in Yeltsin's own words, would not 'shy away from defending our own interests'.

Statehood and the Post-Cold War World

The end of the Cold War has had mixed consequences for statehood. To begin on a positive note, one of its more visible effects has been a massive proliferation in the number of states, a process, which for some, marks a 'springtime of nations' (Howard, 1989–90), or a 'renaissance of the nation state'(Brown, 1995, p. 2). The breakup of Yugoslavia, the Soviet Union and Czechoslovakia into their constituent, usually ethnically defined parts, and the due recognition granted to these nascent states by the international community, seemingly reinvigorated the idea of statehood based upon a defined population or nation. To this process has been coupled a revival in the sovereign powers of previously dominated states. Client states which had formerly been subjected to the imposing influence of the superpowers suddenly lost their utility to Washington and Moscow as the imperatives of East–West global competition diminished. Amongst the former Soviet satellites in Eastern Europe, the consequent re-animation of sovereignty has not only seen the introduction of democratic political structures (and ironically in some cases the free election to office of former communist parties), but a wholesale reorientation of foreign policies. States such as Poland, Hungary and the new Czech Republic, once firmly and forcibly contained within a Soviet sphere of influence, are now at the front of the queue for membership of the historically Western-oriented NATO and the EU.

The end of the Cold War has also had less welcome consequences. The legitimacy given to nationalism has proven a poisoned chalice in some new states which are themselves multi-ethnic. The vicious wars in Bosnia, the secessionist struggle by the Chechens in Russia, and the demands for greater autonomy on the part of Russian minorities in the Soviet successor states of Moldova, Ukraine and Kazakhstan are all testimony to this fact. Moreover, many of the new state entities are strongly redolent of the quasi-states described above. In the former Soviet Union, for instance, the successor states emerged at the end of 1991 with little preparation for self-government and, in the case of the five new states of Central Asia, no historical memory of statehood. All, moreover, had been weakened as a consequence of their removal from the once centralized Soviet economy, military and governmental administration. Some, it is true, have compensated for this by means of nationalizing those structures within their borders, but this has itself presented additional problems. In many cases, military and economic assets have been useless outside the context of the integrated Soviet system or have been the subject of rival claims on the part of Russia, the self-declared 'continuing' state of the Soviet Union. In such circumstances only a few of the successor states have proven capable of developing 'empirical' statehood (Ukraine, Latvia, Lithuania and Estonia). The remainder have either succumbed to civil war (Azerbaijan and Moldova), Russian tutelage (Armenia, Belarus) or both (Tajikistan and Georgia).

As for the more familiar quasi-states in the Third World, here too the end of the Cold War has had its effect as states once propped up by superpower patronage have been forced to cope in a new austere climate. Central governments once reliant on an abundance of aid to prop up their economies and on free military hardware to fight their internal battles have found themselves cast adrift. The resource-rich, for instance Angola, have sought compensation in international arms markets. The poor, however, have gone to the wall, resulting in one case in state partition (Eritrea formally seceded from Ethiopia in 1993) and in others in the further crumbling of empirical statehood (Afghanistan has been engulfed in a near total lawlessness since the fall in 1992 of once Soviet favourite President Najibullah). In fact, the plight of some in the Third World has become so catastrophic that they are now described as 'failed states' – entities totally deficient in internal order and 'utterly incapable of sustaining [themselves] as . . . member[s] of the international community' (Helman and Ratner, 1992–3, p. 3).

More ambiguous than the rise and fall of states have been the apparent modifications of principle that have accompanied the end of the Cold War. An important shift has concerned the notion of non-interference derived from sovereignty. Matters previously excused as the purely domestic affair of a state have in the post-Cold War world been the subject of increased international concern where they involve destabilizing external repercussions or gross human suffering. Recent humanitarian operations of the UN inside Iraq, Somalia and Rwanda have been conducted without the clear consent of the state concerned and thus, strictly speaking, amount to infringements upon sovereignty. These actions are all the more notable in that they are multilateral, endorsed by the UN and, therefore, quite different from both the violations of sovereignty perpetrated by the superpowers during the Cold War and earlier cases of humanitarian intervention noted above, which were unilateral in nature (see also Chapter 7).

This shift has implications that take us back to the core qualities of statehood. The incidence of cases of humanitarian intervention in the post-Cold War period reflect two profound changes: a political one and, closely linked to this, a normative one. The first of these relates to the nature of the 'winning coalition' that emerged victorious at the end of the Cold War. Composed at its heart of the states of the West, this meant a victory of liberal democracy and *ipso facto* a discrediting of communism as a political force (Buzan, 1995, p. 394; Barkin and Cronin, 1994, p. 126). In that the dominant values within the international system have come to be increasingly associated with democracy, a normative context has been formed that renders intervention legitimate when it can be shown that certain states are in clear violation of its principles, specifically those that relate to human rights. In this sense sovereignty is a limited asset. To quote Stanley Hoffmann, 'the state that claims sovereignty deserves respect only as long as it protects the basic rights of its subjects. . .When it violates them . . .the state's claim to full sovereignty falls' (Hoffmann, 1995–6, p. 35).

Yet the degree to which these political and normative changes have resulted in a fairer, more just world can be far from gainsaid. In the first place, some would argue that actions based on a moral claim continue to disguise a less worthy intent. That recent interventions have occurred in the Third World and have been at the initiative of powerful states, notably the US, has led to charges that humanitarian intervention is nothing more than a justification for the pursuit of American and, more broadly, Western interests.

Moreover, recent UN-endorsed operations (both humanitarian and otherwise) have tended to be selective and temporary in nature, something that has a clear implication for the failed states noted above. Saving these either through prolonged involvement or massive resource transfers is not top of the foreign policy agendas of either the European states, the US or Russia. Only in rare cases (Bosnia is a case in point) have determined efforts been undertaken. Take away the lucky coincidence of strategic interests, geographic importance and political prominence that motivated action there, and little or nothing will be forthcoming. Liberia, Afghanistan and Somalia are all cases where in the 1990s international efforts at a restitution of political order have proven to be both unconvincing and short-lived.

More neutral in effect, but no less sweeping has been change flowing from economic forces. As well as a victory for liberal democracy, the end of the Cold War also witnessed the apparent triumph of market economics (Buzan, 1995, p. 393). The communist alternatives to the market in the form of central planning and state ownership were by the late 1980s thoroughly discredited and have since given way to market-oriented economies of varying forms throughout both the former communist countries and in China and Vietnam where communist parties remain in power. While this has not meant an unprecedented exposure to the global economy (the east Europeans, for instance, were heavy borrowers during the 1970s and 1980s and the Soviet Union and China had become increasingly entwined in world markets), the extent of that involvement has undoubtedly deepened. The increased need for sources of external finance (to fund reform), coupled with trade reorientation, and the encroachment of foreign equity has opened up states formerly on the margins of the international capitalist system to those forces of economic globalization that intrude upon statehood.

Economics has made an impact in another sense: it has partly usurped military power as the crucial variable of status. The rise of economic powers, notably Germany and Japan, did, of course, occur while the Cold War was in progress. Yet there is a sense in which the order of priorities has now fundamentally altered. The premium attached to military capability has been downgraded with the end of the Cold War, at least amongst the states of the West (including Japan) in that the territorial defence of territory has become a less pressing concern. Consequently, to use a phrase of Ken Booth, '(p)ower in world affairs is increasingly determined by economic success rather than military statistics' (Booth, 1991, p. 8). Statehood itself has not been altered by this change, but the relative importance of the indices that rank states one against the other certainly has.

States and international organizations

One further and much commented upon consequence of the Cold War's demise has been a process of adaptation on the part of international organizations. The dramatic political changes in Eastern Europe and the former Soviet Union, coupled with the more amicable spirit of East–West relations, has forced a rethink in the scope and rationale of some major organizations. The UN and the Organization for Security and Cooperation in Europe (OSCE), for instance, have taken on board large numbers of new members from the successor states. The EU and NATO have outlined routes to possible future membership among these states and in the interim have begun programmes of association and partnership. Other bodies, meanwhile, have simply fallen by the wayside. The Warsaw Pact and the Council for Mutual Economic Assistance were wound up in 1991, their purpose at an end with the disappearance of communist rule.

Organizational development of this kind is part and parcel of a trend that has a far longer historical trajectory – a 'move to institutions' that has in the twentieth century seen a proliferation and increase in the scope of international organizations and, linked to this, in the evolution of other areas of institutionalized behaviour – international law and international regimes.

The growing prominence of this dimension of international life has had significant consequences for states. At a surface level, it has actually reaffirmed statehood. International organizations, with rare exception, have only states as members, adhere in their documentation to the principles of sovereign domestic jurisdiction, and generally are reliant on voluntary, as opposed to binding compliance on the part of their members. Controversy arises over two major issues: first, the relative importance of international organizations as non-state actors (something alluded to above) and second, the issue considered here – the degree to which international organizations can moderate state behaviour and encourage cooperation.

On the one hand are those, usually referred to as 'neo-realists', who claim that organizations are empty vessels, existing only to the degree that they affirm state interests. Cooperation is not ruled out, but it occurs within a clearly delimited framework. Owing to the existence of a condition of anarchy (the absence of a world government above states), the international system is seen as insecure and characterized by distrust. Self-help becomes the order of the day and cooperation is inhibited by fears of cheating, dependency and 'relative gains' (the suspicion on the part of one state that collaboration benefits other states more than itself) (Grieco, 1988). This is clearly not a propitious environment for the operation of international organizations. Indeed, to the extent that they do carry out important roles, these are largely derivative of the international distribution of power between states. The more powerful create and shape organizations so that they might pursue selfish objectives, a state of affairs at its most obvious in the privileges enjoyed by the Permanent Five members of the UN Security Council. In short, organizations, of whatever type, will only reflect the balance of interests of their constituent parts (that is, states). When states are not in harmony, organizations will have to engage in negotiated compromise. When states disagree fundamentally, organizations will be rendered ineffective (Meirsheimer, 1994–5). Hence, the somewhat limited success of internally divided bodies like the Organization of African Unity and the Arab League, and the frequent impotence of the UN.

Ranked against this rather pessimistic position are the arguments of the so-called 'neo-liberal institutionalists'. This view is willing to accept certain core neo-realist tenets (the position of states in a condition of anarchy and the subsequent pursuit of self-interest), but asserts that even the self-interested state will recognize the lasting benefits of cooperation. Following arguments derived from game theory models such as the Prisoners' Dilemma, it is argued that cooperation avoids outcomes which are 'suboptimal', that is situations in which states will be worse off owing to their neglect of mutual agreement. Organizations offer the means to formalize and facilitate such cooperation in world politics.

International organizations also address structural obstacles to cooperation. With regard to the problem of cheating, for instance, this can be deterred by, first, establishing punishment regimes for transgressors and rewards for cooperative states, and second, by creating expectations that the benefits of future cooperation will be jeopardized if a state seeks unilateral advantage. As for the relative gains dilemma, organizations help overcome this by facilitating an environment of security among states which encourages them to focus on 'absolute gains'. In such a setting, states measure success in terms of their own returns, and not whether their gains are greater or less than those of other states. This allows them to cooperate even in the knowledge that they will not be the only or the greatest beneficiary of cooperation (Stein, 1990, pp. 115–17). Moreover, in a world which has become increasingly interconnected, states are thrown together in a ever greater number of institutional arrangements. Some are entirely without controversy (the Universal Postal Union), while some are slightly more contentious (the IMF and the WTO). Whatever, membership creates a habit of institutionalized contact between states that leads to an awareness that their own interests need not be at odds with those of others. International organizations thus become the vehicles for the pursuit of common concerns and states learn to take the interests of others into account when framing their own policies; they become 'joint-maximizers rather than self-maximizers' (Stein, 1990, p. 53). In sum, states recognize the utility of international organizations and are prepared to invest substantial material resources in them. If not, how else would one explain the longevity and indeed the strengthening of bodies such as the EU, NATO and the WTO? (Keohane and Anderson, 1995, p. 40).

Despite the divergences of opinion within the debate on international organizations, both the neo-realist and the neo-liberal accounts are premised on a core assumption: that the state has an inherent usefulness, either as the vehicle of a self-defining interest or as the basic unit of international cooperation. The same cannot be said for a third, more radical view, the so-called 'global governance' perspective. This confronts the state head on, arguing that it is an inadequate and even counter-productive tool for tackling the plethora of problems – ranging from AIDS, ecological catastrophe and mass poverty to nuclear proliferation and the population explosion – that face the globe at the end of the twentieth century. Since these problems cut across states, they can only be resolved through more directed international cooperation and a fundamental reallocation of state sovereignty and responsibilities. An effective structure of global governance is consequently seen as necessary. This should be anchored in international law and a strengthened United Nations system and ought gradually to 'displac(e) the state as central actor on the world political stage' (Falk, 1995, pp. 79–103).

Many have discounted the claims of global governance. States have proven extremely reluctant to hand over sovereignty under any guise. When it has occurred – for instance, in a limited form within the EU – it has been a luxury of the established, wealthy states. Governments of the weaker states by contrast regard sovereignty as virtually the only protection of their status and would be loath to surrender it to some remotely accountable global structure dominated by the established Western states (Jackson, 1990, pp. 175–6). Such criticisms are not to say that structures of global governance are totally absent (as well as the UN, one could point to other bodies with a global role such as the IMF and the WTO), but these are deficient in the greater legitimacy that still attaches to the state.

Statehood and Contemporary World Politics

At a time of considerable turbulence in the international system it is hardly surprising that the state should be an object of some controversy. In this final section we will consider two perspectives on the future of the state.

First, many have claimed that the state, if not dead, has at least reached the age of retirement (Mann, 1993, p. 115). In the face of urgent global problems and the influence of non-state actors, the state is seen as increasingly anachronistic and insufficient. In much of the Third World, statehood has either a 'quasi' nature or has failed entirely, while in the more economically developed areas of the globe, it is becoming an increasingly irrelevant concept amidst the interconnectedness of economic, cultural and political life, and the consequent drive toward tighter organized international cooperation. While none of these developments is entirely new, and the demise of the state has been heralded more than once before (Dyson, 1980, pp. 282–7) there is a perception that in recent years something of a different order has occurred. Rapid changes in the structure of the international economy, the dramatic pace of advances in technology and communication, the rise of nationalism, and the end of the Cold War – all have challenged the pre-eminence of the state (Horsman and Marshall, 1995, pp. ix–xx).

Yet amidst this turmoil, the state continues to survive and even prosper. In contrast to a view of an embattled state, others have argued the case that it remains both a vital and essential part of the international system. Barry Buzan for one has claimed that '(f)or all its limitations, the sovereign territorial state seems to have no serious challengers as the organizing principle for the political life of humankind. Decolonization has made it virtually universal, and it remains the aspiration of almost every remaining group that is rebelling against the existing structure of power and authority'(Buzan, 1995, p. 392). Robert Jackson and Alan James have suggested similarly that sovereign statehood remains 'the fundamental way in which the world is politically organised' (Jackson and James, 1993, p. 6).

This more sanguine view is rooted in a perception that there exists no real alternative to the state, both as the ordering unit of the international system and as the framework for domestic governance. Most issues around the world tend to be conceived of in state terms. Granted, many do elicit an international involvement, but for every instance of this type there are many, many more in which the state concerned is considered to be the primary agent for action. Squatter camps around Soweto are South Africa's problem, the pollution of Lake Baikal is Russia's problem, and the congestion on Britain's roads is Britain's problem (Murphy, 1994, p. 212).

The state, moreover, can be seen as something more than simply a passive onlooker of global transformation. States, it is argued, have proven adept at channelling many of the forces noted above. Take for instance one of the more pervasive, that of economic globalization. While it would be true to say that in this regard the responsiveness of states may vary (there is a world of difference between the capacity of, say, the US and the poor states of Africa), all are nonetheless privileged to some degree by virtue of the right to sovereign jurisdiction over their domestic sphere. This is not to argue that a state can totally resist the world outside or that it can operate with a limitless menu of policy choices. However, some scope for action still exists. States can tax, regulate, deny access, license; in sum, they 'set the basic rules and define the environment' (Krasner, 1995, p. 279) in which transnational economic forces must operate. Indeed, when properly harnessed many states can actually benefit from these forces. Consider two rather different examples. First, Angola, a state that has been able to finance a civil war of some two decades' duration, partly as a result of tax revenues collected from Western oil companies. And second, Japan, a state that has exploited the desire of foreign companies to win access to its markets by requiring that they transfer valuable technologies to home firms, a stipulation that has helped in the development of world-beating, technologically advanced industries (Krasner, 1995, pp. 273–4).

The true picture of contemporary statehood is probably less clear-cut than the two alternatives outlined in this section suggest. Indeed, to juxtapose them in this rather bald fashion underplays the complexity of the processes at work. It is entirely feasible to argue that the state, in James Rosenau's phrase, is both 'widening and withering' simultaneously (Rosenau, 1988, p. 32). Its competencies have been fatally weakened in some areas, but in others it remains pre-eminent. To observe a diminution of state power in certain instances need not lead to the conclusion that the state in general is in decline. Similarly, one should not extrapolate a general crisis of statehood from specific cases of state failure and collapse. States rise and fall, but nowhere has the form itself been placed in abeyance as a preferred means of political organization. In sum, then, what appears crucial is the remarkable ability of the state as an institution to adapt and to survive (Jackson and James, 1993, p. 25).

Guide to Further Reading

Owing to its centrality in discussions of world politics, the concept of the state has given rise to an enormous and diverse literature. A good starting point is the collections edited by Navari (1991) and Jackson and James (1993). On the state system in international relations, the classic text is Hedley Bull's (1977). Berridge (1992, chapters 1–4) and Hocking and Smith (1995, chapters 4–5) meanwhile provide useful outlines. Discussions of statehood and sovereignty can be found in Hinsley (1966) and James (1987).

An issue that has given rise to much recent debate is the position of the state in the post-Cold War order. This is treated at length in an eclectic collection edited by Sakamoto (1995). The book by Horsman and Marshall (1995) is also worth reading. The state's relationship to international organizations is also the subject of controversy. The articles by Meirsheimer, (1994–5), and Keohane and Anderson (1995) provide a flavour of the debate.

3

Trade, Money and Markets

ALAN RUSSELL

In the mid-1990s, the best estimates put the amount of foreign exchange dealing across national borders, around the world, at about $1.3 trillion daily (The Economist, 1995a, p. 12). In contrast, total government foreign reserve holdings – the money by which governments enter the game of market speculation and intervention – rested at less than the equivalent of two days of this turnover in the foreign exchange market (Walter, 1993, p. 199) and totalled around $640 billion for the rich industrial countries (*The Economist*, 1995a, p. 12). The capacity for this market to create targeted runs on particular currencies is thus fearsome. In late 1987 the dollar plummeted by some 14 per cent in just over three months following loss of confidence in international money markets (Spero, 1990, p. 62). On 16 September 1992 the British Chancellor of the Exchequer authorized the spending of more than one-third of Britain's total foreign currency reserves in a rearguard action in the face of a market-led assault on the pound. By the end of what became known as 'Black Wednesday' the policy had failed and the Quantum fund run by George Soros was $1 billion in profit. Two things stand out. When it comes to international monetary issues, national economies are highly interdependent with each other and vulnerable to the foreign exchange market. Because of this, individual governments face a loss of control over the economic destiny of their countries.

In 1944, the world witnessed the birth of the so-called 'Bretton Woods' economic order. It encompassed the International Monetary Fund (IMF) and the World Bank. Fear of a return to the economic disorder of the 1930s spurred internationally agreed action to address the issues of international currency management and post-war reconstruction. The subsequent Marshall Aid plan for Europe speeded these objectives along, and the success of these initiatives has long been recognized. But in one area there was dismal failure. The planned third organization, the International Trade Organization, was stillborn. Such is the political sensitivity of trade that it took until December 1993 to achieve agreement on a World Trade Organization (WTO). Forty-five years in the making and, in the event, the WTO was finally agreed on the very last day of the Uruguay Round negotiations – themselves of seven years' duration! Again two things stand out. As with international money, interdependence characterizes trade relations. From the perspective of governments, the very issue of economic control over trade gets to the heart of the politics of trade. However, at a crude nationalist level, governments might prefer to maximize their nation's gains from trade at the expense of their national competitors. Where competitiveness is insufficient the alternative may be deliberate intervention to distort markets.

Both trade and international monetary issues suggest interdependence between countries of the world – an interdependence generally considered to be increasing. Moreover, because stable monetary relations are designed to assist trade, and disruptions to trade can seriously affect exchange rates, money and trade are also interdependent. Taking the interplay of forces evident between economic and political systems and between domestic and international levels it is possible to identify a range of linked issues. The key to understanding these linkages is the concept of interdependence.

Economic Interdependence: A Set of Issues

Interdependence is a difficult concept – but a very important one. It refers to the many types of connections between countries around the world. Such connections include: economic links of all kinds; the movement of people across borders; cultural linkages; almost all forms of communication; shared international concerns for issues like the environment, human rights, technological advance and health improvement; and the rapid growth in the number and range of international organizations. Connections between countries have increased dramatically over the course of the twentieth century, largely due to technological advance – with decreasing communications times heralding an associated image of a shrinking world. Yet, interdependence is more than simply the growth in connections, important as they are in themselves.

Interdependence means that economies, societies and governments are affected by events beyond national borders – events which may have origins within the borders of other countries. Strictly speaking, this would imply *dependence*. However, because such effects travel both ways we talk of *inter*dependence. In other words, all societies and economies are potentially influenced, in this fashion, by all others. In reality, it may be more sensible to confine images of interdependence to links among industrially developed states or regional groups of such states. There is a strong case for arguing that less developed countries are *dependent* on the industrialized world. Here, the two-way street is not so evident. Another way of seeing interdependence, again suggesting its two-way nature, is by defining it as *mutual dependence* (Keohane and Nye, 1977, p. 8). The great merit of this latter definition is that it suggests that interdependence can entail national costs inasmuch as future destiny is shaped through external dependence – although, of course, national influence may be extended internationally in issue areas where dependence is reversed.

Especially significant has been the growth of economic connections which generate interdependence. The chaos of the 1930s, when the Great Depression spread like a disease through the Western world, was a manifestation of *economic interdependence*. Lengthening dole queues and resurgent protectionism sent powerful signals to governments about how much their economic prosperity was intertwined. Where the then-new Keynesian economic theory advocated governments intervening in their domestic economies to manage them, it provided simultaneously a rationale to consider *collective* management of economic interdependence at the international level. The post-war Bretton Woods institutions were the pragmatic response. Growth and prosperity were recognized as dependent on international trade, and a suitable economic environment for trade was believed to require a stable international monetary order.

International monetary stability – eventually based on a fixed exchange rate system – was the cornerstone of Western post-war prosperity. But it came at a cost. Each government within the system was faced with a trade-off. They had to abide by the rules of international stability at the cost of a loss of independence in the realm of domestic economic management. Collective management of interdependence was not politically neutral. When governments had to make efforts to ensure their balance of payments balanced, they found that this could compromise preferred economic policies at home. Reducing imports and increasing exports, to avoid a balance of payments deficit, usually meant a government taking measures to affect domestic economic prices, a move that could be unpopular at home if the intervention increased the cost of popular imports and lowered the cost of exports, perhaps with an associated rise in unemployment.

Governments have responded to the problems and potentialities of interdependence in a variety of ways. International institutional arrangements such as those of the Bretton Woods organizations are one response. Other responses which encourage interdependence included deregulating monetary movements, encouraging free trade and promoting cross-investment between economies. Despite such positive measures, which help foster economic interdependence, governments have shown willingness to manipulate circumstances of interdependence to their state's advantage and have rarely held back from using political influence for economic advantage.

The Scope and Intensity of Economic Interdependence

The scope and intensity of important issues derived from inter-dependence can now be considered. The first issue is judging the extent to which interdependence amongst a group of countries is equally reciprocal. If there is significant bias in the relationship then we can talk of *asymmetric* interdependence, a situation which can extend to the political relationships between nations. In the post-war example of the dominance, or even hegemony, of the United States in the Western world, there was clear asymmetry. At the end of the Second World War, the US accounted for around 40 per cent of the world's total economic output (expressed as Gross National Product). It has remained between 20–25 per cent since the start of the 1970s (Huntington, 1988; Strange, 1994, p. 238). In other words, the world economy does not comprise a set of equally important economies.

Nevertheless, the concept of interdependence is still useful. The United States economy may not be as dependent on the Mexican economy as the latter is on the United States economy, but the United States economy is dependent for markets on the other economies collectively. It is easy to fall into a trap of seeing interdependence as if it should only apply to pairs of states: the US and Japan; France and Germany, and so on. The world economy has many national economies with economic connections creating a web of links across the globe. Yet, asymmetries do exist and often lead to political debate over particular bi-lateral links.

A second issue to consider is the extent to which economic interdependence is encouraging a process of globalization. In the words of the song, 'money makes the world go round'. Financial markets allowing the trading of currency and other capital assets have become global. Technology and policies of deregulation have enabled the traditionally important financial markets, such as those of London, New York and Tokyo to become linked through information technologies, effectively allowing twenty-four-hour 'real time', if impersonal, trading. This has heightened international concern over the stability of foreign exchange markets (Walter, 1993). Tremors in one money market could spread rapidly to others, perhaps leading to volatility in national interest-rate policies and volatility in business links across borders. The sheer size of the pool of liquid assets available to the private sector is constantly in the minds of national policy-makers. The consequence has been growing pressure for the world's leading economies to coordinate their economic policies in such a fashion that there is avoidance of excessive divergence in interest rates or inflation rates, bringing some measure of greater certainty in money markets. Unfortunately, as we shall see, the politics of reaching such agreements on coordination have dogged recent meetings of the Group of Seven industrial nations (G7).

Globalization is also evident in the changing nature of production, with fundamental implications for the ways in which we view trade. One author has described a set of changes in the pattern of international production as a 'global shift' (Dicken, 1992). In the nineteenth century, the industrialization of much of the world proceeded with a corresponding growth in trade between national economies. Then, especially since the end of the Second World War, the world has witnessed an immense growth in big firms setting up production operations outside their home economy (creating what is called *foreign direct investment* – FDI). Rather than produce goods at home and then export them, the economics of competition encouraged multinational corporations (MNCs) to take their expertise in production nearer to the foreign markets in which they sold. In particular, highly efficient US firms were in the vanguard (Vernon, 1971).

By the late 1960s, the average number of new foreign subsidiaries being set up was running at ten times the rate of increase in the 1920s, and up until the mid-1970s, US firms accounted for nearly 50 per cent of the total of this foreign direct investment (FDI) (Dicken, 1992, pp. 51–2). The global shift has been to a new development on top of this. It is no longer just the big companies that operate with an international outlook. Globalization in production has brought even small firms to consider their operations in relation to selling in a global market rather than in a national one. Trade is decreasingly an 'arm's length' phenomenon between separate economies. Today it is effectively impossible to quantify real figures for trade, as around half the trade for some industrial countries takes place within the operations of single firms – in other words, subsidiaries of a single firm 'trade' with each other, across national borders, in an activity described as *intra-firm* trade. In addition some three-quarters of all trade by the mid-1980s was conducted within or by multinational companies (Dunning, 1993). Consequently, there has been a relative decline in the percentage of world FDI originating in the United States as the new production links become more global and others have jumped on the bandwagon, including the vibrant economies of South East Asia.

Once again, a significant driving force for the changes in the nature of production is technological innovation. Where Henry Ford's production line set the precedent for exploiting economies of scale through the mass production of near-identical units, in his case automobiles, technology is bringing a startling transformation. High technology and very adaptable production lines are allowing much smaller batches of units with differing characteristics to be produced, without expensive re-tooling. Information technologies guide the production process in an adaptive fashion. Ultimately car production is heading towards 'just in time' methods, whereby the customer enters a showroom, chooses the colour (old Henry Ford would have none of that!) and the specification, all of which the sales person enters into a terminal and the car is manufactured that afternoon.

Globalization can also be seen in the way many firms now market their goods around the world. Marketing strategies have begun to exploit the growing similarity of tastes in many nations. Brand images are used to achieve recognition and identity with a product the world over (Frieden and Lake, 1991, p. 143). Thus Coca Cola 'and McDonalds are commonplace in many countries, including the former Eastern bloc and the developing world (Gill and Law, 1988, p. 61). Automobile manufacturers have turned to using names for their cars that are either recognizable in many languages, or invented and not found in any. Strange but partly familiar words like 'Mondeo', 'Vectra' or 'Laguna' have resulted. The entertainments industry sees the outpourings of Hollywood and the popular music industry eroding cultural differences. The push for common brands and marketing strategies is reinforced by what Robert Cox has described as an emerging transnational management class bonded by a shared image across borders of how business is done and how people train for this world – a culture promoted the world over by prestigious business schools and management training programmes (Cox, 1987, p. 359).

The third issue, in contrast, is the possibility that economic interdependence is at the heart of a recent resurgence in regionalism (see also Chapter 4). If globalization is adding to pressures which erode the borders of national economies, then it raises interesting questions about a growing trend towards regional links between states. For some regions, such as Europe and North America, the characteristics of the overall process of globalization are reflected regionally. There is, for example, considerable economic interdependence in Western Europe and much intra-firm activity encouraged by the Single Market and the institutions of the European Union. Coordination of monetary policy is common practice and a declared intention of the European Union is to establish a single European currency. Moreover, the problems thrown up by the politics of trade and globalization may be more easily managed at a level of regional governmental cooperation rather than in forums such as G7 (Hurrell, 1995). Whatever the relationship with globalization the evidence seems to be suggesting an increase in regional links (Taylor, 1993). Western Europe has long been a focus of policy which has attempted to enhance interdependence in a managed fashion, delivering a process of economic and political integration. Other regions have also shown more awareness of the importance of regional ties, with the establishment of the North American Free Trade Association (NAFTA) and the Asia-Pacific Economic Cooperation forum (APEC) being particularly noteworthy.

A last issue to consider is how we go about understanding the way the global political economy works: this will involve utilizing theoretical approaches. Further, in our search for understanding it is necessary to realize that the policy-makers of the world themselves are applying their own ideological bias – and this in turn affects our perspectives as analysts. Students of International Political Economy (IPE) have identified three broad analytical perspectives applicable to the study. The most established and widespread view, often claimed as the guiding viewpoint in government policy circles and international economic institutions, is the *liberal* perspective. This centres on the ideals of open markets and pluralist democratic political systems. Markets, therefore, are seen to create and distribute economic wealth. Government intervention in markets is modest, with the state tending towards a hands-off approach. The liberal viewpoint in general welcomes the growth of economic interdependence.

A second perspective is associated with *Marxist* views of class conflicts and the spread of global dependence, whereby poorer states of the world are seen to be locked into a relationship with the industrial word characterized as one of dominance and dependence. The FDI activities of large firms have been a particular focus, with attention drawn to their ability to exploit poor economies and to repatriate profits to their home economies (Hymer, 1972). The third perspective focuses on *economic nationalism* (Gilpin, 1987), whereby governments are seen to act to promote the interests of their home economies at the expense of others. Subtle and sometimes very unsubtle measures may be taken to protect areas of important economic activity, including the use of tariffs and quotas, orderly market arrangements, voluntary export restraints and restrictive national standards. Economic nationalism may at times better characterize government attitudes even when they profess to be following liberal principles. From a national perspective, it may be fortuituous if other countries follow policies of economic openness at a time when one's own country is able to avoid economic penetration by others – the basis of many complaints against Japan.

Differences in these perspectives or ideologies (Gilpin, 1987) go to the heart of assessments of the role of markets and the ability of states to manipulate them. The former British Prime Minister Margaret Thatcher once said 'you can't buck the market'. Markets are undoubtedly viewed as powerful distributive phenomena by all of the perspectives. Differences between the perspectives revolve around perceived abilities to shape markets politically – or alternatively, for markets to drive the political domain. Two influential texts summarize the nature of international political economy, in terms of 'states *and* markets' (Strange, 1994) or 'states *versus* markets' (Schwartz, 1994). Capitalism in the late twentieth century, with the collapse of the communist Eastern bloc, is all but supreme as the organizing mode of production the world over. However, capitalism and the global market are host to a range of influential actors: not least the state, the transnational corporation and national big businesses, international finance organizations, labour organizations and a myriad of small businesses. They span monetary, trade, production and investment activities. Whether intentionally or not, their actions also have political consequences.

Thus we face a global economy of high interdependence in monetary, trade and production activities. Understanding the associated issues draws us into attempting to understand a changing environment of political and economic interactions. The impact of interdependence and globalization may ultimately be so far-reaching that the sovereign state may become increasingly anachronistic in the face of regional developments and new and powerful forces of transnational production and money movements.

General Problems of Economic Interdependence

The specific form of issues of interdependence may change but they tend to be symptomatic of a set of general problems. These can be examined under the following headings.

Trade problems

Interdependence in trade has brought a set of general problems underlying many present issues. A fundamental problem is the international agreement of principles. The differing perspectives of international political economy can result in alternative sets of principles. However, membership of the WTO implies a degree of acceptance that trade operates best with minimal governmental intervention, with reciprocity and the gradual reduction of all barriers to trade. Such principles represent a dominance of the liberal perspective. Associated problems include ensuring compliance with these principles, the resolution of disputes over protectionist practices and the inclusion within the set of principles of controversial areas such as agricultural trade. Nevertheless, trade conflicts keep recurring.

Trade conflicts between the United States and Japan, for example, have often been the subject of media headlines, with the United States Congress from time to time threatening economic retaliation against Japan because of the difficulties of penetrating the Japanese market while the United States appears open to Japanese trade and FDI. When the US trade deficit reached $160 billion in the 1980s, some 37 per cent of this was with Japan (Balaam and Veseth, 1996). Even the popular author Tom Clancy has managed to weave a tale of military conflict between the United States and Japan with origins in trade and financial disputes (Clancy, 1994). The European Union has also found itself in trade disputes with the United States, particularly over agriculture. As a consequence, the Uruguay Round trade agreements (see below) required the Europeans to reduce subsidies on agricultural exports by 36 per cent.

International monetary problems

Once again there is a key problem of agreeing principles. International monetary stability, as a principle, may be agreed internationally but there are still disagreements regarding the relative merits of fixed or floating exchange rate systems and the means to manage or police any agreements. Fixed rates have often, in the past, been seen as preferable but with acknowledgement of a problem of a trade-off between the needs of international economic stability and domestic autonomy. Moreover, this trade-off did not apply equally to all states. In the post-war period the power of the United States economy, supported by the role of the dollar as an international reserve currency, ensured that the US could avoid many of the distasteful costs at the domestic level. Indeed, the US deliberately ran a balance of payments deficit to encourage the spread of dollars around the world.

Ultimately the United States' trading partners objected to this US immunity from politically sensitive domestic costs – an immunity gained at their collective expense. Some writers, however, have argued that such a dominant economic and political leader – a *hegemon* – is necessary in order to ensure that all countries abide by the agreed principles and thus maintain stability (Gilpin, 1987, pp. 72–80). Provided the hegemon is seen as 'benign' then its leadership may be collectively recognized and supported. Misuse of its position, an accusation increasingly made against the United States by the early 1970s, may lead to a decline in authority. The whole issue of hegemonic leadership as a means of stabilizing the international economic environment has become quite controversial. Its continued relevance lies in the uncertainties and instabilities that have followed the collapse of post-war Bretton Woods arrangements with a move to floating exchange rates and high levels of market dealings in currencies. The problem has become one of what level of international management is now possible and who should undertake it.

Global production problems

The globalization of production has added to the range of problems associated with economic interdependence. Trends towards production patterns associated with post-Fordist and 'just in time' methods, which avoid the need for huge inventories (such as completed cars sitting in huge car parks awaiting purchase), has meant the 'networking' of component suppliers together. This networking does not stop at national borders. Whatever the technical nature of individual production lines *per se*, there has nevertheless been a widespread increase in cross-border acquisitions and mergers since the 1980s which, combined with less formal links, is blurring the borders of firms as well as the borders of countries (Dunning, 1993; Badaracco, 1991). We thus witness a growing global interdependence between companies evident in intra-firm and intra-industry trade. Such developments of networked links between the businesses of the world, combined with innovations in decentralized decision-making – again cutting across borders – led Robert Reich (1990) to ask the pertinent question of the control of US domestic production activities: 'Who is US?' In other words, if a state is to take action to promote its national economic welfare, it may find itself encouraging foreign-owned firms that provide jobs and investment in its economy in preference to its nationally owned firms that may be more busy beyond its borders, thus assisting employment in foreign countries.

General problems

Taken together there is a general trend towards increased economic interdependence across many areas of economic activity. This has raised complex issues in each case. The changes involved reflect some general problems. In particular there is the question of the autonomy and independence of individual countries. If monetary stability requires high levels of policy coordination, and if trade arrangements require complex negotiations and agreements, and global production methods entail the opening of borders to cross-investment, then economic and political independence is severely challenged. The global context is emphasized, with national borders being simply less important – leading to the popularization of images of a 'borderless world' of high technology communications. In the words of Peter Dicken:

> National borders no longer act as 'watertight containers' of the production process. Rather, they are more like sieves through which extensive leakage occurs. The implications are far reaching. Each one of us is now more fully involved in a *global* economic system than were our parents and grandparents. Few if any industries now have much 'natural protection' from international competition whereas in the past, of course, geographical distance created a strong insulating effect. Today, in contrast, fewer and fewer industries are oriented towards local, regional or even national markets. A growing number of economic activities have meaning only in a global context. (Dicken, 1992, p. 4)

In sum, the most significant effect of this process of globalization is the loss of national independence for states. Governments simply cannot keep track of the complex web of cross-investment that has grown between developed countries and increasingly with developing countries. Intra-firm and intra-industry activities, the movement of financial resources globally, and the general growth of economic uncertainty taxes the abilities of governments to respond. Such is the importance of this interdependence in the calculus of competitiveness that governments have been actively engaged in the liberalization of markets and, in Europe, governments compete to offer the best deals to encourage FDI from Japan and the Asian 'tigers'. The eminent professor of international business, John Dunning, observes:

> In a variety of ways, and to achieve many diverse objectives, governments are increasingly taking actions which, taken as a whole, have repercussions on the competitiveness of markets . . . far in excess of anything that the kind of industrial policies of the 1970s, and which are so much an anathema to right-wing politicians, ever achieved. (Dunning, 1993, p. 326)

Putting Issues of Economic Interdependence on the International Agenda

Part of the character of a transnational, interdependent world political and economic system is the politics of agenda-setting itself. The complexity of economic interdependence gives rise to efforts by many actors to bring issues to international attention and to resolve politically a wide variety of problems. In this respect, Stopford and Strange have highlighted the 'new diplomacy' evident between states and firms (1991). The new diplomacy represents a growing recognition that governments must negotiate with firms as well as other governments, and that firms have also 'become more statesmanlike as they seek corporate alliances, permanent, partial or temporary, to enhance their combined capacities to compete with others for world market shares' (Stopford and Strange, 1991, p. 2). The determination of items for the global agenda can be taken under the following categories.

Government to government issues

Under this category there are high profile issues such as reciprocity in trade, agricultural subsidies, trade protectionism, international intellectual property recognition, trade in services, and strategic trade policies – all of these being key issues within the Uruguay Round trade talks held under the auspices of the General Agreement on Tariffs and Trade (GATT). Governments have also negotiated over mutually sensitive or coordinated monetary policies – a constant issue for G7 meetings and inter-governmental relations within the European Union. Governmental relations between the industrial world and less industrialized countries have in addition included issues of foreign aid, loans, credits and debt, regulation of MNC activity, and access to and protection of resources. Such dialogue between countries is paralleled by traditional inter-state processes such as diplomacy and political negotiations. For the economic nationalist the links between the political and economic areas may in any case be very close.

Government to firm issues

Under this heading, agenda issues include enticements to invest, commercial 'sweeteners', government contracts, subsidies, bribery, protection, technology transfers, transfer pricing, financial market activities, repatriation of profits, environmental sensitivity and development. However, government–firm relationships vary tremendously. Relations with the government of an MNC's home state can be quite different from a possibly more adversarial relationship with foreign host governments. Past activities of some multinationals brought considerable bad press to MNCs, eventually leading to the United Nations and the Organization for Economic Cooperation and Development (OECD) exploring means to set standards of acceptable behaviour for MNCs. Today the situation is less hostile with many governments competing to attract inward investment from MNCs.

In a similar fashion, governments are locked into a complex relationship with the international private sector in financial markets. While tumultuous events like the run on the dollar in 1987 and on sterling in 1992 during 'Black Wednesday' bear witness to government failures, governments still have their influence. At a minimum they have two significant weapons. The first is the ability to manipulate their national interest rates, at least in the short term – a powerful instrument given that it is interest rate differences that primarily encourage the trade in currencies in foreign exchange markets. If governments are reluctant to interfere with interest rates, they have a second weapon. They can themselves become players in the foreign exchange markets, buying and selling currencies, including their own, in order to influence relative prices. Both weapons tend to be reinforced by a psychological game of trying to influence the expectations of the market. It has to be said that the British government used both weapons to no avail on Black Wednesday, when the overriding objective was to hold sterling at a particular value commensurate with it remaining in the fixed European Exchange Rate Mechanism (ERM). The psychological game was also played and lost, as the Chancellor of the Exchequer threatened to raise interest rates by a total of 5 per cent and was simply not believed! Further witness to the difficulties was evident in the bond-market crash in industrial countries in 1994 and the Mexican bail-out of 1995. Recognition of the general problem led the liberal publication *The Economist* to ask in late 1995, 'Who's in the Driving Seat?' (*The Economist*, 1995b).

Firm to firm issues

Under this heading we see corporate alliances, mergers, acquisitions, market sharing and price setting, subcontracting, and joint representations in dealing with governments. The global linkages between firms are changing as we have seen. With complex patterns of sub-contracting and alliances within industries becoming more significant, linkages appear to ignore national borders. With this internationalizing of production, firms have demanded more sensitivity within governmental circles to their collective requirements.

One response to this has been witnessed in the rush to deregulate in the 1980s. The apparent international agenda of liberalization and general removal of restrictions to trade and cross-investment over borders, with greater tolerance of intra-firm and intra-industry trade, was partly encouraged by the activities of large companies. In some respects the changes would level the cross-border playing field for medium-sized and smaller firms which lacked the capacity for intra-firm trade displayed by the larger MNCs. The problem was that the big firms could avoid the constraints of national economic policies by their intra-firm activities where smaller firms could not (Gill and Law, 1988, p. 175). For example, if a country put its interest rates up, a small firm borrowing money to expand faced a higher cost of doing so. In contrast a big MNC could raise the money abroad at lower interest rates and transfer it to the country in which it wished to expand, by internal transfer pricing, thus avoiding the effects of the interest rate increase and in the process getting around national exchange controls. Of course, the reduction of restrictions and levelling of the playing field, in recognition of the growing demands of cross-investment and trading in global markets, has been at the expense of national economic autonomy.

Setting the international economic agenda is no longer something confined to governments (if ever it was), yet inter-governmental negotiations must never be underestimated. They have been of great importance in the likes of GATT negotiating rounds, G7 meetings, forums such as the IMF and World Bank, and in more controversial organizations such as the United Nations Conference on Trade and Development (UNCTAD) and the United Nations Industrial Development Organization (UNIDO). However, intergovernmental agenda-setting is shaped within a broader environment of many economic actors clamouring for a say, either by pressurizing their home or host governments, or through the development of new and often unstoppable trends in their operations.

Economic Interdependence and the End of the Cold War

While international economic issues had gradually been coming more to the fore since the 1960s, the end of the Cold War consolidated their importance. Moreover, a central characteristic of the end of that conflict has been the efforts of the former Eastern bloc countries (including Russia in some measure) to transform themselves into democratic market economies. The ideological split which helped characterize the Cold War was itself founded on radically different world views at the level of international political economy. The apparent 'victory' of Western ideology and practice, encompassed in the democratic market economy, over Marxist-inspired central economic planning is part of what we define as the 'end of the Cold War'. Thus, high levels of economic interdependence have come to characterize relations in the West while the former Eastern bloc is now striving to embrace this very system of economic interdependence. Cold War politics have given way to Western efforts to assist that transformation by encouraging linkages in trade, finance and production. Not least, large-scale loans are involved. At stake is the avoidance of a return to conflict with a potentially isolated Russia.

For some former Eastern bloc states, the escape from the shackles of Communist rule in 1989 was a culmination of popular will to 'rejoin the West' (Batt, 1991, p. 104). In 1938, only 10 per cent of East European exports (including the Soviet Union) went to other Eastern countries while 68 per cent went to West Europe and 4 per cent to North America. Some 15 years later, in 1953, a low point of isolation was reached with 64 per cent of East European exports now remaining in the East, only 14 per cent heading to West Europe and less than 1 per cent to all of the Americas. Import patterns were similar (Spero, 1990, p. 307). However, any economic 'return' to the West would not simply mean a return to the arm's-length trading of the pre-war years (Kearns, 1996, p. 55). While the East remained locked in a timewarp of central planning, the West, as we have seen, moved on and on. A partial cause of the collapse in the East was undoubtedly the inability of those countries to remain at high levels of economic isolation from the West. From the early 1970s trading links and later financial links grew steadily. Strangely, the globalization of production and financial markets now offers both assistance and challenges for the East in their efforts to rejoin the West.

Challenges have included overcoming the lack of stock exchanges and capital markets, privatization of the vast range of government-owned enterprises, relaxing exchange controls, capping inflation, reducing heavy state expenditure, modernizing banking systems and re-creating a culture in tune with capitalism (Rollo *et al.*, 1990). A fundamental problem was the general lack of competitiveness in industrial and commercial activity compared with the West and the relatively low quality of East European goods. The transformation of this situation was to take place in parallel with the establishment of democratic political systems. By any criteria, the changes involved were of huge magnitude.

The forced interdependence of trade between countries within the former Eastern bloc has had to be replaced with a more general establishment of connections with the global economy. The problem for the East and Central European economies was the risk of profound asymmetries in the new connections, suggesting more a situation of dependence than interdependence. Moreover, another form of asymmetry saw Hungary attract nearly half the $18 billion of foreign investment which went eastwards between 1989 and 1995

(*The Economist*, 1995b, p. 12). Yet, at the same time, it has been essential for the former Eastern bloc to attract capital and productivity investment from the West. In this way, the very ability of investment (financial and physical) to move across borders, so characteristic of the global economy, is important in returning the East and Central European economies to the fold. In this way, the financial markets of the West and their firms' capacity for foreign direct investment could help the modernization process. Of course, Western governments and the global economic institutions have a role to play as well: providing loans and credit; transferring technical knowledge and offering policy advice; and generally encouraging the reform process. At the political level the Western governments have encouraged links with NATO, the European Union and other institutions.

Generally the pace of change to the mid-1990s was uneven across the former Eastern bloc countries. Hungary led the field, but was not without its own problems. Of the important countries Russia lagged behind. Privatization programmes everywhere suffered through a lack of accumulated capital in private hands. FDI – a key to embracing the global economy – triggered the following dilemma:

> although Central European countries desperately need foreign capital, their revived sense of identity arouses nationalist qualms about being bought out by foreigners. Poland and Slovenia in effect ban outsiders from owning land. (*The Economist*, 1995b, p. 27)

The issue of economic interdependence thus gained new momentum as a result of the end of the Cold War. First, the relative decline of the high politics issue of security and East–West stability gave added emphasis to the general rise of issues of international political economy. Second, the pattern of economic globalization itself extended eastwards, albeit in an uneven fashion. Third, there was an agenda within Western governments and former Eastern bloc governments actively to encourage the fostering of economic interdependence as a basis to lock-in the process of transformation and to avoid any return to the Cold War. In this respect even Russia received huge IMF loans for economic reform and was invited to join G7 meetings. Fourth, the Central European countries saw economic interdependence as a basis for joining the general European process of integration centred on the European Union and its enlargement. Joining the NATO Partnership for Peace initiative reinforced the overall return to the West. Fifth, with the decline of a Cold War focus on Europe, more attention came to rest on other parts of the world, such as South East Asia and China. In the latter case, even the human rights violations of Tiananmen Square (1989) were soon being forgotten as the realities of economic interdependence with the rapidly growing Chinese economy took hold.

Managing Global Economic Interdependence

As there is no single issue involved in economic interdependence there are various international institutions active. The established institutions of the Bretton Woods system (the IMF and World Bank) have been joined by the new World Trade Organization (which subsumes GATT). Often accused of dominance by the industrially developed (predominantly Western) states, these organizations co-exist with others such as UNCTAD and UNIDO where the less developed states have more voting influence. Despite this, the key organizations remain those associated with Bretton Woods (including the WTO). In addition, G7 and the OECD play significant roles.

The IMF and the World Bank

The Bretton Woods institutions were established with the express purpose of attempting to facilitate the management of economic interdependence at a time when prevalent economic theories justified interventionism. Many of the principles of Bretton Woods were abandoned in the early 1970s leaving a period of great uncertainty. Notably the IMF lost its main role as guardian of the fixed exchange rate system as currencies were allowed to float and find their own value against each other. This effectively encouraged the huge growth in foreign exchange markets, producing figures such as those cited in the opening paragraph of this chapter. The World Bank had long ago turned its attention to the needs of developing countries following the post-war rush to independence from former colonisers. The irony is that in carving out a new role for itself, the

IMF has found its activities overlapping with the World Bank. As many developing states went further into debt with Northern banks, a crisis grew which threatened the financial system. In 1982 the crisis came to a head when Mexico announced it could no longer service its debts. Many banks were faced with the possibility of collapse. In other words, the interdependence of the situation threatened both the lenders and the creditors. The IMF stepped in with assistance designed to enable developing states heavily in debt to continue to make repayments – often by providing new loans. In return, as it also moved further into debt-related issues in the 1980s, the World Bank began to apply conditions on loans comparable to those required by the IMF. Both institutions moved to centre-stage in dealings with developing states (see also Chapter 5).

The nature of IMF and World Bank conditions has brought controversy. Both institutions have required recipients of long-term loans to meet certain conditions in their economic policies (*The Economist*, 1991; Feinberg, 1988; Williams, 1994). Generally the recipient countries have been required to undertake structural adjustments in their economies designed to make them more market based, with reduced government expenditure, less reliance on imports and with more capacity to earn foreign currency through exports. Severe social costs have resulted from some of these conditions as education, health and infrastructure provision have suffered following reduced government spending. Moreover, the repayment of loans and falling economic confidence in many developing countries has created a situation of huge amounts of money moving from the less developed world to the developed countries. Writing in 1992, Susan George estimated that for eight years from January 1982 until the end of the decade the developing world transferred $6.5 billion a month to the developed world in interest payments alone (George, 1992, p. xiv). Consequently the twin institutions have been described as more concerned with saving the Western banks than in alleviating the problem of debt. Critics have associated the institutions with a doctrinaire view of the world founded upon a market oriented, free enterprise philosophy.

The Group of Seven (G7)

G7 was viewed with some optimism in the late 1980s. With the end of the Bretton Woods order based on fixed exchange rates, new issues of interdependence were eventually recognized as requiring 'management'. The growth in foreign exchange markets, within a floating exchange rate environment, created the potential for instability in monetary relations. Following the 1985 Plaza agreement, G7 formally established procedures for policy coordination between them. In particular, there was concern over the, by then, massive US trade and budget deficits. The dollar was seen to be valued too highly by the market and hindering US export potential. G7 planned to monitor their respective economic performances and was prepared to intervene collectively in currency markets to stabilize exchange rates. It offered something of a return to the spirit of Bretton Woods with national discipline being needed for the good of international economic order. The 1987 stock market collapse and the run on the dollar shattered confidence for a time. Ironically, one contributing cause of this was the apparent lack of consensus in G7, at its Paris summit earlier that year, with respect to how much it should intervene in order to lower the value of the dollar, and by what amount. A sharp lesson was learnt and the incentive to achieve real policy coordination was temporarily renewed. A decade on, and following a new Mexican collapse in 1995, it was all but recognized that policy coordination was dead in the water and there was considerable talk in G7 meetings and elsewhere of the intention to strengthen the Bretton Woods institutions. Notably this would entail revamping the role of the IMF.

Trade organizations

The General Agreement on Tariffs and Trade (GATT) began life as an interim arrangement while the world awaited an international trade organization. With the US Congress against the ratification of the ITO, hope for the birth of the institution was lost in the early 1950s. Through this accident of history the GATT acquired a bureacracy and became an organization. It became the centrepoint of a series of international trade negotiations or 'rounds'. The most recent, the Uruguay Round, was completed on 15 December 1993, ratified by late 1994 and came into effect in early 1995. Over the years the GATT has worked under principles of liberalizing trade and, like the IMF and World Bank, has been accused of bias towards the interests of the developed world. Nevertheless, the deal reached in the Uruguay Round involved the developing states much more than any previous round and attracted widespread international support, with membership of the new World Trade Organization contingent on accepting the full Uruguay Round agreement.

The WTO has taken up the mantle of overseeing trade issues and ensuring implementation of the Uruguay Round agreement. Most significantly it has more extensive dispute settlement provisions than the GATT and extends into controversial areas newly established under the Uruguay agreement. These include much greater coverage of agriculture (a major weakness of the GATT), intellectual property protection, trade in services and foreign investment. Unlike the IMF which weights voting in accordance with economic power and allocated quotas, the WTO operates on one vote per member. This opens interesting possibilities for the developing states *vis à vis* the developed world, while the United States keenly watches out for any apparent anti-US bias in decisions and dispute settlements.

Older organizations such as the UNCTAD, host in the past to many calls from the developing countries for a new international economic order, can be expected to lose further ground against the institutions favoured by the developed world. With the establishment of the WTO and with G7 talk of strengthening the Bretton Woods institutions, it is possible that calls from some quarters for the break-up of UNCTAD might come to fruition.

At the regional level there are many organizations around the world that have issues of economic interdependence as part of, or the whole of, their brief (see Chapter 4). These include the European Union (EU), NAFTA, APEC, and the Organization of American States (OAS) amongst others. The most established of these, the EU, acted with a single voice in the negotiations leading to the Uruguay Round.

Whether regional or global, monetary or trade oriented, a key issue in any organizational effort to manage aspects of interdependence is the extent to which the big economies might dominate the decision-making. The United States is no stranger to being accused of dominance and bias. It is worth noting that NAFTA, APEC and the OAS all include the United States. The influence of Japan and Germany must also be considered as very important in various organizations. What may be most significant is that the many organizations could simply be host to growing economic rivalries if policy coordination should fail.

Economic Interdependence and Contemporary World Politics

The collective issues involved in economic interdependence raise serious questions about state sovereignty and the predominance of international politics as traditionally conceived. The activities of many other actors have encouraged the growth of interdependence and in turn have themselves been influenced by the continued increase in interdependence. Governments attempting to achieve economic and political objectives (domestically and internationally) have to give more attention to the activities and objectives of other agents: other governments; international organizations; transnational companies; banks; finance houses; and the behaviour of individuals aggregated through markets.

Economic interdependence as part of the process of globalization has given rise to a much greater complexity of linkage between societies, affecting all aspects of life, including ideology, culture, entertainment, environment, technology, wealth creation and distribution, and implicit in all of this is a growing interdependence in security questions (themselves defined more broadly than in the past). In this context politics is also becoming more transnational or globalized (Luard, 1990).

Concepts such as interdependence and dependence help us to identify issues and attempt to understand their underlying causes. Metaphors such as globalization give us images of an uncertain, but no doubt exciting future. It is a future of benefits as well as costs to most of the main actors, states included. It is a future where politics and economics at domestic and international levels will be increasingly hard to separate. It is a future where the movement of money, the globalization of production and the complexity of trade issues will remain high on the international agenda – alongside other issues such as the environment, security, human rights, religion and poverty.

Guide to Further Reading

Balaam and Veseth (1996) have produced an excellent introduction to all aspects of economic interdependence and the international political economy, covering money, trade and production as well as issues such as energy, the environment and food. Spero's (1990) text is well established as a narrative covering the politics of the post-war development of the international economy. With respect to the globalization of production, more detail and discussion of issues are provided by Dicken (1992), Dunning (1993), and Stopford and Strange (1991). For those particularly interested in monetary issues, Walter (1993) is recommended. On economic institutions in general and their relationship with the developing world, see Williams (1994). More advanced IPE texts include Strange (1994), Gill and Law (1988) and Schwartz (1994). On the development of regionalism, Taylor (1993) and Gamble and Payne (1996) are worth considering.

4

Regions and Regionalism

MICHAEL SMITH

During the 1990s, there has been a notable surge of interest and activity in both regions and regionalism. One manifestation of this has been the renewed salience of regional conflicts such as those in the Balkans and the Gulf region, or in the former Soviet Union. At the same time, there has been a sharpened awareness of the possibilities of regional cooperation and institution-building. For example, a World Trade Organization (WTO) study published in 1995 listed over one hundred regional trade arrangements, ranging from the highly developed institutional framework of the European Union to limited and often specialized agreements between three or four countries (WTO, 1995, pp. 77–91). There has also been an increasing tendency in all parts of the world to search for mechanisms of cooperation in the political and security fields: for instance, in the case of South East Asia, the Association of South East Asian Nations (ASEAN) developed in the 1990s from a loose association of countries with rather unclear regional objectives into a more elaborate and focused set of institutions with explicit aims in the political and security fields. In Latin America, there has also been a revival of the search for a regional identity in both the economic and the security fields (Hurrell, 1992).

Concern with regional patterns and with regionalism did not suddenly begin in the 1990s: it has been a focus of study and political action since the beginning of the twentieth century and, some would argue, for even longer than that. Why, then, has the concern with regionalism fluctuated, and why has it re-emerged with such force in the post-Cold War era? As already noted, regionalism is often linked very strongly with regional organization and institutions. Why do these institutions arise, how have they developed, and how do they relate to other, more global institutions? Not only this, but how do they relate to that most pervasive, if debatable institution, the nation-state? Does regionalism imply the coming together of states and their interests, or does it reflect broader forces of integration that may eventually at the level of the region undermine the predominance of the state itself?

It can be seen from this set of questions that regions and regionalism can act as a kind of 'lens' through which central issues of world politics are refracted and given particular shape. For instance, it is often argued that processes of cooperation and integration are easier at the regional level; but this can be paralleled by the awareness that regional conflicts can have a peculiar intensity and violence. Equally, it is argued by some that regionalism contributes to the broader development of global order, and in the economic sense that it can be seen as a reflection of globalization; but alongside this is often the fear that regional groupings can become introspective and protectionist in their leanings, closing themselves off from the world economy. By focusing attention on such questions at the regional level, it is possible to explore in some detail, whilst still preserving an awareness of the national and the global pictures.

Regions and Regionalism: Characteristics and Driving Forces

Many scholars have attempted to define the essential characteristics both of regions and of regionalism in world politics. The 1960s and 1970s saw a first wave of analysis, focused particularly by the regional impact of the Cold War and by the emergence of regional institutions both in Europe and in the Third World (Cantori and Spiegel, 1970; Nye, 1971; Russett, 1967). During the 1990s, as noted above, there has been renewed interest because of what has been termed 'the new regionalism' of the post-Cold War era, and this has led to further attempts at definition (Fawcett and Hurrell, 1995; Hurrell, 1995; Gamble and Payne, 1996). One of the most concise such attempts has been made by Stubbs and Underhill (1994, pp. 331–5), who identify three central elements to regionalism. First, there is a common historical experience and sense of shared problems among a geographically distinct group of countries or societies: this effectively gives a definition of 'region'. Second, there are close linkages of a distinct kind between those countries and societies; in other words, there is a 'boundary' to the region within which interactions are more intense than those with the outside world: this intensification of interactions has been termed 'regionalization'. Finally, there is the emergence of organization, giving shape to the region in a legal and institutional sense and providing some 'rules of the game' within the region: this element of design and conscious policy is central to 'regionalism'.

Although Stubbs and Underhill are concerned particularly with the political economy of regions and regionalism, their criteria can be extended to cater for all areas of interest and activity. Notably, the criteria do not make judgements about the outcomes of regional activity and organization: these outcomes can as easily be an intensification of frictions as an intensification of cooperation or integration. The key element is proximity and intensity of relationships. Thus, the extent of 'common historical experience and sense of shared problems' could be said to be at its peak in areas such as the Balkans where there has been a history of destructive conflict, not only in areas where there is a long tradition of cooperation, such as Scandinavia. Both areas also show evidence of strong tendencies towards regionalization, with concentration of attention and activity within the boundaries of a certain group of countries. Not everyone would agree, however, that the Balkans and Scandinavia show equivalent levels of regionalism.

A brief examination of the contemporary world arena confirms this initial impression: there are strong elements of region and regionalization, but not always of regionalism. Regionalism is widespread, but it is also diverse. The most formal and wide-ranging expression of regional interactions is undoubtedly the European Union: a highly developed set of institutions expressing not only the economic but also increasingly the political integration of the Western European region, with the possibility that this might be extended into the field of security and defence, or to other parts of Europe. Some have argued that this implies ultimately the construction of a kind of 'regional state', in which the traditional roles of national state authorities are transferred to the European level. This possibility, of course, has also been the focus of intense political debate and often open dissent within the EU itself. At the other end of the spectrum, there is a wide range of regional agreements which focus on a limited number of states or societies and often on very specific problem areas: for example, agreements between landlocked African countries for transit by land or air to the outside world, or between countries in the Middle East over the supply and use of water from rivers running through several countries.

In dealing with this variety, three particular elements seem important. First, there is the spatial dimension of regionalism: how large is the area covered, and how is that area defined or redefined as conditions change? As an example, one can examine one of the most highly developed regional security arrangements, the North Atlantic Treaty Organization (NATO), which was established in the late 1940s and early 1950s. Even then, there was a difficulty in defining the 'North Atlantic area' and adjusting membership to reflect it. By the early 1950s, Greece and Turkey were members of the organization, but no one would argue that this was because of their presence in the North Atlantic: it was a reflection rather of the (equally regional) concern to surround and contain the Soviet Union. By 1996, in the aftermath of the breakup of the Soviet bloc, Poland and other major central and east European countries were being talked of as future members of NATO, and it was clear that political change had impacted again on the geopolitical definition of the 'NATO area'. This also demonstrates that regional boundaries can overlap or interpenetrate: many European countries can be considered as parts of several regions or 'sub-regions' depending upon the criteria used, and of several regionalisms according to their involvement in different organizations and institutions.

A second key feature in the variety of regionalism is its scope: in other words, the tasks or areas of interaction covered by the region or by regional organization. Here, the variety is if anything even more bewildering. NATO, at least, is centred on defence and security; but these have changed their meaning markedly in the 1990s. The EU began as a predominantly economic organization and expression of regionalism, but has developed towards political and security activities. Other expressions of regionalism can take cultural forms, for example in the awareness of shared heritage between Muslim countries in the Middle East, or in the notion of Nordic regionalism which has been present for centuries. Often, there can be unevennesses in the awareness and impact of regionalism: it is sometimes noted that African nations have a well-developed sense of Africanness, but that for a number of reasons they are not very closely tied economically. Africanness has also not prevented large numbers of regional conflicts among the states of the continent. One of the problems entailed in trying to capture the variety of regionalism is thus the need to cater for overlapping tasks and functions. As with the geographical boundaries of regions, so do the functional boundaries shift and overlap or merge.

A third feature of the variety of regionalism is the level and extent of regional organization. It is clear that although the overall level of regional organization has risen over the decades, and particularly in the 1990s, it remains uneven and fluctuating. Some regional organizations are tightly structured, permanent and impose important constraints on their members: this is most true of regional organizations in Europe: not only the EU, but also NATO and the Organization for Cooperation and Security in Europe (OSCE). Others are much looser, depending on the shifting political or economic needs of their members and on the broader political climate in the world arena. The example already cited of ASEAN is a case in point. For many years, this grouping existed as a largely defensive political club designed to express its members' interest in steering between China, Japan and the United States. During the 1990s, it has increased and deepened its organizational structure, but it remains essentially a club of national governments rather than an integrated set of structures and roles. For some of the more extensive and general-purpose organizations, such as the Organization of American States (OAS) or the Organization of African Unity (OAU) there are complex bureaucratic and administrative structures, but it is not always clear how much they express the common interests of very diverse memberships.

The three criteria suggested by Stubbs and Underhill, therefore, are useful as much because they expose the variety and unevenness of regionalism as because they define its essential features. They also demonstrate that in the same way as 'interdependence' and 'development', regionalism is a set of issues rather than a single problem area for the analysis of world politics. Such an impression is further borne out by a study of some of the major patterns of regional interaction as they have been studied in the literature of world politics. Three such varieties can be identified here: regional integration, regional transnationalism, and regional security complexes.

Perhaps the most salient form of regionalism in the contemporary world arena is that of regional integration. Predominantly based on the intensification and organization of economic interdependence, this form of regionalism has become part of the economic orthodoxy of the 1990s. Although it is often identified primarily with the European Union and with the European Economic Community first established in the late 1950s, there is now a wide range of attempts to organize and to institutionalize economic integration in all regions of the world. One of the most notable efforts has been the creation of the North American Free Trade Area (NAFTA) between Canada, Mexico and the USA; this has established elaborate mechanisms for furthering trade, investment and other economic relationships between the three members, and may over time extend to other countries in the Western hemisphere. The Asia-Pacific Economic Cooperation forum (APEC), established in the early 1990s, has developed not only a permanent organizational structure, but also plans to create free trade in its region by the year 2020. In Latin America, MERCOSUR (Southern Common Market), composed of Argentina, Brazil, Paraguay and Uruguay (with Chile as a recent associate member), promises to establish a full customs union and some of the features characteristic of the EU itself. ASEAN, as noted above, has developed plans for economic cooperation and the reduction of trade barriers.

Regional integration is also closely linked with a second form of regionalism, regional transnationalism. Much of the activity directed towards regional integration has not unnaturally been led by states and their governments, but it has been accompanied in every case by an awareness that many of the regional interests and processes on which it focuses are transnational in their scope. They spill over borders, involving contacts between groups who are located in different national societies but who are linked by economic, cultural or political needs. Sometimes, these groupings are directed towards private commercial or other objectives: this is clearly the case for major multinational companies, which are often organized on a regional or continental basis for reasons of efficiency or because of the dictates of the market. Other transnational groupings at the regional level are less concerned with private profit than they are with political influence: they may wish to achieve results in areas such as environmental protection, human rights and other areas which demand governmental action at the national or the regional level. In such areas, there is an intimate relationship between organizations such as Greenpeace, Friends of the Earth or Amnesty International and the regional bodies with responsibility for the specific issue areas in question, such as the European Union or the European Commission for Human Rights. More subversive and sometimes more dramatic are the groupings operating transnationally in specific regions to attack the 'established order': liberation movements or movements for regional autonomy within national states can often take action across national boundaries to destabilize their 'home' governments, as have the Basques in France and Spain, or the contending forces in Afghanistan during the 1980s and 1990s. In turn, this can lead to the development of regional structures to try and control such groupings, through military or police collaboration at the regional level.

This concern for transnational public order within regions links with the third type of regionalism to be explored here: regional security. One of the longest-standing focuses, both of regionalism in general and of regional organization in particular, has been the concern with regional security and stability (Nye, 1971). Traditional analysis of international politics very often focused on the problem of the regional balance of power, and of the ways in which regional stability linked with the broader world order (Bull, 1977, Chapter 5). More recently, Barry Buzan has developed the notion of 'regional security complexes' (Buzan, 1991, Chapter 5). These complexes are seen as expressing distinctive regional security dynamics, which exist between the national and the global levels; in particular, they reflect three key forces, those of proximity, of power relations and of 'amity and enmity', operating between the states within a given region. An example furnished by Buzan is that of South and South East Asia: each region contains often intense security interactions, but there are very clear boundaries between them, and a clear climate of indifference. Thus, the tensions between India and Pakistan are of intense interest to powers in the South Asian complex, but of little direct concern to those in South East Asia, whilst the conflicts involving Vietnam, Cambodia and Laos over the years have had little direct effect in the South Asian sphere. In neither case is it clear that regional organization has developed in such a way as to handle more effectively the underlying conflicts: there is no 'South Asian security community' which might set out rules of the game or apply them to disputes, for example.

Problems of Regionalism

Perhaps the most significant problem posed by regionalism in world politics centres on the linkage between intra-regional relations and the broader world arena. As noted above, one of the key tensions exposed by the study of regionalism is between what goes on within a given regional arena and what goes on between that arena and the outside world. In this section, the focus is on these two dimensions.

Intra-regional relations

The most immediate problem posed by the study of intra-regional relations concerns the role of states. It has already been noted that in many regional arenas and regional organizations, the role of states is either constrained or in extreme cases thrown into fundamental doubt. But national governments often see it rather differently. By entering into regional agreements and organizations, they may be better placed to achieve their national objectives, whether these focus on prosperity or on security. Thus, while the EU undoubtedly limits the freedom of its members to pursue their own independent courses of action, there is no doubt that, in economic and political terms, participation in the EU adds to the strength of each of its members. From a purely rational national perspective, therefore, the gains can very easily outweigh the losses. Likewise, in the case of NATO, there is no doubt that collective regional defence adds to the ability of each of the members to defend themselves.

Often, these generalized benefits of active regional participation on the part of states are underlined by specific gains to individual countries. For example, in the Americas, one of the perennial problems for all countries apart from the United States is the United States itself: a dominant power in both economic and security terms, whose actions if unconstrained can have unpredictable effects on the rest of the hemisphere. From the point of view of countries such as Canada and Mexico, therefore, it makes sense to construct regional arrangements which set out some rules of the game for the conduct of relations with and by the United States, and it is well worth sacrificing some independence in order to achieve this. From the point of view of the United States, this can also have specific benefits, if it forestalls the possibility of defensive actions on the part of its partners and opens their markets to US goods. This example also underlines the fact that, in many cases, regionalism arises from the positive adoption of state policies, and from agreements between national governments. In other words, whilst what is going on in such agreements as NAFTA may look like the sacrifice of national independence, it can also be seen as the exercise of national choice – an expression of sovereignty as well as a sacrifice of national freedom (Leyton-Brown, 1994).

Regionalism, therefore, expresses a constant tension between the demands of statehood and the pressures for collective action or adjustment to regional realities. One of the key realities is the distribution of power between major regional actors, usually but not always states. As noted above, for all states in the Western hemisphere, the dominance of the USA is an inescapable fact of life, all the more telling because of its regional expression. In the EU, the actual or potential predominance of a united Germany has been one of the underlying themes of the 1990s, conditioning all efforts at EU reform and enlargement. Not surprisingly, other regional systems also demonstrate the importance of the regional distribution of power. Thus, in South Asia, the centrality of India and of its conflicts with its neighbours has been a relatively permanent aspect of the regional economic and political orders (Buzan and Rizvi, 1986). In other cases, sudden or radical change in the regional distribution of power can have important catalytic effects: thus, in 1979, the deposition of the Shah of Iran and the installation of a radical Muslim regime reverberated throughout the region and beyond. Likewise, in Afghanistan, Soviet intervention in 1980 had important effects on the regional order, whilst the prospect of a radical Muslim regime there in 1996 led to significant new efforts at regional collaboration among the states of central Asia.

Arising from the interaction of states and regions, and expressing in part the shifting distribution of power within regions, is the broader problem of regional order. As Robert Cox has argued, international orders express a combination of forces including the distribution of power, the role of institutions and the existence of identities and ideologies (Cox, 1986). From what has been said, it is apparent that these are important at the regional level as well as at the global level. Where there is a close 'fit' between the three elements of power, institutions and ideas, there is at least super-ficially a settled regional order. This could be said, for example, of

Western Europe for long periods during the 1950s, 1960s and 1970s or of Latin America during the same periods. Where there is no close 'fit' between the elements, or there are radical shifts in the balance between them, then there ceases to be a settled order (Smith, 1993). Such conditions arguably prevailed in South East Asia for much of the Cold War period, and can be seen in central Asia or the Balkans during the 1990s.

A further problem at the intra-regional level is that of the relationship between economics and security. It has been seen already that this is one of the ways in which regionalism can be defined or described, but it is also apparent that it has significant impacts on the functioning of regions and regional orders. For example, the rise of protectionism and exclusive economic agreements during the 1930s was seen as a strong force in the approach of the Second World War (and incidentally conditioned the post-1945 desire for European economic integration). During the Cold War, one of the underpinnings of the Soviet bloc was the establishment of regionalized economic processes in Central and Eastern Europe through the agency of the Council for Mutual Economic Assistance (CMEA). Whilst the USSR retained its military and political dominance of the region, it was possible to maintain some semblance of a regional division of labour economically. But the decay of Soviet power in the 1980s and its collapse in the 1990s was paralleled by the decay and collapse of the purported regional economic order. Outside Europe, part of the debate about the emergence of a potential East Asian bloc as a competitor for the USA and the EU has been centred on the apparent growth of a regional economic system, but this has been qualified by the frictions between Japan, South East Asia and other regional actors arising from the uneven distribution of economic power and prosperity (Cable and Henderson, 1994; Gibb and Michalak, 1994).

Not surprisingly, it is not always clear to observers that the growth of regionalism is a 'good thing'. This is essentially a normative question, about the way things ought to be as well as the way they are in world politics, and regionalism is not the only issue which raises it: for instance, one could ask whether statehood itself is a good or desirable thing, or whether globalization and certain models of development are to be desired (see, for example, Chapters 2, 3 and 5). As in other cases, though, regionalism focuses the question in a distinctive way, because it combines the demand for specific policies or institutions with broader demands of change in the world arena. Thus it mattered greatly to Americans whether NAFTA was going to bring them benefits or whether they would lose business and their jobs to Mexico or Canada. In the same way, the intense arguments about British membership of the EU have not simply been generalized arguments about world order: they are arguments about jobs, living and working conditions and about local and regional democracy. In South East Asia, it matters intensely what rules are developed for the regional management of resources such as those of the Mekong River, and it matters not just to governments but also to local and regional interests. Regionalism, it might be said, reaches parts that other issues do not always reach.

Regionalism and the world arena

Many of the problems described above as intra-regional intersect with problems in the broader world arena. In a sense, the two arenas are inseparable, but by dealing with them separately one becomes more aware of the linkages and tensions between them. Three particular problems can be identified here: the problem of inter-regional relations; the problem of relations between regionalism and globalism; and the problem of relations between regional orders and world order.

Inter-regional competition and collaboration between regions is an important dynamic in the world politics of the 1990s, and will remain one into the new millennium. The most obvious formal manifestation of this process centres on the EU. At one and the same time, the EU can be seen – and is seen both in Europe and outside – as a formidable competitor in the world political economy and as an attractive partner for other regions of the world. In the first of these guises, the EU has sometimes been presented as a 'fortress Europe' in the making, taking every opportunity to protect its own and to attack the entrenched positions of the Americans and the Japanese (Rosecrance, 1991; Katzenstein, 1993). This fits with the idea that inter-regional relations may give rise to a world of competing blocs, not just in the economic but also in the military spheres (see below). On the other hand, the EU often presents itself as a 'world partner', constructing agreements and initiating dialogue with other regions; in this guise, it has developed a web of inter-regional agreements with groupings such as ASEAN, MERCO-SUR, the Andean Pact and (more loosely) with a wide range of Mediterranean countries. In their turn, many other regional group-ings have initiated a search for inter-regional partnerships, partly as a defensive measure to maintain access to potential 'fortresses' and partly as a conscious attempt to build new forms of world order (Edwards and Regelsberger, 1990).

Attempts to build ambitious inter-regional arrangements thus have a certain ambiguity to them, and this ambiguity is underlined when it is related to a second problem: the relationship between regionalism and globalism. As noted in Chapter 3, there are very strong pressures in the world political economy towards globaliza-tion of processes of production and exchange; these run alongside the awareness of global problems such as those of the environment or of security in the post-Cold War world (see Chapters 6, 11). Given the strength of regionalism in the 1990s, how can these forces be reconciled? In a sense, this is again not a new problem: during the 1950s, the tensions between the search for security in Europe and the broader demands of world order were apparent, and there is a continuing tension between regional economic integration and the multilateral rules of the world trading system (see Chapter 3; also Anderson and Blackhurst, 1993). The pressures of regionalism in the 1990s, though, put a new gloss on these tensions, giving new point to the question once posed by Robert Lawrence (in Fawcett and Hurrell, 1995): are regional organizations 'building blocks or stumbling blocks' when it comes to the search for world order? In particular, the frictions can be seen in two areas: those of institu-tions and rules, and those of identity. Many regional organizations have developed elaborate systems of rules and accompanying institutions, and it is sometimes unclear how these relate to global institutions and rules. The most obvious example here is the World Trade Organization (see Chapter 3; also WTO, 1995), which has to pay a great deal of attention to the ways in which regional rules match up to its global multilateral framework. But the problem is not absent in the sphere of security: the development of elaborate codes for regional conflict resolution has posed a challenge to the United Nations and other bodies in their attempts to manage regional conflicts. More intangible is the tension created by the search in some regions for a 'regional identity', which affects expectations and habits in distinctive ways. A case in point is that of differing attitudes towards Burma (Myanmar) during the mid-1990s. The EU and other 'Western' groupings saw the human rights policies of the Burmese government as an outrage, and demanded that the regime be ostracized and subject to sanctions. ASEAN countries saw the issue differently, and as a grouping were able to resist the demands of the 'outsiders', which were expressed in terms of world order and universal rights. Although ASEAN was aware of the offences committed by the Burmese regime, they concluded that there were different and more regionally appropriate ways of dealing with the problem.

Regions, Regionalism and the International Agenda

One explanation for the fluctuating salience of regions and regionalism on the international agenda is that it reflects in large measure the fluctuating preferences of states. For large states, there is something to be said for regionalism if it can be used as a vehicle for their influence in the international arena: as a result, it may be promoted as a means of extending and consolidating influence. The clearest examples of this are regional efforts sponsored by dominant or hegemonic powers, such as the USA and the USSR during the Cold War. During the 1950s and 1960s, the USA in particular attempted to extend its influence – or sometimes to legitimize the influence it already had – in many regions of the world, particularly through regional alliances. Outside the military sphere, organizations such as the European Economic Community have also been viewed as the expression of US desires to shape Western Europe. It is not always predominant or hegemonic powers that instigate regional cooperation, however. As already noted in the case of ASEAN, it can be argued that regionalism gives weaker countries an outlet, enabling them to avoid either domination by predominant powers or marginalization by them (see also Chapter 5; Gibb and Michalak, 1994; Gamble and Payne, 1996).

Implicit in this discussion of regionalism on the international agenda is the question 'who benefits'? We have already seen a range of potential beneficiaries from the processes and products of regionalism: hegemonic states, weaker states, multinational corporations and others. It is sometimes also argued, for example, that the real beneficiaries of regionalism are domestic political and economic elites in the countries concerned. Rather than having to account directly to their populations for their decisions and any damage that may arise, they can effectively cover their tracks by operating at and through the regional level. Christopher Hill, in studying the foreign and security policies of the EU, has pointed to the 'cover function' whereby responsibility for awkward decisions can be shifted to the European level (Hill, 1983, 1996); others have pointed to the ways in which this can be used to justify unpopular policies, or to escape the blame for them, at the national level. Other beneficiaries from regionalism may include military leaders who can point to regional commitments as the justification for increased defence budgets, pressure groups who can bypass national administrations to try and achieve their aims at the regional level, and commercial or industrial interests who can organize and influence more effectively through regional bodies than through the national process or at the multilateral level.

An evaluation of the place occupied by regionalism on the international agenda thus depends partly on the significance given to the needs and preferences of states, and partly on the significance allotted to the wider range of beneficiaries who can participate and influence processes of regionalization. It is also important to point out that the salience of regionalism has a direct and significant connection with the development and structure of the global arena itself. Where that arena is highly polarized and dominated by major states or groupings, it is likely that regionalism will be subordinated to the dictates of the global balance. Equally, if globalized processes of production and exchange are the dominant patterns of relations in the world political economy, it might be expected that regionalism and regional organization would effectively be a transmission belt for those patterns.

Regionalism in the Post-Cold War World

How has regionalism been affected by the end of the Cold War and its associated divisions or rigidities? The recent upsurge of interest in regions and regionalism clearly has strong links with the collapse of the USSR and of the Soviet bloc, the emergence of many new states and of many new potential focuses for conflict and cooperation. But it would be misleading to trace the upsurge in regionalism solely to this set of events, in particular because the direction and pace of change in different areas of world politics have been markedly different. To put it simply, the onset of economic inter-dependence and associated issues leading to the focus on regional-ism and globalization is not simply a product of the 1990s: nor are the problems of development and inequality which have attended regionalist efforts in the developing areas of the world; whereas the new forms and focuses of regional conflict or of nationalist tensions in Europe and Eurasia in very large part are. This is an important point for the analysis of world politics as a whole: there are different 'timetables' for change and for the onset of novel trends depending upon the particular issues under examination (Fawcett and Hurrell, 1995, Chapter 1).

This said, there can be no doubt that the collapse of the Soviet 'empire' and the radical changes in the global distribution of power associated with it are a profound influence in the 'new regionalism' of the 1990s. Barry Buzan has referred to this as the removal of the 'Superpower overlay' which affected almost all areas of the world and which had the effect of suppressing or distorting processes of regional interaction (Buzan, 1991, Chapter 5). Most dramatically, this process removed the once seemingly permanent division of Europe, throwing into question the tidiness of the regional divisions which accompanied it. At one and the same time, the EU was catapulted into a wider Europe and the countries of Central and Eastern Europe were left without the (admittedly uncomfortable) certainties of Soviet domination. In this situation, it was not clear what the 'region' was: 'Western Europe' and 'Eastern Europe' were contrivances of the Cold War, but they had gained a certain reality because of the adjustment of policies and institutions to the east–west divide (Wallace, 1990).

The result of this transformation was not felt only in Europe, nor only as the consequence of the Soviet collapse. Reference has already been made to the fact that processes of globalization had made themselves apparent during the 1980s, as had the possibilities of intensified competition between regions surrounding the EU, the US and Japan. What the changes in Europe added was a major element of uncertainty about regional alignments and about the relationships between regionalism and the broader world order. As noted in Chapter 7, the United Nations was seen by many as the solution to many of the new areas of conflict which emerged during the late 1980s and early 1990s, but it rapidly became apparent that the UN was ill-suited and poorly resourced to deal with the demands of regional conflict management. Thus, the UN Secretary-General, Boutros Boutros-Ghali, was led to call for a new division of labour between the UN and regional organizations in conflict management and peacekeeping. In some cases regional bodies and their major members were eager to take over the task, but in many cases – for example, in former Yugoslavia or the former Soviet Union – they proved unequal to it. As a result, there was confusion and uncertainty about the roles of different global or regional institutions.

There is thus a strong argument to be made that the end of the Cold War 'took the lid off' a number of intractable regional problems, with an ethnic as well as a national security dimension (see Chapter 8). This may well have led to a stronger emphasis on processes of regionalization and on regionalism as an issue, but it also underlined some of the limitations of regional institutions in dealing with new challenges. Even the strongest of regional institutions, such as the EU and NATO, often found themselves in uncharted territory; NATO planners had spent the 1970s and 1980s planning for what happened when Yugoslavia collapsed, but they had not at all foreseen the prior collapse of the Soviet bloc. Outside Europe, there were also new challenges, or at least familiar challenges in new conditions, such as those in Somalia or – most dramatically – in the Persian Gulf following the Iraqi invasion of 1990. Here, the predominance of the USA led others to expect that it would become a global and a regional police force; but where the USA was unwilling, there were no regional institutions to take its place.

In the security domain, then, the post-Cold War world provides a very patchy picture of regional challenges and regional responses, perhaps because it was in security matters that the Cold War 'overlay' had been most pervasive. Economically, the 1990s were less of a new world than a continuation of marked trends in the old one. As noted earlier, the growth of new regional trading and regulatory arrangements had been going on apace during the 1980s, and major international trade negotiations under the General Agreement on Tariffs and Trade (GATT) had since 1986 been wrestling with the coexisting tendencies towards globalization and regionalization (Anderson and Blackhurst, 1993; Cable and Henderson, 1994; Gibb and Michalak, 1994). There were, though, some major changes in the problems confronted as these processes moved into the 1990s. In the first place, the nature of regional arrangements and of economic processes had changed, with the rise of trade in services and the increased emphasis on regulatory policies which reached 'behind the border' (see Chapter 3). One major question which arose from this set of challenges was whether global or regional institutions were best suited to handle the emerging problems; the result was an often uneasy coexistence of the two, with regional organizations such as the EU or NAFTA introducing new regulatory mechanisms alongside and sometimes in conflict with attempts at global agreement.

It therefore seems that the post-Cold War world has created both fertile new ground for regionalism and a whole set of new challenges. Importantly, these challenges often cut across the national/regional/global divide, creating tensions between different levels of government and administration. This is as true of problems in the sphere of security as it is of those connected with economic and social questions. Sometimes, these questions come together in new and particularly demanding ways: thus, the conflicts in former Yugoslavia exacerbated problems of migration and employment in a number of European countries as large numbers of refugees looked for a safe haven (Waever *et al.*, 1993). This again was not an unprecedented regional problem; the end of the Vietnam war in the 1970s had led to an exodus of large numbers of 'boat people' whose presence imposed heavy burdens on a number of regional actors. But the coming together of post-Cold War conflicts with new economic and social demands certainly gave a new twist to the process.

The most important question arising from this confusion of regional and global processes concerns regional and world order. Is there evidence that in the conditions of the 1990s, regionalism has assisted in the maintenance of stability, the containment of conflict and the maximization of prosperity? There has been a rash of new regional organizations and agreements, particularly in the economic field, but it is open to question whether they have yet generated (or can generate) a settled set of regional orders within a stable world order. If one returns to the earlier discussion of international orders based around the three criteria of power, institutions and ideas, it could be argued that no settled regional orders have emerged from the end of the Cold War, most particularly in Europe and the Middle East, and that world order has proved much more difficult to sustain in the absence of the Superpower 'overlay' for security matters and in the presence of globalization for economic problems.

Managing Regionalism

At the beginning of this chapter, one of the central focuses was on the variety of regionalism and of regional organizations. Reference has been made at many points to regionalism at a number of different levels and centred on a wide range of different activities. In terms of management processes, this variety and range can be seen both as a problem and as a source of potential. When viewed as a problem, it can easily seem that regionalism is a mess of competing tendencies and organizations, often getting in each other's way and sometimes coming into open conflict, with clashing claims to authority and influence. When viewed as a source of potential, it can be argued that the variety of regionalisms is a reflection of the variety and complexities of world politics, and that without a wide range of organizations the world would be short of solutions to important questions about security and economic development.

Not surprisingly, this diversity and untidiness has spawned many different images of regionalism and its management as we approach the twenty-first century. On one level, regionalism itself can be seen as a mechanism through which states and other groupings attempt to manage their involvement in the international arena. The test of effective management, as suggested earlier, is thus the extent to which regionalism expresses and channels the needs of the actors involved in it. At another level, regionalism can be seen as a means by which authority is transferred away from states and other groupings to regional bodies better able to manage the problems that confront them. Often, this transfer is strongly contested, but the test of effectiveness is the extent to which security and prosperity can be achieved through collective action at the regional level. At a third level, regionalism appears either as a contributor to or as an obstacle to world order and the management of the changing international arena – a building block or a stumbling block. During the 1990s, there has been a considerable debate about the relative merits of so-called 'open regionalism' and 'closed regionalism': the first implies an openness to the needs of the broader world order and a readiness to adapt to it, whilst the second implies an attempt to build a fortress and to manage by using regionalism as an insulator against the broader challenges of world politics. On the whole, the late 1990s give a good deal of support to the building of 'open regionalism' both in economic and security questions, but it is not impossible that adverse economic or security conditions could lead to a reversal of this tendency (Rosecrance, 1991; Katzenstein, 1993).

The effective management of regionalism in world politics thus depends to a large degree on how management is attempted through regionalism: the one is in many respects the flip-side of the other. Depending on the extent to which regionalism reflects state strategies as opposed to integrative forces, or is problem-centred as opposed to legalistic in style, it has the potential to be both a bridge and a barrier to the achievement of order. What it does express is the emergence of a multilayered policy environment characterized by the multiplicity of institutions and the need for political action to take account of linkages and complexities in novel ways.

Regions and Regionalism: Implications for World Politics

The implications of regionalism for world politics are as diverse as the forms and features of regionalism itself, but three central strands can be isolated from the discussion in this chapter:

- First, regionalism can be seen both as a force for integration and as a force for disintegration in world politics. At one and the same time, it expresses the desire for collective action and identity and the desire for difference and distinctiveness in the world arena. In doing so, it has some of the properties of other issues dealt with in this book, such as nationalism and statehood. The tension is ultimately unresolvable, since it is of the essence of the drive to regional awareness and regional organization.
- Second, regionalism has profound implications both for statehood and for world order as focuses of aspirations and activity in the world arena. It can be seen as both promoting and dissolving

statehood; it can be seen as a bridge and a barrier to world order. It has two faces, inevitably as a result of its place at the intersection of the national and the global systems. The pursuit of regionalism as a goal thus brings about some very challenging situations for policy-makers, and these have multiplied as the result of the spread of regionalism in the 1990s. The disappearance of such moderating devices as the Superpower 'overlay' has meant that the 'new regionalism' has to be constructed in a new context, and that its implications have not yet been fully recognized.

- Third, there is no one model of regionalism, nor one predominant theoretical framework for the analysis of regionalism. Andrew Hurrell, in one of the most wide-ranging treatments of the subject, identifies three major theoretical tendencies in the study of regionalism: systemic theories which see regionalism as a response to outside pressures and forces; theories focused on the development of regional interconnectedness and interdependence; and domestic-level theories which stress the impact of changes such as democratization on the tendency to regionalization and regional cooperation (Hurrell, 1995). It is clear from the discussion in this chapter that any full analysis of regionalism requires the deployment of all three types of theory. Not only this, but it must recognize that theories of regionalism are themselves part of the debate about the merits and demerits of regionalism itself as a phenomenon in world politics.

In the final analysis, a study of regions and regionalism as an issue in world politics is a way of taking a perspective on virtually all of the major questions of our time. It encapsulates the paradoxes of a world more united yet also in some ways more divided than ever before, and it raises important questions about the future both of the state and of world order.

Guide to Further Reading

The best general collection dealing with regionalism, both in its historical context and, as it has re-emerged in the 1990s, is Fawcett and Hurrell (1995); it covers both the theoretical aspects of the issue and a series of comparative case-studies. The article by Hurrell (1995) is the best short treatment of concepts and theories. Another good treatment is Gamble and

Payne (1996), which focuses particularly on state strategies and has a set of regional case-studies. Classical treatments of regionalism include Cantori and Spiegel (1970) and Russett (1967). Issues of regional security are well covered in Buzan (1991) and in Nye (1971). On regionalism in the world political economy, see Stubbs and Underhill (1994), especially Part III. The relationship between regionalism and the world trading system is described in detail in WTO (1995), which has a wealth of data and looks at the institutional arrangements. For more conceptual analysis of the economic issues, see Anderson and Blackhurst (1993). The specific problems of regional economic blocs are best handled by Cable and Henderson (1994) and Gibb and Michalak (1994).

5

Development and Inequality

CAROLINE THOMAS AND MELVYN READER

A consideration of development and inequality in the 1990s raises a number of matters vital to both students and practitioners of world politics. The twentieth century has witnessed enormous advances in science and technology, accompanied by an unprecedented rise in industrial and economic productivity. Yet almost a third of humanity still lives in conditions of dire poverty, and 14 million people die of hunger annually. This is one of the greatest paradoxes of the modern world.

In the 1950s, before the commencement of the First United Nations Development Decade, the Indian statesperson, Jawaharlal Nehru, declared '[i]t is science alone that can solve the problems of hunger and poverty, of insanitation and illiteracy, of superstition and deadening custom and tradition, of vast resources running to waste, of a rich country inhabited by starving people' (quoted in Midgeley, 1992, p. 24). However, actual observations of the appliance of science to the field of development during the last four decades raises doubts as to the efficacy of this belief. Unbounded confidence in the ability of science to 'save the world' is profoundly misplaced, especially when it fails to take account of prevailing political and social realities.

The enormous power of modern, so-called 'value-free' science and its associated technologies have been unleashed upon a world-system characterized by social injustice and economic inequality. The result has been the development of a situation of 'social apartheid' in which the rich and powerful have been helped to become more rich and powerful, whilst the poor and powerless have been pushed further to the margins. Today, in many Southern countries it is common to find enormous, beautifully designed shopping centres filled with high-priced luxury goods overlooking nearby shanty-towns whose occupants would regard an adequate diet and a change of clothes as luxurious living. Undeniably, economic growth has been a feature of most parts of the South since the end of the Second World War, but whether such growth is an adequate measure of development is highly questionable.

As a general sociological concept, *development* can be defined as a multidimensional process involving change from a less to a more socially desirable state. However, when it comes to specifying the exact content of that process and how it is to be pursued, the essentially normative (value-based) nature of the concept of development is evident. Indeed, any informed analysis of development must necessarily concede that, 'Development can be conceived only within an ideological framework' (Roberts, 1984, p. 7). It is possible to identify two broad perspectives on development in the 1990s: the *orthodox* or *mainstream perspective*, and the *critical alternative perspective*. The former represents the view of development that has been dominant for the last fifty years, whilst the latter has arisen largely in response to the perceived shortcomings of the former and incorporates more marginalized understandings of the development process. The orthodox approach has played an important role in shaping the policies of Western states and key multilateral institutions, such as the International Monetary Fund (IMF) and the World Bank, towards the South. As a result, the approach has had a determining influence on many of the policies pursued by Southern governments. In contrast to this basically elite-driven approach to development, the critical alternative perspective has emerged from grassroots groups composed of the poor themselves and from Southern and Northern non-governmental organizations (NGOs) working directly with them.

The orthodox view of development believes that the best way forward for the South is to replicate the social and economic changes that occurred in the North following the scientific and industrial revolutions of the seventeenth and eighteenth centuries. Consequently, industrialization and scientific technology are advocated as the best means to achieve the goal of generating wealth, whilst success is measured in terms of higher business profits and an increasing Gross National Product (GNP – a measure of a country's total economic output). One of the most influential 'modernization' theories is the 'Stages of Economic Growth Model' put forward by the US economic historian Walt Rostow in the late 1950s. Rostow argued that all countries must develop through a number of stages, starting with a 'traditional' society (characterized as agrarian-based, unscientific and economically unproductive), and culminating with a 'modern' society (industrial-based, scientific, economically productive, and engaged in mass consumption). The key to these changes was seen as the mobilization of domestic and foreign savings for investment in economic growth. Consequently, according to Rostow and the various theories of 'modernization' his model inspired, the most important development indicator is a country's economic growth rate.

Measured by the criterion of high economic growth rates, Southern countries have been notably successful. In the post-war period the South's average annual growth rate was 4.9 per cent, whilst that of the North was 3.5 per cent (Adams, 1993, p. 8). Yet despite the large increases in economic production that these figures represent, the post-war world has not made much progress towards the abolition of global poverty. Certainly it is true that the introduction of improved medical services has led to a decrease in child mortality rates, but often 'these changes have simply enabled people to *survive* their poverty, not to be freed from it' (Clark, 1991, p. 4).

In contrast to the narrow concentration of the orthodox perspective upon economics and technology, the critical alternative perspective argues that true development is about the improvement of global human welfare as defined holistically in terms of human physical and spiritual needs, community relationships, and environmental sustainability. It criticizes the orthodox approach for having created 'a system of production that ravishes nature and a society that mutilates man', and instead puts forward the view that development should be conducted 'as though people mattered' (Schumacher, 1973). A pioneering contribution to the critical alternative approach was the model of development set forth by the Dag Hammarskjöld Foundation in the mid-1970s. This model, referred to as 'Another Development', argued that development should be:

1. *need-oriented* – geared to meeting human material and non-material needs, rather than to supplying the wants of the wealthy.
2. *endogenous* – based upon the self-defined values and goals of each community involved.

3. *self-reliant* – drawing primarily upon each community's own resources, and reducing external dependency.
4. *ecologically-sound* – using resources in a way that does not cause harm to the environment, now or in the future.
5. *based on structural transformations* – taking account of prevailing social structures and the need to alter those that are unjust (Ekins, 1992, pp. 99–100).

A similar conception of development was reflected in the 1974 Cocoyoc Declaration (made by a United Nations committee of experts) which asserted that, 'Our first concern is to redefine the purpose of development. This should not be to develop things but to develop man.' The Declaration argued that the pursuit of '[a] growth strategy that benefits only the wealthiest minority and maintains or even increases the disparities between and within countries is not development. It is exploitation.' Instead the Declaration advocated a 'fairer distribution of resources satisfying basic needs' in a more 'harmonized cooperative world' in which everyone aims to live 'at the expense of no-one else' and the poor are encouraged to 'invent and generate new resources and techniques' so as 'to generate their own way of life' (Cocoyoc Declaration, 1974). Such ideas about a critical alternative conception of development have been around internationally for at least two decades, but so far they have had little effect on the mainstream development model.

Issues of Development and Inequality

In terms of visibility, the issue of development (or its absence) has received relatively little attention in the 1990s. One reason for this is that subjects such as everyday poverty and hunger do not generally make very 'newsworthy' items for the global media industry, largely because they are ever-present, difficult-to-resolve matters, and are unresponsive to the 'sound-bite' treatment. Neither viewers nor advertisers want to see images of poor and starving people constantly projected on to the television screen. Those brought up in a 'modern' secularized culture feel uncomfortable when reminded of their own mortality. Development matters capture the media's attention when they are perceived as sudden, dramatic or catastrophic. Examples might be famines, or the spread of 'killer viruses' such as the 1995 Ebola virus outbreak in Zaire which liquefied its victims' internal organs. However, most people who die of hunger or poverty-related causes are likely to do so in a silent and largely unnoticed fashion:

> The persistence of world hunger is one of those issues that permeates the background of life. With the exception of the occasional news-making event – typically, a famine in which the human disaster is so acute that it cannot be ignored – hunger lives as a process, a persistence, a chronic condition. People die day in, day out; and because this is the norm, it is not 'news'. (The Hunger Project, 1985, p. 2)

During the 1980s, one development-related matter that reached the news headlines was the 1984–5 Ethiopian famine. This was largely as a result of the efforts of the pop-star Bob Geldof, whose appeals for public generosity at the Band Aid and Live Aid concerts gained international media attention. However, when in 1989 the unchanged situation in Ethiopia necessitated further appeals for financial generosity, the media began to talk in terms of 'compassion-fatigue' and, rather than address the fundamental structural problems that underlay the situation, it made much of the views of potential donors who felt that they had already given enough. The lesson that needed to be drawn was not that giving money to end hunger was a waste of time, but rather that ending hunger on a more lasting basis would require a fundamental change in social structures. Unfortunately, the media in general seem less able to focus on development-related issues at this sort of depth. Therefore, as students of world politics, it is necessary for us to realise that:

> Behind the blaring headlines of the world's many conflicts and emergencies, there lies a silent crisis – a crisis of underdevelopment, of global poverty, of ever-mounting population pressures, of thoughtless degradation of the environment. This is not a crisis that will respond to emergency relief. Or to fitful policy interventions. It requires a long, quiet process of sustainable human development. (UNDP, 1994, p. iii)

The course of social change in the 1990s has highlighted the global scope of development-related problems such as poverty, inequality and environmental degradation. Earlier analyses of these problems focused on the existence of an international division between the wealthy, developed countries of the North and the poorer, less-developed countries of the South; a division which continues to be reflected in much of the literature on development (for example, Adams, 1993). However, whilst this approach may be useful for some analytical purposes, it is important to realize that such an essentially state-centric approach may encourage us to ignore the truly global nature of today's development-related issues.

Throughout the 1980s and 1990s it has become increasingly clear that large inequalities exist not only between the North and the South, but also within the North and the South themselves. There is a growing 'South' in the 'North', just as there is a growing 'North' in the 'South', and today one can find large numbers of poor people in the North as well as significant numbers of extremely rich people in the South. In the mid-1980s, the writer Paul Harrison after completing his book, *Inside the Third World*, felt compelled to publish a sequel about Britain entitled *Inside the Inner City* which highlighted some of the similarities that existed between the appalling conditions found in parts of Britain's largest cities and those he had described in the South. At the same time billionaires from the South, such as Roberto Marinho – owner of the huge Brazilian media empire of Rede Globo – began to appear in *Forbes* magazine's list of the world's wealthiest people. In the 1990s it has, therefore, become more and more difficult to map out poverty and hunger in accordance with the constraints of a state-centric model of the world. In large part this has to do with the globalization of the world economy and the stimulus that has been given to this process by the global spread of a political and economic philosophy that privileges the role of the market over that of the state or other actors in determining the distribution of goods and services. This is a matter which will be addressed in the next section.

Problems of Development and Inequality

The issue of development presents us with the challenge of human suffering and misery on a massive scale. Statistics show that, despite

over 40 years of official development plans and projects, 26 per cent
of the world's population continue to live in absolute poverty, 800
million people in 46 countries suffer malnourishment, and 40,000
people die of hunger-related causes every day (ICPF, 1994, pp. 10
and 106). It is important to recognize what these statistics represent
personally to those for whom poverty and hunger are an everyday
reality and not just a nebulous, theoretical concept. We need to
remember that poverty and hunger are primarily things that effect
people: the mother who has to explain to her young children that,
rather than stay at home and starve, it is better that they go and beg
for food in the streets; the families that queue outside the super-
market after closing-time so that they can rummage for food when
the waste-bins are put out; the children who cannot attend school
because they do not have the money to buy writing-paper; and the
newly-born baby who dies of a minor ailment because its parents
cannot afford the price of the necessary medicine. Not surprisingly,
those who are thrust into such situations feel overwhelmed by forces
operating beyond their control.

> [t]he prevalent emotion of underdevelopment is a sense of perso-
> nal and societal impotence in the face of disease and death, of
> confusion and ignorance as one gropes to understand change, of
> servility towards men whose decisions govern the course of
> events, of hopelessness before hunger and natural catastrophe.
> Chronic poverty is a cruel kind of hell, and one cannot under-
> stand how cruel that hell is merely by gazing upon poverty as an
> object. (Dennis Goulet, quoted in Allen and Thomas, 1992,
> p. 122)

What is the cause of the continuing human tragedy that poverty
and hunger represent? The orthodox development perspective
points to insufficient economic growth and, in the 1980s and
1990s, attributes this to the failure of governments to allow the
growth-potential of market forces to have free-rein. Former World
Bank President, Barber Conable, speaking of the 1980s, has
asserted that:

> If I were to characterize the past decade, the most remarkable
> thing was the generation of a global consensus that market forces
> and economic efficiency were the best way to achieve the kind

of growth which is the best antidote to poverty. (quoted in Cavanagh, Wysham and Arruda, 1994, p. 3)

This statement reflects the powerful influence that the political and economic philosophy known as 'neo-liberalism' came to have upon the policies advocated by the world's governing elites during the 1980s. This influence has continued to be of great importance in the 1990s and it is worth spending some time to examine the essential components of 'neo-liberal' thinking.

In essence, the 'neo-liberalism' of the 1980s and 1990s argues that the production, distribution and consumption of almost all goods and services should be determined by market-forces, and that the free functioning of the market should not be distorted by government interference. Consequently advocates of neo-liberalism favour minimum government and *'laissez-faire'* economics. This harks back to the views of the nineteenth-century 'Manchester School' liberals, but owes much of its current popularity to the writings of 'neo-classical' economic thinkers such as F. A. Hayek (1899–1992) and Milton Friedman (1912–). The ideas of these thinkers gained many adherents amongst professional economists in the late 1970s, and subsequently they came to have an important effect upon the policies of the New Right-influenced governments of the United States and Britain. The World Bank and the IMF were also profoundly affected by neo-liberalism via their US-trained economic advisors and the strong role given to the United States government in their management. The neo-liberal approach today provides the backbone to the orthodox perspective on development, which consequently identifies the key to the reduction of global poverty and hunger as the promotion of economic growth through the unfettering of the market from government controls.

However, critics of neo-liberalism argue that its policy prescriptions have helped create the highest levels of global inequality seen in the post-war period (Adams, 1993, p. vii). Data produced by the World Bank shows that in 1960 the share of global income going to the richest 20 per cent of the global population was 70.2 per cent, whilst that going to the poorest 20 per cent was only 2.3 per cent. This high level of inequality subsequently worsened so that in 1990 the richest 20 per cent received 80.8 per cent of the global income, whilst the poorest 20 per cent had to make do with a mere 1.3 per cent. Therefore, in the course of only three decades, the ratio of the income of the richest 20 per cent to that of the poorest 20 per cent increased from 30:1 to 64:1 (Brown and Kane, 1995, p. 46). Such changes provide a potent illustration of the historian Eric Hobsbawm's observation that:

> [t]he belief, following neoclassical economics, that unrestricted international trade would allow the poorer countries to come closer to the rich, runs counter to historical experience as well as common sense. (Hobsbawm, 1995, p. 570)

Even supporters of the free-market model have had to admit its failure to assist the world's poor. For example, the *Financial Times*, despite lauding the 'system of wealth creation . . . now everywhere regarded as the most effective that humanity has yet devised', had to concede that, '[i]t remains . . . an imperfect force . . . [since] two thirds of the world's population have gained little or no substantial advantage from rapid economic growth' and even 'in the developed world, the lowest quartile have witnessed trickle-up rather than trickle-down' (*Financial Times*, 24 December 1993).

Earlier we mentioned that during the course of the 1990s it has become increasingly difficult to map world poverty on the basis of an international North–South divide. A key reason for this has been the adoption of neo-liberal policies by many Northern governments; particularly those of the United States under the Reagan and Bush administrations, and Britain during the prime-ministerships of Thatcher and Major. The powerful influence that neo-liberal policies have had upon the generation of inequality within the United States has been recognized, not only by those on the left of the political spectrum, but by persons as conservative as Jean-Claude Paye, former Secretary-General of the pro-free market Organization for Economic Cooperation and Development (OECD). Recently Paye acknowledged that, 'If you take the United States over the last 15 years, the gulf between the ones who are at the top and the ones who are at the bottom has increased, and is increasing' (*Newsweek*, 29 April 1996, p. 54). In Britain, even the government's own statistics on income distribution confirm that inequality increased rapidly over the period between 1981 and 1992/3, and whilst the real income of the poorest 20 per cent only increased by 1 per cent, that of the richest 20 per cent rose by 46 per cent (Central Statistical Office, 1996, pp. 108–9). However, these statistics exclude some of the poorest sectors of British society (such as those without homes or living in institutions) and the reality is probably much worse (see Rowntree Foundation, 1995).

Since neo-liberal policies have significantly increased inequality in some Northern countries, it should not be surprising if their impact upon Southern states, which already lack effective welfare services, has had even more devastating consequences for the poorer classes. The triumph of the law of the market in the South represents the surrender of the economic realm to the 'law of the jungle', and consequently it ensures that the stronger win in the competition for resources whilst the weaker lose out. The parallel with the competition between species in the world of nature is no coincidence, since one of the strongest justifications for *laissez-faire* economics has come from the philosophy of Social Darwinism, which was popularized in the writings of the nineteenth-century social thinker, Herbert Spencer (1820–1903). It was Spencer, rather than Charles Darwin the biologist, who coined the phrase 'the survival of the fittest'. Spencer believed that making welfare provisions for the poorer members of society (whom he regarded as the 'least fit') would retard the development of human society as a whole, and should therefore be abandoned. The cruel implications of such a philosophy appear shocking, and yet many advocates of neo-liberalism in the 1980s and 1990s have come close to adopting such a position: the welfare state should be 'rolled back' in order to eradicate the 'culture of dependency' that it breeds, and all areas of life should be opened up to economic competition.

Other negative implications of the neo-liberal development orthodoxy have also been noted. For example, the driving force of the *laissez-faire* economy is the profit motive, and this encourages the production of consumer goods which can command a high sales value, to the neglect of needed public goods such as education, health and welfare services, recreation facilities, public amenities, safe working conditions, environmentally sustainable production processes, and so on. The end result is a social situation characterized by 'private affluence and public squalor' (Ward and Dubos, 1972, p. 20). Furthermore, the neo-liberal approach encourages individuals to pursue their own self-interests to the detriment of the interests of the broader community (this was reflected in Prime Minister Margaret Thatcher's view that 'there is no such thing as society') and thereby causes the decline of social altruism in human relationships.

Advocates of the critical alternative view of development there-fore believe that the continued existence of global development-related problems, such as poverty and hunger, represent the out-working of a neo-liberal philosophy which, like the biblical princi-ple in regard to faith, ensures that 'to everyone that has shall more be given, and he shall have an abundance, but from the one who does not have, even what he does have will be taken away' (Matthew 25:29). Consequently it is believed that whilst neo-liberal-ism holds sway, it will remain true that although 'humanity shares one planet, it is a planet on which there are two worlds, the world of the rich and the world of the poor' (Raanan Weitz quoted in Todaro, 1989, p. 3).

Development and Inequality on the International Agenda

For most of the post-war period, the status and handling of the issue of development at the international level has been determined by Northern governments, and the intergovernmental organizations which they dominate, especially the IMF and the World Bank. Since the beginning of the 1980s, as we have already seen, the policies of these actors have all been strongly influenced by the neo-liberal agenda. The principal manifestation of this at the interna-tional level has been the Structural Adjustment Programmes (SAPs) supported by the IMF and the World Bank. These programmes have similar aims and components for all countries to which they are applied: a reduction in government expenditure through the removal of subsidies, the cutback of welfare spending and the privatization of government-owned industries and services; the removal of restrictions on the import and export of goods; the deregulation of the economy; the promotion of foreign investment; and the devaluation of the exchange rate in order to encourage exports and reduce imports. The IMF and the World Bank claim that such policies are essentially apolitical in nature and simply reflect the 'value-free' principles uncovered by 'positive economics'. However, such a claim must be regarded as disingenuous, since SAPs clearly adhere to the neo-liberal political agenda of minimal government, a *laissez-faire* free-market economy, international free-trade, and the promotion of private business interests. Indeed, the IMF and the World Bank must be regarded as the principle instruments through which the doctrine of neo-liberalism has obtained its current hegemony in the global order (Broad and Landi, 1996, p. 15).

The IMF and the World Bank believe that, although SAPs may in the short term have a deleterious effect on the economies to which they are applied, they will eventually secure long-term prosperity for Southern countries. In support of this view they cite the cases of the economic 'tigers' of South East Asia, such as Hong Kong, Taiwan, South Korea, and Singapore, which secured high economic growth rates during the 1980s on the basis of their export-oriented policies. However, these countries – which represent only 2 per cent of the total population of the South – should be regarded as the exception rather than the rule and, as one commentator observes, 'few of the countries undertaking structural adjustment have turned into tigers. Most have turned into turkeys' (Michael Massing, quoted in Kegley and Wittkopf, 1993, p. 273). Further-more the policies of these newly-industrializing countries (NICs) in Asia placed heavy reliance upon state-intervention and investment in targeted sectors of their economies and cannot be regarded as models of free-market orthodoxy. Certainly, for much of the rest of the South, SAPs have had detrimental consequences for the poor and socially marginalized. In 1990, for example, the Report of the South Commission noted that,

> the complete disregard of equity in prescriptions for structural adjustments . . . had devastating effects on vital public services like health and education, with especially harmful consequences for the most vulnerable social groups. (South Commission, 1990, p. 67)

Consequently, whilst development defined according to the ortho-dox perspective – that is, the generation of economic growth through the promotion of free-market principles – has occupied a relatively high position on the international agenda, the view of development held by the critical alternative perspective – essentially the promotion of human welfare – has, until recently, been hardly considered at all.

In the post-war era another set of actors, besides governmental and inter-governmental organizations, that have begun to influence the way development is treated at the international level are multinational corporations (MNCs). These, along with transnational banks (TNBs), have been of growing significance throughout the last two decades and, given current trends, it is probable that in the future their activities will become more important in determining the course of development than the policies of governments, the World Bank or the IMF. In large part this can be attributed to the very success of the latter in promoting the development of a neoliberal global order in which the role of the state is minimized and that of the market is maximized. Indeed, according to one analyst, rather than assisting countries to achieve higher living standards for their poor, '[t]he main role of the IMF and the World Bank is the construction, regulation and support of a world system where multinational corporations trade and move capital without restrictions from nation states' (Laurence Harris, quoted in Vallely, 1990, p. 185).

The rise of MNCs has undoubtedly been a key aspect of the latest phase of economic globalization. In the late 1960s, there were only about 7,000 MNCs, whereas in the 1992 there were over 37,000 of them and they were responsible for 5.8 trillion dollars worth of sales – more than the value of all the world's trade exports put together (*Newsweek*, 26 June 1995, p. 35). In the 1990s investments by MNCs in the South have become much more significant in monetary terms than official development aid (which for most Northern governments has never reached the UN target figure of 0.7 per cent of their GNP). For example, whilst US foreign aid declined from 11.4 billion dollars in 1990 to 9.7 billion dollars in 1993, the outflow of US foreign investment rose from 423.2 billion dollars in 1990 to 548.7 billion dollars in 1993 (*Newsweek*, 26 June 1995, p. 35). The declining importance of foreign aid relative to foreign investment is set to continue into the next millennium for two main reasons. Firstly, government-to-government aid is regarded by the prevailing neoliberal orthodoxy as a form of state-intervention in the market which should be eradicated (it is noteworthy that the World Bank increasingly prefers to channel funds to private organizations rather than to states). Secondly, the adoption of neo-liberal inspired privatization programmes by Southern governments is providing further opportunities for MNCs to expand their sphere of operations.

Whilst MNCs are today generally welcomed by the governments of the South because of the financial capital, technology, managerial skills and elite career opportunities that they introduce into the economy, the consequences of their activities are sometimes detrimental to the interests of the poorer citizens of Southern states. Some of the most important criticisms of MNCs are that they

> typically produce inappropriate products (those demanded by a small rich minority of the local population), stimulate inappropriate consumption patterns through advertising and their monopolistic market power, and do this all with inappropriate (capital intensive) technologies of production. (Todaro, 1989, p. 477)

In other words, the profit-maximizing objectives of MNCs, if not restrained by ethical concerns, can have highly deleterious social and environmental consequences in Southern states. Instances of this include the following: agribusiness operations which have encouraged the production of cash-crops for export at the cost of decreased food production for the domestic market (for example, Brazil is the world's second largest exporter of food products, and yet is estimated to have 30 million people hungry); the merchandising of unsafe commodities, such as pesticides, cigarettes, and pharmaceutical products, which have been banned in the North; and the encouragement given to governments to switch funds from grassroots development projects to huge infrastructure construction schemes.

The activities of MNCs have encouraged the emergence of a worldwide affluent, consumption-oriented class, so that the lifestyle of an elite in the South has far more in common with their North American and European counterparts than with most of those living in the South. Too often in the past, MNCs have represented both the products and agents of a materialistic culture which encourages the pursuit of self-gratification and the wasteful consumption of global resources. Certainly, the more recent adoption of ethical mission statements and community involvement programmes on the part of some MNCs are hopeful signs of change and, if widely implemented, they could significantly alter the impact that MNCs are having in the South.

Developmental NGOs and grass-roots development organizations (GDOs – these are distinguished from NGOs by being made

up of the poor themselves) represent another set of non-governmental actors that in recent decades have attempted to influence the
international agenda with regard to development. Whilst most
MNCs are headquartered in the North (with the exception of a
few based in NICs, such as Daewoo of South Korea), there are now
many NGOs headquartered in the South, as well as in the North.
Prominent Northern NGOs with developmental concerns include
Oxfam, the Save the Children Fund, the Catholic Fund for Overseas Development (CAFOD), World Vision, and Christian Aid.
Examples of Southern NGOs include the Malaysian-based Third
World Network, the Campaign against Hunger in Brazil, the
Sarvodaya Shramadana Movement in Sri Lanka, the Grameen
Bank of Bangladesh, and the Freedom from Debt Coalition in
the Philippines. Southern GDOs include landless peasants movements, rural workers' unions (such as the rubber-tappers' union
founded by Chico Mendes), tribal peoples' rights groups, food
cooperatives, credit and savings groups, and the base ecclesial
communities associated with the Roman Catholic Church. These
groups have access to considerably less resources than those available to MNCs, Northern governments or multilateral development
banks (although, as a result of debt-repayments, net-transfers of
financial resources to the South by Northern NGOs exceed those of
the World Bank). However, they have made important contributions to meeting the needs of poor people around the world. They
have also played an important role in campaigning for change in the
policies of the World Bank. It is chiefly from amongst NGOs and
GDOs that the critical alternative perspective on development has
arisen, and although, as we will see in the next section, this
perspective has yet to make major inroads on the development
orthodoxy, there have been some successes.

Development and Inequality in the Post-Cold War World

The end of the Cold War has had a number of important repercussions on the way the development issue is currently being presented.
At the time of the destruction of the Berlin Wall in 1989 there was
much talk of a 'peace-dividend' and the possibility was voiced that
funds previously assigned to military budgets could be diverted to

provide a larger source of funds for development-oriented projects in the world's poorer countries. This optimistic prospect has proved to be illusory. Although some analysts still feel that 'bipolarity's demise will allow the long-dormant seed of North–South cooperation to germinate as previously stymied North–South alliances emerge to forge solutions to common problems' (Richard Feinberg and Delia Boylan, quoted in Kegley and Wittkopf, 1993, p. 152), it now appears that the South is highly justified in feeling 'profound anxiety that the termination of the East-West struggle will cause the industrial democracies to forget about it' (ibid., p. 263).

Before the Cold War ended, some Southern governments had certainly become 'Accustomed to an age where conflict provided a magnet for . . . foreign policy attention', but now the competition between the two superpowers to secure allies in the South has finished it should not be surprising that the latter 'now fears falling off the North's agenda' (ibid., p. 263). Such a situation is made even worse because the South faces competition from the former Eastern bloc for a diminishing pool of inter-governmental aid. Consequently, Southern governments have had to turn to other sources, primarily foreign investors and foreign-owned MNCs.

The changes associated with the end of the Cold War mean that the special development needs of the South are increasingly being ignored by the North, which is putting forward an essentially Western localized worldview as a universal truth. This is made clear in Francis Fukuyama's view that we are today witnessing

> not just the end of the Cold War . . . but the end of history as such: that is, the end point of mankind's ideological evolution and the universalization of Western liberal democracy. (Fukuyama, 1989, p. 4)

According to Fukuyama, the collapse of the state-controlled, centrally-planned economies of the former Eastern bloc symbolizes 'the triumph of the West, . . . an unabashed victory of economic and political liberalism . . . [and] the total exhaustion of viable systematic alternatives to Western [neo-]liberalism' (ibid., p. 3). The arrogance of this claim is astonishing, as is the ignorance of other possible modes of social and economic organization that may better serve humanity.

In the South, the adverse effects of the prevailing market-oriented development model have stimulated the generation of a critical alternative model of development amongst grassroots communities who have been obliged to engage in cooperative 'self-help' practices to secure their access to basic resources. We have already examined some of the main elements of this alternative model and mentioned some of the groups involved. In the next section we will see the role that this alternative perspective on development has played in the institutional management of development-related issues at the international level during the post-Cold War era.

Managing Issues of Development and Inequality

In the 1990s, one of the most important institutional mechanisms for dealing with development-related matters has been the convening of global summits under the auspices of the UN. Most noteworthy are the United Nations Conference on Environment and Development (UNCED) or 'Earth Summit' held at Rio de Janeiro, Brazil, in June 1992, and the United Nations World Summit on Social Development held at Copenhagen in March 1995.

The Earth Summit was important for familiarizing a wider audience with the concept of 'sustainable development'. This concept had first come to public attention in the early 1980s in an International Union for the Conservation of Nature (IUCN) document. It received further emphasis in the influential Brundtland Report of the World Commission on Environment and Development (WCED) in 1987, which defined sustainable development as a process that 'meets the needs of the present without compromising the ability of future generations to meet their own needs' (WCED, 1987, p. 8). Embracing the new terminology of sustainable development, the official inter-state UNCED gathering gave public acknowledgement to the idea that the environment and development are inextricably linked, and it encouraged important actors such as the World Bank to assert their commitment to a 'new environmentalism, which recognizes that economic development and environmental sustainability are partners' (World Bank, 1995, p. ii). Most significantly, however, the conference gave further legitimation to market-dominated development policies. The

UNCED linked environment and development in name only and the agenda of the conference was dominated by the entrenched interests of Northern and Southern elites.

Consequently, the inter-state conference failed to identify the global environmental crisis as part of a larger developmental crisis. It ignored the major issues of debt, terms of trade, aid, and the consumption of resources, which formed a central part of the discussions conducted at the parallel NGO summit at Rio. Some critics have therefore concluded that, despite the apparent 'mainstreaming' of environmental concerns that occurred at UNCED, 'the old thinking about economic growth [still] prevails' and 'the old establishment that had made a living out of such economic growth has [merely] repackaged itself in green' (Chatterjee and Finger, 1994, p. 162).

The task of the 1995 Copenhagen Summit was to address continuing and widespread poverty, inequality, and unemployment. However, despite the dissent voiced earlier by some Southern governments, the inter-governmental *Summit Declaration and Programme of Action*, concluded that the best method for alleviating development-related problems is the pursuit of economic growth through the continued promotion of free-market policies and individual initiative. Effectively the declaration called for a further extension of the neo-liberal model of development, and whilst there were a few very watered-down references to structural adjustment, debt and the need for dialogue between the UN and the IMF/World Bank, no mention was made of the social responsibilities of MNCs or the possibility of new transfers of finance from the North to the South.

In contrast to the inter-governmental deliberations, the *Alternative Declaration*, produced by the parallel NGO Forum at the Copenhagen Summit, severely criticized the prevailing neo-liberal development model for aggravating rather than alleviating the global social crisis, and put forward its own alternative model of development based on the principles of environmental sustainability, social equity, and community participation and empowerment. The NGOs specifically identified the policies of government privatization and trade liberalization as being responsible for growing global inequality, and called for the immediate cancellation of debt, improved terms of trade, greater transparency and accountability of the IMF and the World Bank, and international regulation of the activities of MNCs.

UNCED and the Copenhagen Summit highlight two major shortcomings in current strategies to manage development problems. First, both meetings incorporated some of the language of the alternative development model into the development orthodoxy. By so doing, opposition to the orthodoxy was effectively neutered and neutralized. There was a complete failure to address the underlying cause of the continuing development/environment crisis and so no appropriate ways out of the crisis were put forward. Secondly, the global scope of the development crisis requires a response which transcends the limitations of inter-state agreements. The state is simultaneously too small to deal with some development concerns, and too large to deal with others. The global nature of the crisis requires the involvement of a whole range of non-state actors, not simply in pre-conference discussion groups, as happened prior to the Rio Summit, but also at the decision-making, implementation, and monitoring stages. The NGO community received a massive impetus in the run-up to the Rio and Copenhagen summits. However their role in implementation is negligible. For example, the Commission on Sustainable Development, created to monitor the implementation of the UNCED output, is composed of state representatives; NGOs can speak at meetings only at the discretion of the chairperson. And local governments, on whom so much depends in terms of implementation of sustainable development policies, do not get a voice there at all.

Before closing this section it is important to mention the efforts of the United Nations Development Programme (UNDP) to legitimize a different set of indicators of development. In 1990 the UNDP published its Human Development Index, and every year since it has built on the ideas contained in this concept. Recognizing a need to move away from conventional indicators of development based on measuring the rate of economic growth, per capita income and industrialization, the UNDP set itself apart from the World Bank and IMF and suggested measuring life expectancy, adult literacy, and local purchasing power (see UNDP, 1994). As an institutional mechanism, this yardstick is gaining ground within the UN system, but until it is accepted by the IMF and World Bank its impact on altering the fundamental parameters of the development experience of the poor will be very limited.

Development, Inequality and World Politics

Consideration of the issue of development in the 1990s raises a number of important challenges to some prevailing conceptions of world politics. The dominant state-centric approach has focused on external military threats to a state's territorial boundaries. Scant attention has been paid to the activities of non-state actors and to issues such as poverty, hunger, and environmental degradation.

Chapter 1 in this volume pointed out that practitioners of world politics have traditionally categorized issues relating to the security of the state as matters of 'high politics', whilst issues relating to the economic and social welfare of its citizens have been consigned to the relatively less important realm of 'low politics'. Development-related matters, unless they have implications for state security, have been placed into the relatively marginalized category of 'low politics'. Furthermore, since the most influential practitioners and analysts of world politics have tended to be residents in the 'developed' North, the issue of development has generally not been high on the agenda even when 'low politics' have been considered. Consequently, students of world politics have tended to give low priority to the issue of development.

To put into perspective the relative importance that traditional security concerns and development-related matters represent to global humanity, it is worth noting the total number of people killed during the First and Second World Wars is estimated as having been about 30 million, whilst the number of people who currently die of hunger-related causes each year is nearly 15 million. Consequently we can say that every two years the number of people who die of hunger is roughly equivalent to the number killed in eleven years of world war.

The expansion of the market into all areas of human life means that global resources are increasingly being channelled to meet the wants of the wealthy, whilst the needs of the poor are being ignored. In other words, human security is being eroded. The capacity of the state to meet food security needs and basic welfare is being undermined, and responsibility is being transferred to the impersonal operation of the market. The ability of the world's poor to secure their families and communities in terms of basic needs is diminishing. Economic globalization is narrowing choice and opportunity for the vulnerable. The eradication of poverty is being removed from the public domain. Indeed, with the acceptance of the market as the determining factor in entitlement, the issue of poverty appears to have been removed from the international agenda altogether!

In response to this disempowerment, a new type of politics is evolving – a participatory, emancipatory politics of empowerment. We are witnessing the resistance of community groups across the South and the development of a global civil society committed to a different vision of society and citizenship. Coalitions are developing within states and across states, and groups are gaining a voice in politics which they have been denied hitherto. The Chipkos in India and Brazilian rubber-tappers are but two examples. NGO coalitions, Northern activists pursuing Shell Oil, Nigerian social activists campaigning for the rights of the Ogoni people and human rights generally are all part of the evolving global civil society. While the power of the economic orthodoxy seems overwhelming, history suggests that the pendulum will swing in the other direction. There is evidence that the counter-force is already apparent.

Finally, as students of world politics it is necessary for us to realize that we can make an important contribution to the development debate, and that

> being among the world's privileged, you and I have a special obligation to think and act as a global citizen, to be a steward of whatever power we hold, to contribute to the transforming forces that are reshaping the world. The future of human society, of our children, depends on each of us. (Korten, 1990, p. 216)

Guide to Further Reading

An excellent starting point for beginners in this area is B. Jackson (1990). This is a straightforward, lucid and compelling account of the problems of poverty and underdevelopment. Building on this foundation, readers should then consult Thomas (1996). Thomas and Wilkin (1996) provide a number of clearly written chapters on a range of issues touched on in the chapter here. The book has the specific aim of understanding the impact of economic globalization, and the neo-liberal agenda, on the lives of marginalized peoples throughout the world. Its chapters address a range of topics including contending views on development, the global political economy of food, and the environment.

6

Arms and Arms Control

JOANNA SPEAR

In this chapter two main categories of weapons are discussed: so-called *weapons of mass destruction* (nuclear, chemical and biological weapons) and *conventional weapons*. In each case the weapons are discussed in the context of security, economic and ethical issues. What quickly becomes apparent is that conventional weapons are the 'odd man out'. Weapons of mass destruction (WMD) have traditionally been the targets of national and international arms control efforts, are regarded as having important implications for international security, have consequently been subject to export controls, and are the subject of considerable ethical concern. By contrast, conventional weapons have rarely elicited such attention.

With respect to both WMD and conventional weapons, there are tensions between the economic benefits of sales and the security problems that may result from such transfers. However, whereas in the realm of WMD the balance is weighted towards controls, with conventional weapons there is much less consideration of the security implications of sales and a greater focus on the economic advantages that result. This neglect of the long-term security implications of conventional arms transfers is potentially problematic. With both WMD and conventional weapons, but particularly the latter, the balance has tilted more towards commercial criteria. As discussed later in this chapter, the striking of compromises between exports and controls has proved particularly problematic in the post-Cold War period.

WMD have long been subject to debate on ethical grounds. The manner and scale of their operation singles them out as something different, and these ethical concerns in part account for the significant number of initiatives which have been introduced aiming to control or eliminate these weapons. By contrast, there has been much less attention paid to the ethical consequences of conventional weapons deployment and use. However, as we shall see, that is now beginning to change.

The Significance of Arms and Arms Control Issues

Weapons of mass destruction

Fear of nuclear war dominated security planning during the Cold War. The end of the Cold War has led to a decrease in concern about the dangers of thermonuclear war between the superpowers. This concern has been replaced in some quarters with a tendency to think that the major security problems are 'over' because of the demise of the Cold War. This is ironic because the majority of the nuclear weapons that were perceived to cause the problem are still in place (Dean, 1994, pp. 34–41). Nevertheless, because of the decreased threat, there is less inclination to do anything about these nuclear arsenals. This means that those interested in arms control and disarmament are having a hard time convincing governments and publics that existing nuclear arsenals are an issue that needs to be tackled. The new problem that arms controllers face is complacency.

If the danger of nuclear war between the superpowers has declined dramatically, other nuclear issues have increased in importance. In the post-Cold War period there is greater concern about nuclear proliferation, that is, the spread of nuclear weapons and the technology and knowledge required to build them. This was a less significant issue on the security agenda during the Cold War when there were two different perspectives on nuclear proliferation. First, those states who were already acknowledged as possessing nuclear weapons (The United States, The Soviet Union, Britain, France and China) were concerned to prevent other states from obtaining nuclear weapons, thus preventing what is called *horizontal* proliferation. A different perspective was taken by non-nuclear states such as India, Indonesia and Egypt who were concerned about the build-up in the arsenals of the five nuclear powers, and particularly about the nuclear arms race between the superpowers. They were more concerned about what is called *vertical* proliferation. Reflecting the power positions of the nuclear weapons states, however, the concerns about horizontal proliferation always received much greater attention. This is illustrated by The Nuclear Non-Proliferation Treaty (NPT) of 1968 which placed great emphasis on stemming horizontal proliferation with barely a mention of vertical proliferation.

In the post-Cold War period this situation has been reinforced: concerns about nuclear proliferation are now almost exclusively about horizontal proliferation, reflecting the successful agenda-setting of the nuclear weapons states. The only time when the issue of vertical proliferation was raised was when China and France conducted underground nuclear tests in 1995–6. These tests were heavily criticized, particularly by states such as India, Australia and New Zealand who championed the end of nuclear testing. Following the tests, France (rather hypocritically in the eyes of some) joined the US and Britain in calling for a Comprehensive Test Ban Treaty (CTBT). The effect of the tests was to return the question of nuclear proliferation to the international agenda, albeit briefly.

It appears that the end of the Cold War has not diminished the significance attached to nuclear weapons, as many had hoped (Woollacott, 1996). Indeed, the incentives for states to acquire nuclear weapons would appear to have increased in the post-Cold War period (Carpenter, 1992, pp. 64–5, 71). Three comments are relevant here. First, the fact that nuclear weapons states have substantially maintained their nuclear arsenals shows that they consider that nuclear weapons play some positive role in providing security. Moreover, the continued reliance on nuclear deterrence sends a signal to the rest of the international community that nuclear weapons are still useful. This contradicts the explicit message that these same states are pushing: that horizontal proliferation should be prevented.

Second, there are now greater incentives for those non-nuclear states to acquire nuclear weapons who have lost the guarantee of extended deterrence previously provided by the superpowers. Extended deterrence, or the 'nuclear umbrella', exists when a nuclear weapons state promises to come to the aid of a non-nuclear state should it be attacked. With the retreat from extended deterrence these states feel vulnerable. For example, even Japan has suggested that should the US withdraw its nuclear umbrella, she would feel obliged to become a nuclear weapons state (Rafferty, 1996).

Third, the combination of the loss of extended deterrence with regional dynamics appears to have increased the incentives to proliferate. For example, Pakistan now perceives itself to be vulnerable to attack from India because the US has scaled back its support. India, who has lost the backing of the Soviet Union, in turn feels vulnerable to both Pakistan and China. In such situations, the instability caused by the breakdown of Cold War alliances can be seen as an incentive to states to acquire a nuclear deterrent.

Two events have increased fears about horizontal nuclear proliferation in the post-Cold War world. First, in the aftermath of the Gulf War, United Nations' Weapons Inspection Teams discovered alarming evidence of the extent of the Iraqi nuclear programme. It was found that Iraq had made significant progress towards a nuclear weapons capability (and had also developed chemical and biological weapons) and had been assisted in this by the purchase of equipment and technologies from both Eastern and Western states (Zimmerman, 1994). This led to the recognition that existing non-proliferation strategies had failed because Iraq – a signatory of the NPT since 1968 – was covertly developing nuclear weapons (Kay, 1994). Without Saddam Hussein's miscalculation over Kuwait, the world would not have known about the Iraqi nuclear programme.

Second, the threat of horizontal proliferation has, ironically, been heightened by one of the consequences of the end of the Cold War, the demise of the Soviet Union. The emergence of a clutch of new states who retain sectors of the Soviet military industrial complex and who face severe economic problems, has led to increased fears that their nuclear technologies, fissile (radioactive) materials and scientific knowledge will be sold off to the highest bidders (Potter, 1995). These fears are heightened because many of these new states have very rudimentary or non-existent export controls. There have already been several instances of attempts to sell fissile materials on the international black market, and there is mounting concern about the ability of intelligence agencies in the East to prevent these transfers (van Ham, 1994, p. 54).

With greater opportunities for obtaining weapons and fissile materials there are also fears about 'nuclear terrorism', a term that describes the possibility of state-sponsored or non-state terrorist groups obtaining nuclear weapons and holding the world to ransom (Potter, 1995, pp. 13–14) To date, these seem somewhat fanciful speculations, but they are already informing moves towards new 'counter-proliferation' policies in the United States and are therefore assuming international importance (Bowen and Dunn, 1996, pp. 132–5).

To turn briefly to other WMD, chemical and biological weapons (CBW) were always considered to be illegitimate weapons of war. Indeed, in the aftermath of of the First World War, it was agreed – in the 1925 Gas Protocol of the Geneva Convention – that nerve gas would not be used in the future because the injuries and suffering it caused were unacceptable (Best, 1994, p. 296). During the Cold War, attention centred primarily on the CBW of the Superpowers, but in fact, more ominous developments occurred outside of the superpower relationship. Chemical weapons were used in the war between Iran and Iraq in the 1980s, and Iraq employed nerve gas against Kurdish villages in 1988 (Black and Pearson, 1993). Although some of the inhibitions on the development and use of CBW remain, these events indicated that existing control measures were inadequate.

Concerns about CBW proliferation were significantly heightened during the 1991 Gulf War when there were fears that Iraq would use *Scud* missiles armed with chemical and biological warheads against the alliance. There was consequently a realization that existing conventions were being eroded and that something needed to be done about these weapons. This was a spur to efforts to reach international agreements banning the use of CBW. With CBW, however, control measures are difficult to devise and implement because the components have legitimate commercial uses. There is therefore a tension between security interests (which favour controls) and economic interests (which favour trade). CBW proliferation continues to pose problems of great concern. This is in part a consequence of the ethical issues that they raise, but also reflects the fact that they are a potential security threat to all states and are difficult to eliminate because they are easily manufactured.

Conventional weapons

The fact that the proliferation of conventional weapons has rarely received great attention within world politics reflects the fact that, unlike WMD, they are considered legitimate tools of defence and statehood. During the Cold War, conventional weapons were regarded as a premier tool of superpower diplomacy and supplied freely to key allies and neutral states. The Cold War has bequeathed two important legacies in the realm of conventional arms. The first is the vast amounts of weapons which were stored up by the two alliances in anticipation of war between East and West. The end of the Cold War has meant that many countries are left with vast arsenals of weapons which are both more numerous and more sophisticated than required for the types of security threats that they now face. Many states – but particularly those formerly part of the Soviet bloc – are seeking to sell off what are now regarded as 'surplus weapons' from their arsenals. Because of the financial situations of such states, these sales are considered a necessity to obtain hard currency. Although these states may consider their weapons surplus or obsolete, they can nevertheless have a significant impact upon security when supplied to states or non-state groups further down the arms hierarchy.

The second legacy are the economies of the two alliance blocs, geared towards military production. During the Cold War, conventional arms transfers were justified in geo-strategic and political terms, with little attention paid to the economic side of the equation. However, supplier states became dependent on arms transfers abroad for maintaining their defence-production-oriented economies. With the end of the Cold War there has been a sharp decrease in military procurement in both East and West. This means there is now even greater pressure to sell abroad to maintain defence industries (and therefore prosperity and employment) at home. The key point here is that, in the aftermath of the Cold War, the trade in conventional weapons has been largely depoliticized and is now regarded primarily as a commercial venture.

Together these trends of continued production and the selling off of surplus weapons have led to significant changes in the international conventional arms market which is now characterized by overcapacity. This move to a 'buyer's market' is having important effects upon the international trade in conventional weapons. First, the increasing commercialization of the trade – and its consequent deregulation – has brought in a whole new range of players, both individuals and companies, legitimate and illegitimate, all involved in trying to secure conventional weapons sales.

Second, a consequence of the permissive market and the desperation to secure sales is that existing (minimal) ethical standards governing weapons sales are being eroded. The depoliticization means that issues such as human rights are being increasingly marginalized in the search for sales opportunities. For example, British Aerospace (BAe) has been engaged in selling Hawk aircraft to Indonesia. The human rights record of the Indonesian government is very poor and the sales have been criticized as 'an outrageous deal' supporting a repressive regime (Campaign Against the Arms Trade) (CAAT, 1996). BAe and the British government have said that the deal is acceptable because the aircraft could not be used against local populations. However, this is disputable as Hawks could conceivably be used in counter-insurgency activities in East Timor, an island illegally occupied by Indonesia. The fact that BAe is going ahead with this ethically controversial sale is an indication of the commercial importance of sales abroad. This pattern of the primacy of economic over ethical considerations is repeated in many other supplier states.

Third, the buyer's market allows would-be purchasers to play suppliers off against one another to obtain the best deals and the most sophisticated weapons. For example, there has been a scramble to sell advanced fighter aircraft to the United Arab Emirates (UAE). The UAE wishes to procure fighters supplied with sophisticated AMRAAMs (Advanced, Medium Range Air-to-Air Missiles). Initially the UAE requested fighters and missiles from the US, but was refused on the basis that AMRAAMs were only available to NATO allies and that such a sale would have the undesirable effect of introducing a new level of technology into the region. However, after the UAE flirted with France and Russia – who both agreed to supply fighters with AMRAAMs – the US acceded to UAE demands. This is a clear instance of a recipient playing the buyer's market to its advantage. The same sort of bargaining is happening at lower levels of the trade and is ensuring that quite sophisticated weapons are obtained for bargain prices.

Fourth, the buyer's market has led to erosion of the convention that weapons are to be sold only to governments. Although not completely adhered to, this norm did inform commercial arms transfers made during the Cold War. Now, however, such sales are actively sought and non-state groups are able to obtain weapons with apparent ease. Increasing supplies of weapons are now reaching sub-state groups involved in battles against their governments or involved in inter-ethnic conflicts (Spear, 1996, pp. 383–4). A good example of the primacy of commercial considerations comes from Russia, where the Chechen rebels have obtained weapons from *Russian* manufacturers more interested in earning money than supporting their government (*Agence France-Presse International News*, 1995).

Finally, during the Cold War it was the case that supplier states would not provide weapons to states engaged in conflict – unless they had a direct strategic interest in the outcome of the conflict. In the post-Cold War period there seems to be confusion amongst suppliers over how to behave. For example, in Rwanda, after the Rwandan Patriotic Front (RPF – the Tutsi-dominated group) began an insurgency against the Hutu government, the Belgians banned all weapons supplies to Rwanda (even though it was their client state). By contrast, the French government stepped up its transfers in support of the Hutu government (Goose and Smyth, 1994). Policy is also changing in the United States. At the end of 1994, the US was providing military goods and services to 26 countries involved in internal or external conflicts (Hartung, 1995, p. 10).

Although considered non-controversial during the Cold War, conventional weapons issues are now forcing their way on to the international agenda. There are three areas of concern. First, there is increasing concern about ballistic missiles as delivery systems for WMD payloads. Ballistic missiles are conventional weapons, but their importance stems from the fact that they can be armed with nuclear, chemical or biological warheads. The advantage of ballistic missiles is that they can deliver payloads to distant targets relatively cheaply and they are hard to detect and destroy in flight (unlike most bomber aircraft). Concerns about ballistic missiles in the hands of Third World states were first raised in 1988 when Iran and Iraq used these weapons to terrorize each others' civilian populations in the 'war of the cities' (Bowen and Dunn, 1996, p. 117). However, it was not until the Gulf conflict that fears about the combination of ballistic missiles and WMD payloads became acute.

Second, conventional weapons proliferation is being recognized as one of the factors fuelling inter-ethnic conflicts (see also Chapter 8). Although rarely the sole cause of such conflicts, the transfer of conventional weapons – and particularly the easy availability of light weapons – has prolonged and intensified existing inter-ethnic conflicts and helped to ignite new conflicts (Goose and Smyth, 1994; Hartung, 1995; Spear, 1996).

Third, an ethical debate about conventional weapons has re-ignited with a focus on 'inhumane' weapons. 'Inhumane weapons' seems an odd term as the whole point of weapons is to debilitate enemies by inflicting pain, suffering and death. It is nevertheless the case that at several points in modern history, particular weapons have been outlawed – by mutual agreement – because the suffering they cause is considered unacceptable. During the First World War, for example, so-called dumdum bullets (soft-nosed bullets which spread out into the victim's flesh doing massive internal damage) were outlawed by common agreement. During the Second World War, in addition to the ban on dumdum bullets, the 1925 nerve gas Protocol was observed.

During the Cold War the attention given to the question of inhumane weapons was minimal. The demands of establishing and maintaining nuclear deterrence were thought to override such minor considerations. Nevertheless, as the Cold War thawed, interest in this category of weapons increased and there have been attempts to extend the category of weapons internationally acknowledged as 'inhumane'. In the 1990s, campaigns have been mounted to elim-inate two types of weapons – anti-personnel landmines and blinding laser weapons (Leahy, 1995).

Despite the higher profile of conventional weapons for the reasons outlined above, one proliferation issue that has arisen since the end of the Cold War remains largely unacknowledged: the surplus capacity in the defence industries of East and West (Mar-kusen and Yudken, 1992). Ironically, at a time when many security commentators have been searching around for 'new' security issues, this form of proliferation has received insufficient attention. Never-theless, this issue has long-term implications for security. The failure to dismantle and reorient the defence-production-biased Cold War economies of East and West could contribute to a new round of insecurity in three ways.

First, if a less benign political force came to power in Russia (such as the communists or the ultra-nationalists) then the existing Russian military industrial complex could lead to increased US perceptions of a military threat from Russia (Nye, 1996, pp. 11–14). Similarly, new Russian leaders may also perceive a threat from the still extensive US military-industrial complex. Second, the desire to secure sales agreements in a competitive market is leading states to agree to the transfer of production technologies alongside (or as a substitute for) weapons sales. This has important implications for the likely proliferation of advanced conventional weapons in the future. This highlights the tensions between short-run economic needs and long-term security threats. Third, the desire of states with defence industries to preserve them through securing overseas sales may have unintended consequences. Uncoordinated sales relying upon the market as the only regulator may serve to create the security threats of the future. Thus the short-run economic policies of today may create the long-term security threats of the future.

The dilemma can be illustrated by looking at the issue of the next generation of fighter aircraft. Five different states or state consortia are now designing and producing fighter aircraft: the United States is producing the F-22; France is producing the Rafale; Sweden has produced the Gripen; a consortium of Germany, Britain, Italy and Spain is producing the Eurofighter 2000; and Russia is thought to be producing the SU-34 multi-role frontal bomber and the SU-27M fighter bomber (Forsberg, 1994). Several important issues arise from this.

At the moment there are no international security threats that demand the acquisition of next generation combat aircraft. The only potential peer threats are the other supplier states and at present relations between these states are quite benign. Nevertheless, production seems set to go ahead and may help to create future tensions between these supplier states – particularly the United States and Russia. Secondly, for domestic procurement (that is, purchase by the supplier states themselves) of the next generation of combat aircraft to be viable, sales abroad are a necessity. This illustrates that short-run 'economic security' issues are driving the production of the next generation of aircraft, even though this will lead to the creation of the security threats that the producer states will then face. Sales to states further down the arms hierarchy would stimulate new domestic procurement as suppliers seek to ensure that they maintain their technological superiority.

The inattention to this issue reflects several factors. First, there is an unwillingness to acknowledge the extent to which during the Cold War the needs of security affected the economies of the protagonists. Second, there is a desire to let the market sort out the problem, rather than arms control, reflecting both a lack of faith in the latter and too much faith in the former. Finally, as noted above, the silence reflects the fact that too little attention is paid to conventional weapons despite their implications for security.

General Problems of Arms and Weapons-Related Issues

The continuing significance of arms and weapons-related issues, even after the end of the Cold War, points to several deep-rooted problems which continue to drive the production and trade in both WMD and conventional weapons and lead to the consequent security, economic and ethical dilemmas examined in this chapter.

To deal first with the question of security, the fact that states continue to seek both WMD and conventional weapons points to the fact that they feel insecure. The search for security has for centuries involved the acquisition of weapons. However, as Robert Jervis has noted, getting weapons does not always bring security as it can have unanticipated consequences. To illustrate, State A acquires weapons (through production or transfer) in order to ensure its security. However, what State A regards as a defensive action may not be perceived in that way by State B, which feels threatened by State A's weapons and decides that it requires more firepower itself. Jervis calls this the 'security dilemma' and notes that it has often resulted in arms races (Jervis, 1978).

It is clear that some states regard getting WMD as a means of escaping the security dilemma because they would then be protected by nuclear deterrence or by possession of the 'poor man's bomb' as chemical weapons are often called. However, as the Cold War arms race between the superpowers illustrated, getting WMD is not an end to the problem, but an upward ratchet in the arms race. The key question remains, then, how to escape the security dilemma. One answer would seem to lie in arms control initiatives.

The international community – dominated by the great powers – is willing to tackle these proliferation issues only by the supply-side route. There is a general unwillingness to deal with the demand side of the equation, that is, to look at the problems that lead states to seek WMD and advanced conventional weapons. This unwillingness to look at the causes of the security dilemma is a traditional approach to security in an anarchic, self-help-based international system. However, it means that responses to the proliferation problem are inevitably one-sided and will at best control the problem, rather than solve it.

Turning to the interaction between economics and security in the realm of arms, it is in debates over export controls that the tensions between the two become most obvious. The problem arises because many of the technologies and techniques necessary for the creation of WMD and conventional weapons also have civil (non-military) uses. These dual-use technologies are regarded by would-be recipients as necessary for the development of various industries (such as nuclear power, pharmaceuticals, satellite launch facilities, electronics and bio-technology) which in turn are regarded as essential to economic development. There are also potentially profitable transfers which supplier states are unwilling to forgo.

During the Cold War, the Western allies were fairly unified in a desire to avoid technology transfers that would aid the Communist bloc in developing WMD and advanced conventional weapons. Export controls were agreed through an organization called The Coordinating Committee on Multilateral Export Controls (Co-Com) founded in 1949. However, as the Cold War thawed, there were increasing disputes within CoCom over the desire of European states to tilt the balance in favour of greater trade. The extent of the disputes were such that the allies were unwilling to retain the CoCom structure, but nor were they able to negotiate a follow-on export control regime for over two years.

The post-Cold War forum for export controls is called the Wassenaar Arrangement on Export Controls for Conventional Arms and Dual-Use Goods and Technologies. Thus far its name is one of the few things on which the supplier states have been able to agree. Because the regime is not East–West focused, states such as Russia are being included as full partners. However, this creates problems. It has proved very difficult to gain agreement amongst the 28 governments as to the balance to be struck between economic and security issues. Also, recipients object that the regime has a North–South focus.

When looking at the issue of export controls the question arises as to whether states in the South are being kept in an economically subservient position – though justified on the basis of security – by being denied access to key technologies. This is certainly the perspective of many Southern states. The example of satellite launch facilities will serve to illustrate this. There is a very close relationship between the civil technologies necessary for launching satellites into space and the technologies that provide a ballistic missile capability. The 1987 Missile Technology Control Regime is designed to prevent the spread of technologies that would aid the development of ballistic missiles. However, this agreement is regarded by many Southern states, particularly India, as also designed to prevent them from gaining access to the lucrative satellite launch market, keeping them dependent upon Western launch facilities and therefore stunting their economic development.

Arms and Arms Control on the International Agenda

The United States is certainly in an 'agenda setting' position on issues of security through its seat on the United Nations (UN) Security Council, its leadership of NATO, the security guarantees it extends to many important states (for example, Japan) and its economic and political connections to other key states. The US and its allies are also very influential within the international fora at which specific issues are addressed, for example, the NPT and Convention on Conventional Weapons (CCW) review conferences, and the negotiations over chemical and biological weapons. In all these fora, the US is able to play a prominent role in proceedings both because of the resources it can invest in preparing for meetings and because of the alliances it is able to draw upon. The US is also one of the few states willing and able to invest the resources required for action on these issues.

The US can be described as a 'unipolar power' indicating that its defence capabilities are now unchallenged. This unipolar position allows the US a determining role in global security issues. Because of this dominance, US security priorities, such as the threats posed by 'rogue' states, the leakage of fissile materials from the former Soviet Union, the horizontal proliferation of WMD, and ballistic missile proliferation, are the issues that the US raises and the issues that become the major global security issues addressed by the international community. This is in part because many of these issues are a general threat to international security, but they are also, importantly, those issues that could threaten US pre-eminence.

The prominent role of the US can on occasions mean that US domestic politics intrudes on the international security agenda.

Similarly, changes in the US presidency can lead to changes in security priorities. For example, in the aftermath of the Gulf War, President George Bush briefly made the control of advanced conventional weapons transfers into the Middle East a security priority. While the issue remained important to Bush, some progress was made in negotiations between the permanent five members of the UN Security Council. However, once Bush decided – for reasons connected to his domestic campaign for re-election – to downgrade the issue, it quickly disappeared from the international security agenda (Spear, 1994, p. 98).

It is very difficult for a state that lacks the military and political power of the US to get issues on to the international security agenda. Even potentially influential organizations such as the European Union do not have sufficient 'clout' in the security field to set the agenda. Forums such as the UN General Assembly (where all states have equal representation) are not very effective in this context. The UN Security Council is much more influential, but even here the fact that permanent members have the power of veto means that initiatives can easily be derailed.

Nevertheless, despite the power of the US and its allies, Third World states can on occasion influence, if not set, the international security agenda. Examples of this are the moves towards the establishment of nuclear weapons free zones (see below). These are an attempt by non-nuclear weapons states both to increase their security and to question the legitimacy of nuclear weapons as a tool of state power (Davis, 1996). In this way they can be seen as aiding the fight against horizontal proliferation, but they are also a challenge to existing nuclear weapons states because they question the legitimacy of *all* nuclear weapons. They are therefore a source of some discomfort to nuclear weapons states.

Another example of agenda-setting concerns the case of landmines, which shows that, on occasion, weak actors can influence the security agenda. In this case the weak actors are non-governmental organizations (NGOs). Globally, landmines are thought to kill 10,000 civilians per year and maim a further 20,000. Landmines are being sown at a rate of 2–3 million per year and are a tremendous problem in countries such as Cambodia, Laos, Angola, Mozambique, The Falklands Islands and the states of the former Yugoslavia (Human Rights Watch and Physicians for Human Rights, 1993). As noted earlier, a campaign was launched in the

1990s to ban the production, trade and deployment of anti-person-nel landmines. The campaign was initiated by a group of US NGOs headed by the Vietnam Veterans of America Foundation and including Human Rights Watch and Physicians for Human Rights. These groups were concerned about the human, economic and environmental costs of the millions of landmines sown around the world. These NGOs gathered the support of other groups such as Oxfam and the International Red Cross and together they lobbied governments to ban landmines.

The campaign has gathered significant support, but has yet to achieve its objectives. Despite the agreement of 30 countries to support a ban on production, trade and deployment, the campaign was unable to prevail in the Convention on Conventional Weapons (CCW) review conferences of 1995–6. Despite the support of prominent states such as the US and most NATO members, there was opposition to the proposed ban from producer states such as China (and to a lesser degree from Russia, India and Pakistan who consider that the weapons have military utility). This opposition succeeded because the CCW works by consensus. The next chance to review the CCW is in 2001, by which time former UN Secretary General Boutros Boutros-Ghali estimates that 'an additional 50,000 human beings will have been killed and a further 80,000 injured by landmines' (Bennett Jones, 1996).

The momentum which this issue has gathered indicates that it is possible to get issues on to the international security agenda. Nevertheless, three salutary facts are worth noting. First, the anti-landmine campaign is primarily a Western campaign and has been able to enlist the support of these states: by contrast, in non-democratic states, its success has been very limited. Second, as indicated above, the campaign has yet to succeed, indicating the primacy of economic and security issues over ethical concerns. Finally, even if the ban were introduced immediately, the UN estimates that there are already 100 million mines laid in at least 68 countries, so the clearance task would be massive.

Arms Control Issues after the Cold War

In the immediate aftermath of the Cold War, there was great optimism that a new era of collective security was about to begin.

This seemed to be reflected in the action against Iraq in the Gulf War, which led US President George Bush to talk about a 'New World Order'. As part of this, the US championed a series of moves designed to place new limits on the horizontal proliferation of WMD and on the transfer of high technology conventional weapons. However, within a short time the initiative was in trouble. Indeed, within a year, the conventional weapons trade had resumed 'business as usual'.

Despite this, the way that weapons issues are discussed in the post-Cold War world is different. One of the key changes in the agenda, reflecting changes in fact, is that now the debate has a clearer North–South element, whereas before this was obscured by the pervasiveness of the East–West dispute. There is now agreement between the old enemies about the desirability of controlling certain types of weapons, which has significantly circumscribed the room for manoeuvre of many Southern states. This new 'Superpower' agreement has led many Southern states to call for a more targeted approach to export controls. They fear that their legitimate security and economic needs will be casualties of this new approach to proliferation issues. These concerns do seem to have been taken seriously as the US now talks of 'rogue states' in an effort to differentiate these troublesome states from the law-abiding Southern states.

It is clearly the case that despite efforts to outlaw nuclear weapons, some states are still seeking nuclear weapons and regard them as the only effective guarantor of their security. This is particularly true for the category of states which have recently been labelled 'rogue', a reference to the nature of the regimes (which tend to be authoritarian and to abuse commonly accepted standards of human rights) and their rejection of many of the (predominantly Western) values underpinning the international system. Examples include Iran, Iraq, North Korea and Libya. With the tide of democratization apparently sweeping the globe, many of these 'rogue' regimes find themselves isolated in an increasingly hostile international system. During the Cold War these states were supported by one or other of the superpowers on the basis of geo-strategic necessity. With the end of the Cold War, 'rogue' states have lost their major international backers. This has the effect of making the security dilemmas they experience more intense and inclines them more towards the acquisition of WMD.

With the end of the Cold War there have also been clear changes in the balance between economic and security issues in the realm of arms. There is now greater acceptance of the economic benefits (such as employment and balance of payments) as legitimate grounds for making sales. At the same time, whereas during the Cold War ethical concerns were often subjugated to security issues, in the post-Cold War period ethical concerns are now often eclipsed by economic interests. For example, the British government allowed the supply of weapons manufacturing technologies to Iraq in 1987–8 despite evidence of Iraqi human rights abuses against their Kurdish populations (Norton-Taylor, 1995, p. 16).

International Control Mechanisms

The international arrangements which exist are dedicated to limiting the horizontal proliferation of WMD and conventional weapons through a variety of means. To date, there has been no holistic approach adopted to these issues, despite the urging of arms control advocates. This reflects the fact that security agreements are very difficult to negotiate. Because of suspicions about other states it is very hard to entrust a state's security to an international arrangement, so the agreements that do exist are limited in scope. This means that the coverage which these various mechanisms provide is incomplete. In the aftermath of the Gulf War there were efforts to close gaps between the various regimes to more effectively inhibit horizontal proliferation. However, as is shown below, this aim was not achieved before the momentum behind the moves was lost, leaving a patchwork of initiatives which are not stitched firmly together. Three types of initiatives are briefly discussed here in the context of both WMD and conventional weapons: export control regimes, treaties and conventions, and finally, confidence and security-building measures.

Export controls

There is a strong tradition of export controls over WMD and their components, and a much weaker thread of controls over conventional weapons exports. In the realm of WMD two export regimes are particularly important. The Nuclear Suppliers Group (NSG, also known as the 'London Club') was established in 1975 and provides the guidelines that underpin the inter-state trade in nuclear materials and technology. The Australia Group of supplier states was also formed in 1975 and monitors and restricts exports of chemicals and dual-use equipment. In addition, the 1987 Missile Technology Control Regime (MTCR) has proved an important inhibitor of transfers of both complete missiles and missile technologies and components.

Several export control regimes have covered both WMD and conventional weapons, and the key organization here was The Coordinating Committee on Multilateral Export Controls (CoCom, 1949–94), which instituted export controls over nuclear equipment, munitions and dual-use equipment. As noted above, CoCom was unable to survive the end of the Cold War. Its successor regime The Wassenaar Arrangement is designed to cover much the same range of goods as CoCom, but is directed against a limited number of 'rogue' states and places a more explicit emphasis on preventing transfers of advanced conventional weapons to these states. However, the Wassenaar Arrangement is not yet operational and there are disputes between its members over the balance to be struck between security and economic interests.

All of these export regimes have limitations which inhibit their effectiveness. Three limitations are particularly noteworthy. First, these export control arrangements do not include every supplier state and therefore the coverage they provide is incomplete. For example, the refusal of China to participate in the NSG, the Australia Group and the Wassenaar Arrangement means that this key supplier is free to make transfers (with implications for the security of all) whilst all the others have agreed to forgo them.

Second, each of these export control regimes relies upon national interpretation and implementation of the rules, and as van Ham noted when examining the NSG:

> the level of enforcement of the export controls differs markedly among the various countries . . . [and] non-proliferation concerns regularly take a back seat to commercial and foreign policy goals. (van Ham, 1994, p. 17)

National interpretation of export controls can also lead to disputes over whether or not a transfer is breaking a regime's guidelines.

Thus, there have been disputes between China and the US over Chinese missile sales to Pakistan which the US claims break MTCR guidelines.

A final limitation of export controls is that because they are supplier led they tackle the symptoms and not the causes of insecurity. Nor are they designed to gain the support and acquiescence of recipient states. Rather, recipient states are treated as targets, not partners, and this gives an adversarial air to export control regimes.

Treaties and conventions

Treaties and conventions are the international legal arrangements designed to limit proliferation. The key treaty covering nuclear proliferation is the 1968 Nuclear Non-Proliferation Treaty (NPT). As noted earlier, there have always been concerns about the discrimination inherent within the treaty which prioritized horizontal over vertical proliferation and was perceived to give all the duties to the non-nuclear states and all the rights to the nuclear weapons states. In 1995 these concerns were given a new prominence because a collective decision had to be taken by the NPT state signatories as to whether to end the Treaty, extend it for a limited amount of time, or extend it indefinitely. Whereas the nuclear weapons states wanted the Treaty to be indefinitely extended (without any alteration of the balance established between horizontal and vertical proliferation), some states wanted the Treaty extended for no more than 25 years (with future renewal dependent upon the nuclear weapons states instituting deep cuts in their nuclear arsenals), whilst a minority wanted the Treaty abandoned altogether (Simpson, 1995).

Reflecting the influence of the US and its allies, some confusion in the ranks of the Treaty's sceptics and the constructive diplomatic role of the South African delegation, the NPT was indefinitely extended at the 1995 conference. Thereafter, the diplomatic battleground shifted to negotiations in Geneva over a Comprehensive Test Ban Treaty (CTBT), with key non-nuclear states again attempting to tie any progress on this issue to vertical disarmament by the existing nuclear weapons states.

In 1993, 130 states signed The Chemical Weapons Convention (CWC), reflecting concerns about chemical weapons elicited by the

Gulf War. However, by early 1996, only 52 states had ratified the Convention, so it had not yet entered into force. This shows that in the intervening period there was a loss of momentum on this issue (Moodie, 1996). A similar story can be told in the case of biological weapons, although in this case there was even less successful action before the issue lost its momentum. There is a convention, The Biological and Toxin Weapons Convention (BWC), which opened for signature in 1972. The BWC has important shortcomings, some of which were dealt with at the 1991 BWC review conference which agreed a number of politically binding confidence-building measures intended to strengthen the regime. Despite this, the Convention does not have a verification regime, that is, provisions for inspection and investigation designed to verify that biological weapons are not being manufactured.

It is recognised that the CWC and BWC are in themselves insufficient to deal with the chemical and biological weapons threat. However, they do gain strength from being paralleled by the export controls discussed above, and from moves towards intrusive verification regimes (Pearson, 1993). One problem remains, however: how to reinvigorate these two conventions after the momentum provided by the Gulf War had been dissipated.

The Convention on Conventional Weapons (CCW) came into force in 1983 and is designed to ensure that certain types of weaponry are not employed on the battlefield. Since the end of the Cold War, there has been increasing interest in the CCW as a means to rid the world of certain types of weapons which do great damage, notably anti-personnel landmines and blinding laser weapons (Leahy, 1995). Nevertheless, at the 1995 and 1996 CCW review meetings, it proved impossible to gather sufficient support for an automatic ban on landmines, but some progress was made with respect to blinding laser weapons.

Confidence and security building measures

Notable initiatives here are the multilateral agreements to establish nuclear weapons free zones. These fulfil several purposes. First, they are confidence-building measures designed to prevent the operation of the security dilemma by showing that no state in the region will destabilize the situation by seeking nuclear weapons. Second, they are designed to safeguard the region from the nuclear weapons of outside powers (who are invited to become signatories). Third, they are intended to boost efforts towards nuclear disarmament by questioning the legitimacy and desirability of nuclear weapons. Four treaties establishing nuclear weapons free zones exist. The 1959 Antarctic Treaty was the first to establish a nuclear weapons free zone. The Treaty of Tlatelolco covers Latin America and the Caribbean. It was established in 1967 and since then its membership has steadily increased. The Treaty of Rarotonga established a nuclear free zone in the South Pacific, and its membership has increased since its inception in 1985, with the nuclear weapons states becoming signatories in 1996. The Treaty of Pelindaba is the culmination of a 35-year effort and is expected to come into force in 1997 (Fischer, 1995–6). It declares Africa to be a zone free of nuclear weapons and nuclear testing and has been given moral authority by South Africa's renunciation of its nuclear weapons programme (Stumpf, 1995–6). Recent activity on the Pelindaba Treaty has been designed to boost the negotiations for a ban on all nuclear testing.

One of the few surviving initiatives in the realm of conventional weapons is the United Nations Register of Conventional Weapons. The Register was established in the aftermath of the Gulf War on the crest of a wave of concern about the proliferation of conventional weapons. Plans for the Register came from the UN General Assembly and pre-dated the Gulf War, but up until that time the idea had received little support from the crucial supplier states who were also members of the UN Security Council. The Register was intended to begin to tackle 'excessive and destabilizing' accumulations of conventional weapons. The Register is a transparency regime designed to throw light on the murky world of the arms trade and performs several functions: to increase the confidence and security of states by showing them (through openness) that the military procurements of their neighbours are not threatening; to increase the degree of difficulty experienced by black marketeers trading in illicit weapons and the difficulty and costs to recipients of illegally procuring these weapons; and to provide information on conventional arms transfers in order to initiate debate about the security, commercial and ethical consequences of such sales (Laurance, 1993). The Register currently requests transfer data on seven categories of weapons: Battle Tanks; Armoured Combat Vehicles; Large Calibre Artillery Systems; Combat Aircraft; Attack Helicopters; Warships; and Missiles and Missile Launchers.

By the mid-1990s, adherence to this (entirely voluntary) regime was not complete, with only approximately 80–90 states returning details of their sales and acquisitions each year (Chalmers and Greene, 1995). Also, many of the major recipients of weapons have steadfastly refused to participate – for example, Saudi Arabia. Adherence to the regime has been particularly poor in the Middle East which is, ironically, the region the Register was designed to help.

Like the NPT, the Register has been criticized as discriminatory. It demands information about exports and imports but makes no mention of domestic procurement (that is, weapons indigenously produced) and hence discriminates against states without their own defence industries. In an attempt to blunt this criticism, states are now offered the opportunity to report domestic procurement in their submissions to the Register. To date, few states with defence industries have chosen to do this.

Arms, Arms Control and Contemporary World Politics

The international community is sending out mixed signals about the utility of nuclear weapons in the post-Cold War world. On the one hand, states such as the US are championing the cause of non-proliferation and seeking to strengthen the regimes that deal with these issues. On the other hand, however, the declared nuclear weapons states are doing little to diminish their nuclear arsenals, and still talk in terms of deterrence. In this situation, actions speak louder than words and horizontal WMD proliferation remains a problem.

It is clear that although the era of global tensions may be over, the security dilemma is still a reality for many states. The regional arms races in South East Asia and the Middle East are evidence of this. The eternal question seems to be how to break the cycle of the security dilemma. The existing institutional mechanisms designed to build confidence and enhance security are very weak compared with the security problems that they are designed to overcome.

This chapter has shown that ethical concerns remain marginal in decisions over the production, trade and deployment of weapons. Whereas during the Cold War ethical concerns were swept aside for reasons of security, in the post-Cold War world they are more likely to be overshadowed by economic justifications for production and trade. Indeed, given the economic importance of defence sales to many supplier states, selling weapons is now discussed as though it was itself an ethical act.

Guide to Further Reading

For readers interested in keeping up with current developments in this field, the best sources are the yearbooks produced by the Stockholm International Peace Research Institute (for example, SIPRI, 1966). In addition, SIPRI has a very useful Internet (web) site which is regularly updated (http://. sipri. se). Another useful web site is that of the US Center for Defense Information (http://www. cdi. org/). To learn more about Cold War defence economies and the problems of converting them, see Markusen and Yudken (1992).

Two books on recent developments in nuclear proliferation are recommended. The problems of controls are examined by van Ham (1994), while Reiss and Litwak (1994) provide a useful review of individual state perspectives on nuclear proliferation issues. For a more detailed examination of US attitudes to proliferation, Bowen and Dunn (1996) is both readable and comprehensive. Readers might also like to contact the US Department of Defense's web site (http:// www. dtic. dla. mil/defenselink/).

7

Peacekeeping and Humanitarian Intervention

MICHAEL PUGH

We can hardly fail to be aware of the international community's involvement in internal conflicts that threaten international peace and security or expose brutality and extensive human suffering. Whether we are conscious of the International Tribunal in The Hague, set up by the United Nations to try alleged war criminals from former Yugoslavia, or of the public appeals by international non-government organizations, such as Oxfam, for money to send assistance to a war-torn country in Africa, there is no avoiding the predicaments that confront international organizations. This chapter focuses on those predicaments as an issue in world politics.

The main argument is that issues of peacemaking, peacekeeping and humanitarian activities reflect failures in world politics. They try to put right what has gone wrong and deal with the manifestations of problems. Not only do these activities fail to address deepseated problems; they may even become part of the problem, by prolonging conflict. Moreover, the roles played by the chief actors mirror the structure of the international system. Much of the impetus for peacekeeping and humanitarian relief comes from the wealthier, more powerful states. The victims of civil war and disasters, whether natural or man-made, are overwhelmingly from less developed parts of the world. In other words, those who organize the intervening are mainly, though not exclusively, from the part of the world that benefits from the maintenance of inequalities. The objects of intervention and hosts to peacekeepers are people who have already been marginalized and who are now to be rescued or policed. There is never any possibility of the reverse occurring, even when industrialized states experience civil unrest.

No one seriously entertains the possibility of the Sudan being called upon to maintain peace in Northern Ireland any more than one would expect a Liberian charity to assist the homeless of Paris.

Before going further, it is essential to devote some attention to the definition of terms which can seem confusing. The term *intervention* can be used to mean either any kind of involvement (such as beaming a media broadcast to another state) or, in the stricter sense used here, as the use of force to interfere in another state. It is rather like *enforcement*, meaning collective action under Chapter VII of the UN Charter which in effect allows states to go to war against aggressors in order 'to maintain or restore international peace and security'. *Peacekeeping* in its original sense is an activity of military and civilian units, using force only in self-defence, and operating in a neutral and impartial way with the consent of the parties to disputes. Increasingly, however, peacekeeping operations have been stretched, not only to perform a range of new tasks from election monitoring to the removal of mines, but also to permit the use of force, for example against bandits and factions in order to protect relief supplies or to induce factions to abide by peace agreements. *Peacebuilding* refers to measures taken in the transition from war to peace, to identify and support structures designed to minimize the risk of a return to violence. *Humanitarianism* is a neutral, impartial and non-coercive method of alleviating human suffering. As only to be expected, the concept of 'humanitarian intervention', the external use of force to stop genocide or widespread human rights abuse, is highly controversial. Imposing aid or going to war to save lives implies a contradiction. Nevertheless it has a long-standing legal and political pedigree and is often associated with the seventeenth-century Dutch jurist, Hugo Grotius, hence it is often referred to as the Grotian doctrine. A useful general phrase to cover all the above types of activity is *peace support measures*.

International Peace Support as an Issue

International peace support has become increasingly important as an issue in world politics. In 1996 there were about 30 conflicts in progress around the world, and whereas only 13 UN peacekeeping missions were started between 1948 and 1987, in the period 1988–95 there were 25 new operations. At their peak in 1994, UN peacekeeping operations involved nearly 80,000 military personnel around the world, seven times the figure for 1990 – though this had declined to 26,000 by 1996 after withdrawals from Cambodia, Bosnia and Rwanda (Fisas, 1995, pp. 89–103). To this we have to add thousands of civilians attached to the missions and thousands of humanitarian relief workers. Unlike Cold War peacekeeping, which in the main was limited to observation and interposition along ceasefire lines between states which had been in conflict, the later operations involved many sorts of activities, more often than not attempting to address conflicts within states.

To a large extent the increased attention paid to this issue after the Cold War reflects two things. First there has been a continued failure by international organizations to address underlying structural problems in the global system. Second, there has been a 'can do' spirit in the industrial and post-industrial states which promotes intervention in war-torn societies, motivated by moral concern for human suffering or, more cynically, by a desire to contain problems and prevent them from affecting the interests of industrialized societies.

At first sight these two developments may seem contradictory. How can the international community foster, ignore, or wrongly diagnose the causes of civil conflict, and yet also assume that the manifestations of conflict are internationally significant and even expend enormous energy and resources in attempting to fix the problems? Why did the UN instruct the UN High Commission for Refugees to coordinate a humanitarian operation in former Yugoslavia and why did the UN send peacekeepers to Croatia and then Bosnia?

The failure to prevent, and the desire to fix, may both stem from processes of globalization. On the one hand, the global spread of capitalism, Western media, cultural influences and democratic ideals may have fostered economic, social and political tensions to the point where some states are regarded as having collapsed or failed. This has been referred to as 'structural violence', meaning the built-in disparities which ensure that societies are forced to struggle for bare survival (Galtung, 1976). On the other hand, there is a potent mix comprising technological power, a sense of universal human values and obligation to relieve suffering, and a perceived ability to provide assistance and policing as measures to improve global security.

From time to time the issue has gained extreme urgency and intensity, when for example states have gone to war in the name of upholding international peace and security (the 1991 Gulf War); when communities of innocent civilians have suffered genocide or 'ethnic cleansing' (in Cambodia, Rwanda and former Yugoslavia); when famine and collapse of government has led to widespread suffering and death (Somalia). The continuing importance of the issue has been reflected in the attention which international actors of all kinds have had to devote to peace support measures since the end of the Cold War. The issue has also generated a great deal of intellectual argument, for example about whether peacekeeping faces a crisis and whether intervention on humanitarian grounds is justifiable. However, the intensity and scope of the issue has fluctuated dramatically according to three factors: the interests of states, the ability of the Western-controlled media to move public opinion and the risks to (Western) lives.

When ruling elites have identified their own state's interests with international security, they have taken an active part in developing peace support measures and have accorded significance to the issue. For example, the member states of the European Union played an active, if ineffective, role in attempting to prevent the disintegration of Yugoslavia, in part because they were concerned about outflows of refugees that would affect their attempts to curb immigration. The UK's despatch of peacekeepers to far-off Cambodia in 1993 could underpin its claim to hold on to its permanent seat on the Security Council at a time of debate about changing the membership to reflect global changes in relative power. The counter-claims of states from the Indian subcontinent for a seat on the Security Council helps to explain their highly visible involvement in post-Cold War peace support operations, providing more than a third of infantry for such operations between November 1992 and September 1994 (Fisas, 1995, p. 98).

Peacekeeping and humanitarian issues have had high visibility in the popular media, though usually on a very selective basis. The famines in Ethiopia, the Sudan and Somalia in the 1980s and early 1990s, and ethnic cleansing in Bosnia in the mid-1990s are obvious cases where dramatic news stories mobilized public opinion and outraged the liberal consciousness of people in wealthy states. The famine relief campaign for sub-Saharan Africa in the mid-1980s led to world-wide audiences for 'Live Aid' pop concerts, which themselves became huge media events. Television coverage of the Somalia famine in 1992 can be said to have influenced US public opinion and US policy to intervene on humanitarian grounds.

The attention of policy-makers, the media and the public has been further heightened when the lives of peacekeepers and aid workers are at risk or deaths occur. Television pictures of a US soldier being dragged through the streets of Mogadishu and UN soldiers held hostage in Bosnia caused a flurry of diplomatic activity, media coverage and public debate which led to changes in policy.

What has to be remembered is that the significance of problems requiring peace support are heavily filtered by our perceptions of national interest and risk, and the way in which the problems are presented. For much of the time, the industrialized world ignores emergencies and the daily quest for survival in the poorer states. The richer states have sometimes dropped their involvement when things go wrong, pulling out from Somalia and Rwanda, for example. Objectively speaking, the deaths of ten Belgian peace-keepers in Rwanda in 1994, tragic though they were, pale in numerical significance beside the mass slaughter of Africans in the Great Lakes region. Ultimately, perceptions of the relative signifi-cance of issues are moulded by the structure of the international system itself. What this in effect means is that attempts to engineer global security are constantly thwarted by the persistence of struc-tural violence.

International Peace Support: General Problems

In addition to the fundamental structural problem discussed above (also discussed more explicitly in Chapter 5) the problems presented by the issue can be analyzed under five sub-headings: legal con-siderations, conceptual difficulties, operational issues, political-fi-nancial issues, and accountability.

Legal considerations

Of the 11 new UN operations set up between January 1992 and 1995 all but two dealt with internal civil conflicts (Boutros-Ghali, 1995, para. 11). This would appear to challenge the doctrine of non-intervention, upheld in Article 2(7) of the UN Charter, which states that nothing authorizes the UN to intervene 'in matters which are essentially within the domestic jurisdiction of any state', though without prejudice to action under Chapter VII, which can only be authorized by the Security Council. International enforcement is legalized by Chapter VII. UN member states have attempted to keep these two conflicting norms of international relations in balance: respect for the non-intervention principle, set against responding to the human needs of those exposed to suffering in complex emergencies. This balancing act has led to an ambiguous situation in international law and the customary behaviour of states. As one might expect, governments which are most likely to be the objects of intervention have been the most vociferous about maintaining the non-intervention principle. In deference to nervousness in the developing world about establishing a trend, resolution 794 (3 December 1992) which authorized the use of force in Somalia, referred to 'the unique character' of the situation and its 'complex and extraordinary nature'.

Over several decades, UN declarations on strengthening humanitarian assistance have stressed the principle that states are sovereign, though, of course, they can give consent for outside involvement. An uneasy compromise was reached in the phrasing of the General Assembly resolution (48/182, 17 December 1991) which established a high-level coordinator for humanitarian emergencies (who was in turn to set up the Department of Humanitarian Affairs as part of the UN Secretariat). The ambiguous phrasing reads:

> The sovereignty, territorial integrity and national unity of States must be fully respected in accordance with the Charter of the United Nations. In this context, humanitarian assistance should be provided with the consent of the affected country and in principle on the basis of an appeal by the affected country.

The phrases 'should be provided', rather than 'must be', and 'in principle' rather than 'without exception,' leaves room perhaps for putting a dent in the sovereignty of states. The phrasing enabled the victors of the Gulf War to impose a Kurdish 'safe haven' on Iraq, and allows for situations where control of a government is violently contested and there is no clear authority to give consent, as was subsequently apparent in Somalia.

The Grotian view (deriving from Hugo Grotius's ideas) justifies forcible intervention to protect people from genocide or other outrages against humanity (Vincent, 1990; Knudsen, 1997). The French doctor, Bernard Kouchner, who witnessed the Nigerian civil war in the 1960s and set up the aid organisation, Médecins sans Frontières, argues that it is nonsensical for governments to have the right to do whatever they like to their own populations, without a right of intervention to protect people (Bettati and Kouchner, 1987). However, a Grotian right of intervention is hardly a custom in world politics. It gives rise to several problems. First, there is an inherent contradiction in trying to preserve human life by going to war, mitigated only by the precept that greater evil would be done by not using force. Second, it can lead to an abuse of the humanitarian principle by disguising ulterior motives, such as protecting oil supplies. Third, delivering relief with the barrel of a gun is generally unwelcome by civilian aid workers because it threatens to damage their intention to work impartially among all victims. The International Committee of the Red Cross (ICRC) depends on the cooperation of signatories to the Geneva Convention for protecting the rights of all people in war, including those being attacked by an international intervention force. Fourth, it challenges the foundations of a state-centred international order which, however much it is undermined by attempts to establish universal human rights, remains very persistent.

The balance between the international community doing nothing and intervening with force is currently reflected in the continued emphasis on gaining consent for assistance and in the formula that people have a right to receive assistance and that states have a duty to assist. However, a right to receive assistance does not mean that the assistance will be forthcoming, and a moral duty to provide it is not as forceful as a legal right (Bettati, 1991; Greenwood, 1993).

Potential 'losers' in the system are likely to be extremely suspicious of bodies such as the UN if Grotian intervention becomes an instrument of control by the most powerful states. China, concerned to prevent foreign attention being directed against its occupation of Tibet and its own human rights record, abstained from voting on Security Council resolution 688 authorizing the Kurdish safe haven in northern Iraq. Since the Clinton administration announced in May 1994 that, in effect, the United States would only support UN operations which advance US interests (as discussed later), it is not surprising that states are extremely concerned about any development of international law and practice in this direction.

Conceptual difficulties

A second set of problems relates to the ideas of collective security and peacekeeping. Neither collective security nor peacekeeping address underlying structural problems in the international system. Nor do they possess sufficient benefits to outweigh the preferences of states for narrowly defined, national, military security solutions to problems.

Originally, the founders of the UN envisaged that the financial benefits of pooling defence resources and the political benefits of having a global security structure to maintain world peace would work in accordance with Chapter VII of the UN Charter. This section of the Charter specifies that member states will make arrangements to provide the UN with a large armed force that could be used against an aggressor. The provision of a veto power to the United States, the UK, France, Russia and China (the permanent members of the Security Council), however, meant that collective security could never be directed against one of themselves since they would veto it. One of the major difficulties with such a collective security arrangement, in which the emphasis is on the use of force for defence only, is that without a predetermined enemy, participants cannot readily make advance commitments to use force against any aggressor declared by the Security Council. The aggressor could turn out to be an important trading partner, a close ally or be able to muster so much military force that to join a fight against it would be national suicide. A system of collective security is therefore inherently unreliable. Moreover, a global system carries the risk of turning local disputes into much larger ones.

Alliances also carry this risk but, by contrast with collective security, systems of alliance security, such as NATO, are purpose-directed against an identified adversary because all the participants already feel threatened by that adversary. In fact the Cold War put an end to the idea of a UN force. Instead, enforcement under Chapter VII of the Charter was arranged not on a collective security basis, but by devising temporary alliances such as that formed against Iraq.

The concept of peacekeeping, by contrast, is based on the idea that there is no enemy except conflict itself. Peacekeeping is not even mentioned in the UN Charter; it was invented as a practical response to the need for international supervision of troop withdrawals at the end of the Suez War in 1956. The principles, devised at the time by the Canadian Minister of Foreign Affairs, Lester Pearson and the UN Secretary-General, Dag Hammarskjöld, emphasize that peacekeepers are impartial towards the parties in a dispute and indifferent as to the outcome of a dispute. They represent a lightly armed, inoffensive, international presence which has the consent of the parties to supervise a ceasefire or political settlement. Because consent has generally been a minimum requirement, UN peacekeeping operations during the Cold War tended to deal with relatively small-scale problems and had no effect on the big Cold War confrontation, except perhaps to insulate problems from becoming part of superpower rivalry. Furthermore, it is a long-standing criticism that peacekeeping freezes hostilities rather than resolves them. There may be an incentive for sides in a dispute to agree to a ceasefire, perhaps because they are militarily exhausted, but no real incentive to reach a long-term solution to their dispute. In this situation, peacekeepers merely cement political divisions in a dispute. One only has to remember that the UN has been in Cyprus since 1962 to understand the point. But peacekeeping could be conceived in a more active way, linking it to conflict resolution and helping in the recovery of war-torn societies (Fetherston, 1994; Pugh, 1995).

Since the end of the Cold War a different sort of criticism has emerged: that peacekeeping is inadequate to meet the problems encountered when civil wars are still in progress and where consent for a peacekeeping presence is fragile and parties to a dispute see peacekeepers as biased against them. A lively and inconclusive debate raged in the 1990s about whether peacekeeping within states rather than between them was a 'dead end' (James, 1994), and whether the answer was to enable peacekeepers to be more forceful in dealing with bandits and paramilitary forces – not to win a war but to act as a kind of tough police force (Gow and Dandeker, 1995; Roberts, 1995–6; Ruggie, 1997). More cautious commentators believe that peacekeeping forces could use coercion only to sustain peace agreements, or would apply such strict conditions on coercion that they are unlikely to be fulfilled (Annan, 1997; James, 1997;

Goulding, 1996). Still others regard robust peacekeeping as counter-productive, likely to become part of the crisis itself and to
jeopardize humanitarian activities (Berdal, 1993; N. Morris, 1995;
Pugh, 1996). States supplying troops to enforcement or robust
peacekeeping missions are also more likely to be concerned about
costs, about deflection from other commitments and about casualties. Since the Cold War, peace support operations have been
more dangerous for personnel than serving on the European central
front during the Cold War. No military hostages were taken in
Germany during the Cold War as they were in Bosnia in 1995.

Operational issues

The absence of a common doctrine of peace support measures has
operational as well as conceptual significance. The participation of
relatively new and inexperienced actors has produced problems.
Some of the militarily powerful states, such as the United States,
France, Russia and Britain, have entered the arena with a desire to
find a new role after the Cold War, and with a history of warfare
where there is a defined enemy (though Britain did have previous
peacekeeping experience in Cyprus). Confusion and lack of understanding about the concepts of peacekeeping were reflected in the
message of a US serviceman involved in the rescue of a pilot shot
down over Bosnia which ended: 'pray for the UN leadership to get a
clue and let us blow these . . . [Serbs] back into the stone age!'
(Zobrist, 1995). He ignored the fact that the international community was not trying to win a war and that his 'solution' would add to
the political and social causes of the problem.

Germany and Japan are also new to peacekeeping but have been
more circumspect in their approach because legal constraints and
historical legacies of aggression have prevented them from sending
military forces abroad. These constraints have been gradually lifted
especially for peacekeeping. Smaller novices have pursued national
goals, too. Argentina has participated in peacekeeping to secure
international respectability after the Falklands/Malvinas War.
Others have participated for the income which it brings in. Sometimes, they have been poorly equipped and ill-disciplined, as in the
case of the Bulgarian contingent in Bosnia. Misbehaviour is not
confined to novices, however. Canada, with its considerable experience and a national culture which accords peacekeeping a high

status, had to disband an airborne division after some of its members murdered Somalis.

All commentators agree, however, that it is a grave mistake to use the wrong kind of force in the wrong situation, to send lightly armed peacekeepers into combat, for example. It is also dangerous for the UN to allow 'mission creep' to occur, that is, to extend the mandate of a blue-helmet peacekeeping force so that it subsequently gets involved in combat. As Lt.-General Sir Michael Rose reportedly commented in Bosnia: 'I'm not going to fight a war in white-painted tanks' (see Dobbie, 1994; Wesley, 1995; Pugh, 1996) The use of soldiers in civil emergencies where there is no political unrest, such as earthquakes, is perfectly viable. But switching between roles, from the modestly armed and transparent peacekeeper to the camouflaged combat soldier, is problematic. This has raised the question as to whether a new type of force is needed for situations where local consent is fragile or unreliable (Childers and Urquhart, 1994; Kinloch, 1997). UN members are unlikely to want to spend money on a new type of force, such as a UN Guard, and its character would have to be carefully thought out, as there is unlikely to be an ideal type that would suit all situations.

At the other extreme – peacebuilding in war-torn societies when conflict is winding down – there is a case for having more civilians in peacekeeping. There are already many civilians engaged in election monitoring, policing and human rights monitoring. Clearly soldiers have to conduct certain duties, such as demilitarizing guerilla forces and removing mines. But humanitarian relief and development agencies should be the principal agents in fostering economic recovery, rebuilding services, refugee protection, psychological counselling, and the rehabilitation of health, education and legal systems. However, relations between military and civilian personnel in responding to emergencies are often tense and suspicious. The two groups have contrasting cultures and traditions of discipline, and they draw their authority from different sources. Whereas soldiers are sent by governments, civilian workers in NGOs attempt to remain independent of governments (even when governments supply them with funds). Coordination of effort among the many and varied actors who participate in peace support measures is fraught with difficulty, largely because each organization involved has its own mandate, ethos, funding and political 'turf' to protect. Although considerable improvements were made with the creation of the Department of Humanitarian Affairs (DHA) as a coordinating body within the UN, it has no power to direct operations, merely to facilitate cooperation between those involved.

Just as charities and agencies are reluctant to submerge their identities and power within a centralized system, so are states reluctant to relinquish control over their armed forces and to make commitments to multinational operations. Developments in international management are considered below, but two problems at the operational level need to be mentioned here because they have often bedevilled peace support measures.

First, it often takes the UN a long time to respond to emergencies because of the *ad hoc*, reactive arrangements which have to be made with individual states. Delays in sending troops have been blamed for allowing human tragedies to unfold, notably in Rwanda. Calls for a permanent UN force have fallen on deaf ears because governments are concerned about the cost and how it would be controlled. Efforts by the UN to establish commitments to stand-by forces, and studies, notably by the Netherlands and Canada, to improve the UN's rapid reaction capability, have had a more promising reception. Second, command and control of UN forces has become an issue, especially when operations are likely to involve combat. The UN does not have a large military staff of its own, and some states, especially the United States, have been concerned about putting their troops under a non-US commander. The problem came to the fore in Somalia, when US marines took orders from their own headquarters in the United States (Ruggie, 1996). Slowness in reaction and problems over who commands the force reflect the general problem in world politics that states are very reluctant to lose any control over their military security.

Political and financial issues

Another general problem is that UN Security Council policy is heavily influenced by the foreign policies of its permanent members who can each veto decisions. The Security Council has determined that some issues are a 'threat to peace, breach of the peace, or act of aggression', while others are not. A clear example of convergence of interests in the Security Council, and indeed beyond it, was the UN's decision first to impose sanctions and then to authorize enforcement after Iraq invaded Kuwait in 1991. Iraq's action was a blatant act of aggression which would have been difficult to ignore. However, its threat to the oil supplies of industrialized states gave added impetus to the belligerent response of many states. More dubious was the success of the United States in persuading the Security Council to consider the government of Haiti to be a threat to international peace and security and to permit the United States to invade in 1994. Hitherto, US administrations had ignored the human rights abuses of the Duvalier regime and had sustained it economically for decades until it lost control in the mid-1980s. Only when a military coup in 1991 gave rise to large numbers of refugees heading for the US and Caribbean coasts did the Bush and then Clinton administrations regard Haiti as a threat (J. Morris, 1995). By contrast, the civil war in Sierre Leone in the mid-1990s was virtually overlooked. Selectivity on the basis of national political interests may guard against the UN becoming overstretched but it leads to inconsistency and reinforces national rather than global security interests.

In addition, 'band aid' humanitarian relief with UN military support has become a substitute for resolving conflicts politically. In fact there were signs by the mid-1990s that Western states were increasingly wary of involvement in central African conflicts. Reduced interest in resolving conflicts through global security afflicted the United States in particular. The Clinton administration adopted an increasingly hostile view towards the UN, and in May 1994 issued Presidential Decision Directive 25 (PDD 25) which laid down criteria for US involvement in UN operations, including the need for clear US interests to be at stake and a limited period for each engagement. The United States also decided unilaterally to reduce its assessed share of peacekeeping costs from just over 30 per cent to 25 per cent of the global cost. This is not to say that the United States actually paid its dues. On the contrary, it continued a habit of refusing to pay up. The effect was to cause a budgetary crisis in the UN in 1995–6 which threatened its ability to continue with existing tasks. Yet the cost of peacekeeping is less than the annual expenditure of the New York Fire Department and is much cheaper in manpower and equipment than the NATO-run Implementation Force (IFOR) in Bosnia. In sum, the United States exercises a quadruple veto: its Security Council veto, its ability to deny political leadership, its ability to deny intelligence or material assistance for operations, and its financial veto through refusal to pay its contributions.

Accountability

Finally, the issue of peace support measures and humanitarian activity generates a problem of accountability. To whom are peacekeepers and humanitarian workers accountable and responsible, and how is accountability implemented? Military peacekeepers are, of course, responsible to their commanders and governments, but there is no mechanism for accountability to the Security Council, which ultimately decides the mandate, the budget and the force structure. Only in 1995 was a 'Lessons Learned Unit' created in the UN Department of Peacekeeping Operations for assessing the performance of completed operations. Humanitarian workers are accountable to their agency committees, donors and contractors, and their headquarters are often driven by the need to raise funds for their own survival. Relief is big business (Hancock, 1989; Stockton, 1994). Moreover, performance is often measured by the numbers of blankets issued, people fed, wells dug – and not by whether the activity fulfils a mandate. The media, too, is highly selective in its coverage and can be irresponsible in its quest for sensational news, ultimately to earn profits for a small number of Western entrepreneurs and shareholders.

In some 'host' countries, notably Rwanda, Burundi and the Sudan, there has been a reaction against the 'invasions' of NGOs and journalists and an attempt to regulate their activities. Most behave ethically and follow a code of conduct, such as that elaborated by the International Committee of the Red Cross. However, the large foreign presence can have a bad effect on local economies. They may also become embarrassing because they reveal continued abuse of human rights. At the cost of adding a layer of bureaucracy to humanitarian assistance, some NGOs have considered setting up a common system of monitoring and self-regulation.

The last people in a complex emergency to be consulted about their future are usually those being protected or assisted. Yet local communities usually know what measures work best for their own survival and can offer rational assessments of their needs. Médecins sans Frontières now sends personnel to a complex emergency in order to discover the requirements of local communities. This is not as simple as it sounds. Survivors may no longer have a functioning decision-making structure, their spokespersons may be unrepresentative, and they may include war criminals and human rights abusers. Nevertheless, the most highly-praised relief organizations are often those which listen to local advice and which, like the UN Children's Fund (UNICEF), try to employ as many local people as possible. 'Whose disaster is it anyway?', the theme of the *World Disasters Report* (IFRC, 1997), is a question that has to be addressed as part of the wider issue of the place of peace support measures on the international agenda.

The Location of Peace Support on the International Agenda

The responsibility for peace support measures and humanitarian assistance being placed highly on the international agenda does not lie with any single event, person or school of thought. Structural violence has been a long-standing feature of the international system which was fostered, ignored or denied by policy-makers in the rich industrial states until confronted by a crisis which affected them, such as the international debt crisis.

However, even before the end of the Cold War, new thinking about global security by academics and international statespersons, carried increasing weight. Theories of international relations which place states and military power at the centre of the international system, came under renewed scrutiny in the light of the US withdrawal from Vietnam in 1975, the oil crises of the 1970s and heightened superpower tension and arms racing from 1979 to 1986. Commentators observed that security was not just a military issue, that human rights abuse was of international concern and that new actors and economic interdependence were challenging the state-centred analysis of security (see also Chapter 3).

Particularly interesting in the context of humanitarian relief was the new thinking about security by geographers and disaster researchers. They drew attention to the links between so-called 'natural disasters', such as floods and earthquakes, and human factors. They argued that natural phenomena led to disaster only when human beings were made vulnerable to them. Disasters and 'complex emergencies' affected poorer countries more frequently and with greater severity because people were made vulnerable by economic marginalization, lower safeguards against hazards and political negligence. Civil war often added to the vulnerability of communities. Such situations were not rare but an enduring part of the fabric of life to be regularly confronted, like the monsoon, literally so in the case of Bangladesh (Hewitt, 1983; Cuny, 1983; Blaikie *et al.*, 1994).

Moreover, the international community's responses to complex emergencies were badly conceived and disorganized. Efforts to strengthen the UN's emergency responses fell foul of Cold War rivalry and many governments were reluctant either to admit the existence of an emergency in their territory (indeed they were sometimes responsible for it) or to allow external involvement. In the 1980s, donor governments also resisted funds being channelled into relief work rather than economic development which, so it was believed, would provide a foundation for Third World debt repayments. Relief agencies and NGOs were at times overwhelmed and cooperated with the Western-controlled media to report on emergencies in Africa and to influence public opinion. Dissatisfaction among humanitarian relief workers with the UN's inability to respond to emergencies came to a head over famines in Ethiopia and the Sudan in the 1980s and over refugees from the Gulf War in 1991, and eventually prompted the creation of the Department of Humanitarian Affairs (DHA).

The end of the Cold War also presented new opportunities for dealing with old, intractable disputes in Cambodia, Namibia, Angola and Central America. The emergence of new crises (in Liberia, Rwanda, Yugoslavia and Somalia) also demanded attention. Former adversaries were now willing to cooperate in the UN Security Council, and the veto power of permanent members virtually fell into abeyance. The near-universal response to the challenge posed by Iraq and the military victory of the Coalition gave a higher priority to multinational operations and the UN's role in security. At that time, the United States discovered the usefulness of the UN for underpinning and legitimizing what President George Bush called a 'New World Order', and in January 1992, for the first time ever, UN Security Council states held a summit with the aim of giving direction to the post-Cold War international security system. At this meeting, the leaders requested the Secretary-General Boutros-Ghali to define the UN's new role. He seized the chance to promote the UN's standing, and his report for the Security Council, *An Agenda for Peace* (1992), was a widely cited contribution to the debate about peace and security. To the extent that Boutros-Ghali was instrumental in providing a document that examined peace support concepts and made recommendations for strengthening the UN's capacity, it can be said that he made *An Agenda* virtually *the* international agenda. It stimulated a rapid growth of academic research on the issue: new journals, pages on the Internet, conferences, new university and military courses, all broadened awareness of the issue. But the growing significance of peace support measures also owed much to crises in the international system and new thinking about security issues in general.

Peacekeeping and Humanitarian Intervention after the Cold War

The end of the Cold War increased the sense that barriers to improving global security were being lifted. The Gulf War increased the sense that in the absence of the old East–West divide, international law could be applied universally and could be used to legitimize international force. However, the end of the Cold War also increased our exposure to the problems of insecurity in areas which had been economically and politically marginalized by the former preoccupation with the strategic balance between the capitalist and socialist systems.

Boutros-Ghali's presentation assumed that the UN could only do as much as the member states allowed it to. But it was also a liberal, internationalist perspective which recognized the problems of structural violence and attempted to foster a global security approach. *An Agenda for Peace* did not in fact present many new ideas; it was rather a re-packaging of old ones, many of which had been around since the UN's problematic intervention in the Congo in the 1960s. However, it did reflect a sense that the changed international context with the end of the Cold War had presented new opportunities to revive and implement reform proposals. Traditional peace-keeping had often been presented as a minor issue in world politics, the most that states engaged in the Cold War could agree to do in tackling interstate disputes. Now, it seemed, a lot more was possible.

An attempt to categorize and define peace support formed the skeleton of the Secretary-General's report, the chief categories being preventive diplomacy, peacemaking, peacekeeping and peacebuilding. The UN's main purpose – conflict prevention – was also its greatest weakness. Boutros-Ghali emphasized the need for more fact-finding missions, early warning and deployment of forces, to prevent conflicts arising or spreading, as in Macedonia, rather than have the UN attempt to correct matters when it was too late and more costly to deal with. However, as the Yugoslavia crisis indicated, any amount of early warning is no substitute for the political will to act. In any case it can be argued that conflicts may have a creative function in the international system and that efforts to prevent them are bound to maintain a status quo which disadvantages people in revolt. Peacemaking was presented as a range of activities, including enforcement, to resolve conflicts which had already broken out. Peacekeeping was presented as action which *hitherto* had the consent of the parties concerned, thus opening the possibility of contested missions in the future. Peacebuilding to restore war-torn societies was barely examined. Boutros-Ghali emphasized the importance of establishing democratic processes such as elections. Recommendations reiterated the need to strengthen UN management mechanisms, to improve the budgetary situation and to secure greater commitment to global security by member states.

Subsequently, in various reassessments, including a *Supplement to an Agenda for Peace*, published in 1995, Boutros-Ghali scaled down the UN's ambitions. Enforcement operations were hardly mentioned, except as something that could be delegated to regional organizations. Thus the post-Cold War presentation of the issue fluctuated from near euphoria in early 1992 to despondency in mid-1995 as the operational problems of peace support measures overwhelmed the intervening agencies. On the one hand, the increased number of peace support operations and humanitarian activities were presented as a challenge to the doctrine of non-intervention. On the other hand, the problems in achieving success have been presented as confirmation of the inadequacy of global security and/or its vulnerability to US domination.

International Management

The purpose of international management has been to contain conflict and end suffering, sometimes to prevent refugee outflows. In the period 1987–96 there were more than a hundred legally binding resolutions under Chapter VII of the UN Charter requiring decisive action to deal with breaches of peace and security (Ciechanski, 1997). The corresponding increase in the number of international peace support measures and the changing quality of peacekeeping operations, put international management mechanisms under great strain.

The main organization involved, because it has unrivalled authority, has been the UN. Management responsibility lies with the Secretary-General, who is responsible for supervising the implementation of Security Council mandates. He is assisted by a secretariat, a small team of military advisers (seconded from national armed forces) and three key UN departments: the Department of Political Affairs, Department of Peace-keeping Operations and the DHA. Cooperation between the departments slowly improved after the Cold War, with better information exchange and more consultation to try to ensure that the bureaucrats were not following divergent policies. As already noted, similar efforts were made to coordinate responses to humanitarian emergencies. However, there remained management weaknesses which reflected partly the competition between departments and agencies, partly the budgetary crisis and partly the suspicion of some states, particularly the United States, of the UN becoming too independent of the Security Council. Ultimately the UN's management abilities depend on what the member states, especially the Security Council members, permit and what they are willing to fund. They can undermine the management of peace support measures by failing to provide the means to accomplish tasks and denying authority to the UN. Nevertheless, some of the blatant inadequacies of the UN in managing operations have been corrected by such reforms as opening a 24-hour operations centre (when previously UN commanders in the field could only contact the Department of Peace-keeping Operations in New York during office hours). These have been refinements to improve the management of multinational cooperation rather than a wholesale attack on the *ad hoc* approach to international security (Berdal, 1995).

The reluctance of states to provide the necessary back-up to Security Council mandates has contributed to damaging the UN's credibility as a management mechanism and paved the way for peace support measures to be farmed out to other bodies – or looked at another way, hijacked by the old cold warriors. A delegation of responsibilities has been an important trend in managing the issue. This is sometimes called 'subcontracting' or 'sphere of influence' management because it means that regional organizations, or those states within whose sphere of influence the problem arises, are authorized to manage the issue. Regional bodies are actually encouraged to tackle problems, under Chapter VIII of the UN Charter, provided it is done in a way which is compatible with the spirit of the Charter. Given that the UN is itself under-resourced it also makes practical sense to delegate responsibility to groups of states which are willing and able to undertake peace support missions.

Among the European states there are various options: the European Union, the Organization for Security and Cooperation in Europe (OSCE), the Western European Union (WEU) and NATO. Of these, only NATO has the military structure and forces at its disposal to engage in enforcement operations or large-scale peacekeeping enterprises. NATO's old Cold War posture has been changed quite dramatically, and its political strength increased as a consequence of giving associate membership to East European states through the 'Partnership for Peace' programme and France's full participation after a period of aloofness. One of the issues on which all NATO partners could readily agree has been peacekeeping. It is relatively uncontroversial and places limited demands on the neglected military capabilities of the East European states. Consequently NATO has devoted attention to planning, joint training, the development of common approaches and, of course, it established the large-scale IFOR operation for implementing the military part of the 1995 Dayton Peace Agreement for Bosnia. The management appears to have worked well in this instance, though much depended on the willingness of the United States to participate and the willingness of Russia to place its forces under American (not NATO) command because it distrusted NATO's intentions towards Eastern Europe.

The other European security organizations have less management capacity, though the WEU played a significant part in managing naval contributions to the Gulf War and in checking merchant ships for sanctions busting in the Adriatic. However, both the OSCE and EU have been heavily engaged in peace support at a diplomatic level, though with mixed success. For example, the EU was engaged in conflict prevention negotiations in the former Yugoslavia, and its chief negotiators arranged various peace plans. But without a more unified foreign and security policy, the EU suffered from the fact that its member states pulled in different directions. The German government, for example, took independent action to recognize the separate existence of Croatia, thereby precipitating, some have argued, the break-up of Yugoslavia. The OSCE has provided negotiators and ceasefire observers in the Caucasus region of the former Soviet Union, such as Nagorno-Karabakh. It has the great advantage over the other European organizations of being a pan-European body, including Russia, in which all members are equal partners. However, it has a small bureaucracy and no muscle to back up its decisions.

It seems likely that the subcontracting approach, as seen in the Gulf War and Bosnia, is the way in which the UN will try to manage enforcement in the future, utilizing existing capabilities within regions. However, three main difficulties place limits on this solution (see Rivlin, 1992).

First, little thought has been given to the need to manage the relationship between the UN and the regional organization concerned. If the UN delegates authority, it loses control over an operation. This was most obvious during the Korean War and the Gulf War which the United States managed with barely any effort to inform or consult with the UN. This facilitated military operations but at the expense of US dominance. The dual management arrangement made for Bosnia, by contrast, resulted in controversies between the UN and NATO, particularly over the use of force.

The lack of managerial expertise and military capacity other than in NATO means that few regional organizations are equipped to deal with peace support. The Organization of African Unity (OAU), for example, provided little leadership or management in the early 1990s, and the Economic Community of West African States (ECOWAS) could make little impact on the civil war in Liberia which broke out in 1991. In effect, delegation of responsibility is not a panacea for global security.

Third, using a subcontractor can raise political sensitivities. If NATO becomes the main enforcer it will raise suspicion among non-NATO states, just as suspicion was raised that the West was protecting oil rather than maintaining international peace and stability in the Gulf War. Political controversy is even more likely when a state is authorized to police its own sphere of influence, such as UN authorization of Russia's enforcement action against Chechnya in the mid-1990s.

In sum, unless UN management is strengthened, particularly in managing relations with subcontractors, peace support measures will be little more than a part of the control mechanism exercised by the rich and powerful states over the poorer states. The richer states already provide the best equipment for peace support operations and soldiers who are generally well prepared and well trained.

Peace Support and Contemporary World Politics

Peace support measures do not address the root causes of social, economic and political problems which are embedded in the structure of the international system. Peace support measures merely deal with the manifestations of problems and mark the extent to which international cooperation has failed to provide security for large parts of the world. States and intergovernmental organizations like the UN can become part of the problem, because of their lack of accountability to recipients of intervention and the lack of attention they give to achieving lasting political solutions to disputes.

To many theorists, the end of the Cold War has made little difference to the way the international system works. The deployment of multinational forces depends upon a coincidence of interests among the rich and powerful states. Dramatic interventions, such as the protection of the Kurds in northern Iraq, do not represent precedents or an extension of global security, partly because each intervention is unique, and partly because governments, especially in the developing world, are anxious to cling to non-intervention principles.

At the same time, the issue of peace support reflects a major concern of contemporary world politics: the fact that the victims of complex emergencies are often victims of state policies and that humanitarian needs are a global concern. The concepts of peace-keeping, peacemaking and intervention are having to adapt to this situation and to the fact that states are inadequate to deal with many international security issues. The UN's operations have been a relative success in many instances (Central America and Cambo-dia), and a relative failure in others (Somalia, Bosnia) either because the principles of peacekeeping have not been properly adhered to, or because they have not yet adapted to intra-state conflicts. Furthermore, reform of international peace and security is required, not least in curbing the veto powers of hegemons like the United States.

Finally, in answer to the question, who benefits from peace support measures?, many communities have benefited in the short term from protection, relief assistance and a transfer of resources from rich to poor. There is little doubt that shattered communities are assisted, but they may pay a price for that assistance in their weakened voice in world politics. The imperfections of global security mean that peace support measures underpin the depen-dency of poorer parts of the world on decisions made in the richer parts of the world. In so far as the rich and powerful states and organizations of the world control the major decisions affecting peacekeeping and humanitarian assistance, peace support measures can also be seen as mechanisms for attempting, not always success-fully, to police the rest of the world.

Guide to Further Reading

The most useful thematic analysis of peace support measures is by the Spanish academic, Fisas (1995). For case studies of operations, see Durch (1994) and James (1990). Stimulating essays which chart the development of thinking about peace support measures since the end of the Cold War are to be found in Pugh (1997); the second edition of Roberts and Kingsbury (1994); Rodley (1992); and Thakur and Thayer (1995). There are many publications by organizations engaged in humanitarian relief, including the annual report by the International Federation of Red Cross and Red Crescent Societies (IFRC). Academic analysis of complex emergencies is to be found in Macrae and Zwi (1994) and Minear and Weiss (1995).

8

Nationalism and Ethnic Conflict

STEPHEN RYAN

Ever since the start of the age of nationalism at the end of the eighteenth century, there have been tensions between the concepts of the *state* and the *nation*. Where the political borders of the state and the cultural boundaries of the nation do not coincide, as is the case with the vast majority of so-called *nation-states*, friction develops between the principles of territorial integrity and national self-determination. For two hundred years these competing claims have introduced a basic fault line into world politics and there is every indication that the consequences of this tension will continue to bedevil the international community.

However, the significance attached to this tension has varied considerably. When the study of International Relations emerged in 1919, 'national, religious and linguistic' minorities were considered to be of major importance. The Versailles peace settlement, influenced by President Woodrow Wilson, identified this as a key issue for post-war reconstruction. Two approaches were forced on the defeated German, Austrian and Russian empires. First, it was proposed that the principle of national self-determination should be applied in a systematic manner in Central and Eastern Europe. In fact, this was an impossible goal. Gellner notes that these new states were 'just as minority haunted, but they were smaller, unhallowed by age and often without experienced leaders, while the minorities whose irredentism they had to face included members of previously dominant cultural groups, unused to subordination and well-placed to resist it' (Gellner, 1994, p. 26). Second, where national, linguistic or religious minorities remained, the newly created states were legally bound, under League of

Nations supervision, to protect them. In the inter-war period, therefore, interest in what we now call ethnic conflict was high on the agenda of international relations (Royal Institute of International Affairs, 1939).

This was not the case after 1945, largely because the main conflict was based around two ideologies that did not attribute high significance to ethnic and national groups. Indeed, between 1945 and the late 1970s, in a world dominated by the conflict between capitalist and Marxist societies, there were only a handful of studies that examined ethnic conflict in international relations, and one can look in vain in the textbooks of the period for any reference to ethnic issues. This is despite the fact that Gurr and Harff show that there has been a steady growth in the magnitude (not the same as the number) of ethnic conflict since 1950, and that this increased fourfold between the period 1950–5 and 1985–90 (Gurr and Harff, 1994, p. 11). Yet it was only in the 1990s that the significance of 'ethnic conflict', as opposed to certain ethnic conflicts, has been recognized in the study of world politics and has been seen as an important issue in its own right.

Before we can go any further, however, we need to define what we mean by the concepts 'ethnic' and 'nation'. Smith (1991) makes the important distinction between ethnicity and nationalism. The former is a way of thinking about the world that is evident throughout recorded history. It is based on the attachment we feel for people who share the same culture as us but, as Smith (1991) also notes, there is more to an *ethnie* than a group's awareness of cultural difference. It also needs a myth of common descent, a shared history, a sense of solidarity, and an association with a specific territory.

The nation, on the other hand, is a modern idea and it is the ideology of nationalism which turns ethnic difference into a major political principle. So, nationalism 'is a very distinctive species of patriotism, and one which becomes pervasive and dominant only under certain social conditions, which in fact prevail in the modern world, and nowhere else' (Gellner, 1983, p. 138). According to Smith (1991), the core doctrine of nationalism is based on the following set of assumptions: the world is divided into nations; the nation is the source of all political and social power and loyalty to the nation overrides all other allegiances; human beings must identify with a nation if they want to be free and realize themselves;

and nations must be free and secure if peace and justice are to prevail in the world.

Smith also points out that nationalism can be defined in different ways. The two most significant forms are *civic-territorial nationalism* and demotic *ethno-nationalism*. The former is found where pre-existing states try to build a sense of 'official' national identity through bureaucratic incorporation on the basis of equal citizenship. Demotic nationalism, on the other hand, emerges from oppressed ethnies and is more likely to be exclusive because it places much more emphasis on cultural difference. Therefore, nationalism does not have to take an ethnic form, though Smith believes that most successful nations are constructed around an ethnic core.

This is a theme taken up by Hobsbawm (1990), who agrees with Smith that when American and French revolutionaries stated their commitment to the 'nation,' what they were referring to was not ethnicity but citizenship. The emphasis on ethnicity, Hobsbawm believes, only becomes significant after 1870. It emerges, in particular, from oppressed groups such as the Irish, the Catalans, the Zionists and the Armenians, who start to create a modern nation out of an oppressed and distinct cultural group. Whereas civic nationalism is used in an integrative way, this demotic ethno-nationalism is usually associated with separatism. It is this ethnic definition which is more of a threat to international stability, since it is less easy to integrate it within the existing framework of sovereign states.

Of course this does not mean that all nationalisms are now only ethnically based. Smith (1991) is surely correct to argue that most modern nationalisms contain both civic-territorial and demotic-cultural elements. Many of us seem to carry with us multiple identities. Research in the West suggests that the majority in Scotland see themselves as both Scottish and British, that over three-quarters of Catalans identify with both Spain and Catalonia, and about half of the people in Brittany feel themselves to be both Breton and French. It is clear, then, that 'identity' and 'culture' are complicated words, and we should be careful to avoid over-simplifications when we use them.

There is another reason to be cautious about the use of the term 'ethnic conflict', for there has been some resistance to this term from some parties in certain disputes. The problem is that when we use the term we may be promoting some preconceptions. It seems to imply that the main causes of the conflict are internal to that society, that it arises out of the inability of two or more cultural groups to live together, and that the best solution may be some form of separation. Very often it is assumed that all the parties are to blame for the conflict. External factors and structural factors like bad governance or social injustice may therefore be ignored or undervalued.

Many Bosnian Muslims, for example, have resented the way that their conflict was characterized as 'ethnic'. They argued that the 'Muslim' side contained Catholic Croats and Orthodox Serbs and that it would have been more accurate to describe the war as a multi-ethnic society under attack from the forces working for a Greater Serbia. Shaw argues that to describe the Bosnian conflict as 'ethnic means an implicit acceptance of the ethno-nationalist description of events. However, this merely assumes what has to be explained, which is the 'disintegration of a largely multi-ethnic and in some sense pluralist society into ethnic fragments' (Shaw, 1994, pp. 102–3).

Some African writers also argue that the label 'ethnic' over-simplifies and misdirects. Khiddu-Makubuya (1994), for example, whilst not denying that recent violence in Uganda has an ethnic aspect, argues that there are other factors that have to be taken into account. These include the colonial legacy, religion, different levels of development, poor leadership, militarism and foreign interests and the external debt burden.

Because of these dangers, it is important to stress that the term 'ethnic conflict' is used in this study only to refer to the form a conflict takes. It does not say anything about the origins of a particular conflict, which will be the result of a complex interplay of factors. The term really tells us very little about the causes of inter-communal violence. To understand these we have to look at factors such as political inclusion and exclusion, social injustice, insecurity and respect for cultural difference.

Ethno-Nationalist Conflict as an Issue

Although ethno-nationalist conflict is found in all parts of the world, any particular ethnic conflict will vary in its scope, urgency, intensity and visibility. Gurr (1993), in the most significant empirical analysis of global minorities, reveals that in 1990 there were 900 million individuals who were members of politically active communal groups and that three-quarters of the 127 largest states in the world had at least one politicized minority. In 1993 there were 22 wars being waged and 'communal rivalries and ethnic challenges to states contributed to conflict in all but five of these episodes' (Gurr and Harff, 1994, p. xiii). In the same year, 25 million refugees were fleeing from communal conflict and repression (Gurr and Harff, 1994, p. xiii).

Sollenberg and Wallensteen (1995) found that in 1994 there were 31 major conflicts (where there had been at least 1,000 battle deaths during the entire life of the conflict) and none of these could be described as a classic inter-state conflict. Although the authors do not attempt to estimate how many of these internal conflicts were ethnic, this writer, using the descriptions they provide, estimates that at least 19 of them deserve this description. Most of the others are made up by conflicts in Latin America. Ethnic conflict is therefore the major cause of large-scale group conflict in contemporary world politics and a major cause of complex 'humanitarian' emergencies.

One indication of the contemporary significance of ethnic conflict is the way that international organizations have become involved with this issue. Boutros-Ghali has noted that four of the five UN peacekeeping operations in existence in early 1988 related to *inter*-state conflict (1995, para. 11). However, thirteen of the twenty-one operations created since then related to *intra*-state conflict. Of the eleven operations established since January 1992, all but two relate to *intra*-state conflict. (There is a more detailed discussion of peacekeeping in Chapter 7.) In Europe, the Organization for Security and Cooperation in Europe (OSCE) created a High Commissioner on National Minorities in order to respond quickly to ethnic tensions. It also sent monitors to various ethnic trouble spots, including the former Yugoslavia, Estonia, Chechnya and Moldova. With the creation of the Implementation Force (IFOR) in Bosnia, NATO also became heavily involved in the most significant ethnic conflict in Europe.

Although ethnic conflict now has a high visibility, specific ethnic conflicts have a varied impact on the global conscience. Gurr (1993) reveals that in the 1980s there were 233 'sizable groups' that were the targets of discrimination or were organized for political assertiveness or both. About one-third of these groups supported autonomy movements between 1945 and 1990 (Gurr and Harff, 1994, p. 153). Yet very few of these have become an important feature of the international agenda. Most seem to have had only a local or regional effect. The scope, urgency, intensity and visibility of particular conflicts will depend on a number of factors which will combine in different ways in different situations. Some of the most important will be examined later in this chapter.

General Problems of Nationalism and Ethnic Conflict

Although the Treaty of Westphalia (1648) is viewed as the starting point of the contemporary sovereign state system, it is easy to forget that, about one hundred and fifty years later, the ideology of nationalism introduced an important qualification to the legitimacy of this system. Sovereign states, nationalists believe, have to be *nation-states* in order to represent their people and gain general acceptance. Yet, as Gurr (1993) points out, although there are only about 180 states in the world there are between three to five thousand 'nations' and 575 'potential' nation-states. The world political system, therefore, retains a high potential for ethno-nationalist conflict.

These conflicts impact on world politics in a number of ways. First, there is the problem of how to respond to secessionist movements. The inter-state system, fearing 'balkanization' or an 'epidemic' effect, has been reluctant to accept such claims when these claims are resisted by the state concerned. This is why so many secessionist attempts have ended in failure, including those in Katanga, Biafra, Punjab, Tamil areas of Sri Lanka and the Southern Sudan. Indeed, between 1945 and the end of the Cold War, Bangladesh was the only state to obtain general recognition after Indian assistance allowed it to defeat the government of Pakistan in 1971. Despite the recognition of some of the former Yugoslav republics against the wishes of the government of Yugoslavia there are still no signs that the general opposition to secession has weakened since the end of the Cold War. There has been a reluctance, despite human rights concerns, to recognize the secessionist movements in the Kurdish areas of Turkey and Iraq or in Chechnya. However, this does not mean that individual states may not attempt to aid particular secessionist movements either because of an affective link (see later) or because they wish to obtain a strategic advantage.

There are also what are called irredentist claims, where one state wants to reclaim fellow nationals living in neighbouring states. Until the 1990s, many of the most serious irredentist movements since 1945 had been based in the Third World, but the rapid collapse of both the Soviet Union and its control of Eastern Europe may give rise to irredentism in several parts of the post-communist world. Already there has been a bloody war between Armenia and Azerbaijan over possession of Nagorno-Karabakh. Dissatisfaction with existing political boundaries may give rise to irredentism in Russia (several million Russians live outside Russia in the 'near abroad'), Hungary (about 20 per cent of Magyars live outside Hungary in Vojvodina, Transylvania and Slovakia) and parts of the former Yugoslavia. How long will the Dayton agreement be respected and will the idea of a Greater Serbia emerge again to haunt the Balkans?

Ethnic conflicts often cause major human rights abuses. These can include genocidal actions (East Timor, Rwanda, Burundi, Southern Sudan and Bosnia), forced assimilation (Tibet, Iraqi Kurdistan until the Gulf War, the Chittagong Hill Tribes of Bangladesh) and a wide variety of other actions that can cause international concern, such as Israeli actions in the Occupied Territories or the execution of the Ogoni leader and writer Ken Saro-Wiwa by the Abacha regime in Nigeria. International concern is also raised in situations of violent ethnic conflict because they create serious refugee problems and humanitarian emergencies. Sometimes, as in Bosnia, these are produced by a deliberate policy of 'ethnic cleansing'.

Given the significance of all these issues it is not surprising that Rupesinghe (1990) has noted a 'disappearing boundary' between internal and international conflict and that many other recent studies have identified the growing internationalization of ethnic conflict (de Silva and May, 1991; Midlarsky, 1992).

Putting Ethno-Nationalist Conflict on the International Agenda

For reasons already discussed, ethnic and nationalist conflicts have
become increasingly visible in world politics. But we have also noted
that the extent of the internationalization varies considerably from
conflict to conflict. We should remember that ethnic groups,
because they are not states, do not have an automatic right of
access to international bodies like the UN, and can therefore find it
difficult to bring their grievances before world opinion. This has
been a problem for the people of East Timor, who have been
fighting against Indonesian occupation of their country since 1975.
Because Indonesia was an important ally of the West during the
Cold War, and remains an important market, few states were
willing to take up the issue of East Timor in international gatherings.

A number of factors are likely to determine the location of the
ethnic question on the agenda of world politics. Premdas has listed
the ones that he considers especially important (1991, p. 16). They
are: the international dispersal of at least one of the ethnic groups
in conflict; the strategic location of the strife-torn country; the
organizational and communication capabilities of the adversaries
and their allies; and the presence of international and voluntary
organizations sensitive to the atrocities that tend to occur in
communal conflict. We shall make use of these categories in this
analysis.

Affective links, where one or more of the parties has cultural links
to groups in other states, can contribute to the international
significance of a particular case of ethnic conflict. In the former
Yugoslavia, outside involvement has been linked to affective sym-
pathies. Thus many Moslem states sided with the Bosnia Moslems,
the Russians tended to support the Orthodox Serbs and some of the
Catholic states of Europe identified most with the Croat cause. The
Cyprus conflict offers another case of affective intervention, with
Turkey supporting the Turkish Cypriots and Greece supporting the
Greek Cypriots. The Tamils of India have played an important role
in supporting the minority Tamil population in Sri Lanka. The role
of diasporas (literally, dispersed peoples) is also of interest here,
though most of the literature is focused on the influence of
'hyphenated Americans' on US foreign policy. It seems undeniable
that Jewish-Americans, Irish-Americans and Greek-Americans

have had an important role to play in influencing US attitudes to the Israeli–Palestinian, Irish and Cypriot conflicts respectively.

Second, the geo-strategic interests of the larger states, and especially the permanent members of the UN Security Council, can affect the international significance of ethnic conflicts. Howard notes that in responding to ethnic conflicts

> Other powers may, if they see it in their own interests, or under pressure from interested elements within their own communities, espouse contending causes and so both widen and intensify the scope of the conflict. Palestine is of course a case in point. They may also recognise that it is in their common interest to constrain them, as have the British and Irish governments in Northern Ireland and as have most major powers in the former Yugoslavia; or they may feel it best to ignore them altogether. (Howard, 1995, p. 289)

The geographical location of a conflict is also an important factor. The high profile given to the conflict in the former Yugoslavia is in part due the fact that this occurred on the margins of Western Europe. The security and refugee problems this raised had to be taken seriously by the European Union. Premdas (1991) also points out how a location close to a major metropolitan centre will make it more likely that the global media will pay attention to a conflict. On the other hand, 'orphaned conflicts' such as those in Fiji, Irian Jaya, Abkhazia, Southern Sudan and Liberia, are likely to pass unnoticed by those not directly affected because they are far from metropolitan centres.

Media coverage of the humanitarian problems caused by particular conflicts can be important in forming international agendas. A CNN reporter with a satellite up-link can create enormous global interest. Pressure can then build for something to be done to help the victims of violence even when governments may be reluctant to get involved. The global media was a catalyst for intervention by the UN in Iraqi Kurdistan and Bosnia (as well as in non-ethnic conflicts like Somalia). There are, however, certain problems with the role of the media. Coverage can be rather superficial, biased towards the interests of the audience (the British media, for example, tended to concentrate on the British contribution to Unprofor – United Nations Protection Force). It can also be

over-dependent on sensationalist images. Some have even com-
plained of an over-reliance on what has been called war pornogra-
phy and a lack of any attempt to explain the underlying causes of
particular problems. The attention span of the media in specific
cases can also be quite short. A huge interest may be built up by
intensive coverage, but when the coverage stops, so does the
concern.

Finally, some non-governmental organizations can bring specific
cases to the attention of the international community. Aid and
charity bodies, human rights organizations and church groups may
investigate and publicize abuses during inter-communal conflict.
Some of these bodies may also have consultative status at the UN,
where they can take up the cause of communal groups that may not
otherwise have an international voice.

Two other points about the significance of the ethnic issue on the
agenda of world politics can be made. First, one of the reasons why
ethnic conflict was ignored for so long in the study of International
Relations was the state-centric assumptions of the dominant realist
approach. As this was challenged, attention was directed at non-
state actors, including ethnic groups. Here, pioneering work was
done by John Burton and by those who have been influenced by his
world society ideas. This world society approach encouraged analysts to 'consider also the linkages between domestic and international conflict, the successful record of conflict management in
domestic contexts, and the academic literature on problems of
deviant behaviour, perception, human needs and political socializa-
tion' (Banks, 1984, p. 20).

Nationalism, Ethnic Conflict and the End of the Cold War

A final reason for a growing awareness of ethnic conflict is the end
of the Cold War. As the superpower confrontation ebbed, the
international community came to see how many of the conflicts it
had viewed in terms of the conflict between liberal-democratic and
Marxist social systems had an ethnic core. Indeed, there are many
writers who specifically link the growing importance of ethnic
conflict to the end of the Cold War. Brown, for example, refers
to an 'epidemic' of internal violence during the post-Cold War
period (1996, p. 26). On the other hand, Gurr and Harff point out

that 'we cannot entirely blame the explosion of ethnic conflict in the 1990s on the end of the Cold War' (1994, p. 10). This is because, as we have already noted, there has been a steady increase in the number of such conflicts since 1950.

It may be more accurate to say that the end of the Cold War has allowed us to become more aware of the significance of ethnic conflict. As Carment points out, 'no longer can potential or on-going strife be subsumed within the ideological competition between East and West' (1994, p. 551). In Angola, for example, the site of a classic Cold War confrontation between the Soviet-supported Marxist MPLA and the US-backed UNITA, it was often forgotten that this conflict had a strong ethnic dimension. For the MPLA was composed mainly of the Akwambunda, whilst UNITA was backed by the Ovimbunda. Howard takes up this theme and claims that the West, and especially the US, 'remained for far too long blind to the extent to which ideological concepts were used to mask conflicts that were basically ethnic . . . Only the failure to recognize this made it possible to believe that with the collapse of communism . . . a New World Order based on the secular, rational and universal values of the West was now about to dawn' (Howard, 1995, p. 293).

The end of the Cold War has had a mixed effect on tensions between states and ethnic groups. During the period of superpower confrontation, both the US and the USSR, either directly or through regional clients, would intervene and counter-intervene in ethnic conflicts, often making them more protracted as a result of their competitive involvement and arms sales policies. Though, as Smith notes, the superpowers 'rarely sought to re-draw existing state boundaries . . . [because] . . . this could all too easily destabilise their own client system' (1981, p. 148). Mayall agrees and points out that, although the superpowers refused openly to support secessionist movements, 'their ideological rivalry often led them to support ethnic separatism covertly and manipulatively' (1990, pp. 66–7).

The end of the Cold War, therefore, made it easier to resolve some of these conflicts where the superpowers had been engaged in competitive interventions in pursuit of their own strategic aims. These would include the Israeli–Palestinian conflict and the war in Angola. On the other hand, the collapse of the USSR also provided an opportunity for suppressed ethnic conflicts to resurface in various parts of the former Soviet Union. So we have witnessed violent conflicts between the Armenians and Azerbaijanis over Nagorno-Karabakh, between Georgia and Abkhazia and between Russia and Chechnya. The Soviet threat to the former Yugoslavia was also a factor which tended to unite Serbs and Croats. When this was removed, centrifugal tendencies were increased.

Another consequence of the end of superpower rivalry was that the United Nations Security Council found that it was able to reach a consensus about how to react to some of the high visibility ethnic conflicts. This was a novel situation, and it generated excessive optimism about the ability of the organization to respond constructively to the ethnic challenge. The high point of this optimism was *An Agenda for Peace*, which set out an impressive plan to improve the role of the UN in promoting international peace and security (Boutros-Ghali, 1992). Since then, after Bosnia, Rwanda and Somalia, expectations of the UN have slumped.

This reminds us that there is a powerful, destructive dynamic behind many ethnic conflicts that may, in fact, have been held in check by the Cold War. Now that the danger of superpower confrontation is over, it is unlikely that a specific ethnic problem could detonate a global conflict. Nevertheless, the phenomenon of crisis management by the superpowers, which may have controlled specific conflicts, is no longer with us. The UN has tried to take on this role through the more grandly titled technique of peace enforcement. Unfortunately, unless the US is willing to provide it with military support, the organization lacks the leverage over the parties to a conflict which the superpowers used to possess and anyway it is frequently too divided about how to respond to specific cases of ethnic conflict to formulate a satisfactory strategy (see also Chapter 7).

Managing Ethnic Conflict

Much of the analysis of ethnic conflict and world politics has centred on the issue of intervention in complex emergencies. This is understandable given that between 80 and 90 per cent of the victims of inter-ethnic conflicts are non-combatants and that civil war contributes to a wide range of problems that include hunger and displacement. Furthermore, bitter ethnic violence can result in the collapse of the state and the paralysis of effective government (Boutros-Ghali, 1995, para. 13). In such circumstances there is a greater need for outside help. We should not forget, however, that humanitarian intervention is a short-term, technical response that only deals with the symptoms of ethnic conflict. Indeed, the need for such action is a sign that the international community has failed to respond adequately to the causes of such conflict.

A number of mechanisms have been suggested to deal with these underlying causes. First, there have been attempts to develop new international legal norms. One obvious area here is the legal protection of individuals belonging to ethnic minorities. In December 1992, for example, the United Nations General Assembly finally adopted a Declaration on the Rights of Persons Belonging to National or Ethnic, Religious and Linguistic Minorities (UNGA Resolution 47/135). Ironically, the first draft of this Declaration was introduced by Yugoslavia in 1978. It is the most significant UN document on the protection of minorities since the 1948 Convention on the Prevention and Punishment of the Crime of Genocide and is a major step forward beyond the relatively weak Article 27 of the 1966 Covenant on Civil and Political Rights. This Article stated that

> In those states in which ethnic, religious or linguistic minorities exist, persons belonging to such minorities shall not be denied the right, in community with the other members of their group, to enjoy their own culture, to profess and practice their own religion, or to use their own language.

Unlike the 1966 article, the 1992 Declaration *expects* states to adopt appropriate legislative and other measures to protect the existence of minorities within their territories and to encourage conditions for the promotion of their identity. It also recognizes the right of persons belonging to minorities to participate fully in decisions which affect them.

Nevertheless the Declaration has several weaknesses. The most obvious one is that it is not a legally binding document. It only has moral force. Furthermore its inability to define what it means by 'minority' and the use of imprecise language such as 'appropriate measures', 'wherever possible' or 'where required,' makes it easier for governments to evade its proposals. Finally, no mechanism was created to monitor the implementation of the measures suggested in the Declaration.

Another promising move to promote the legal protection of ethnic minorities concerns the 1948 Genocide Convention. This makes it illegal to undertake actions with the intent to destroy, in whole or in part, a national, ethnical, racial or religious group. The problem, however, has been in implementing this Convention. Experts point out that although there have been several examples of genocide since 1948, the Genocide Convention has never been invoked to punish those responsible (see Fein, 1992). This has led to a withering attack on the UN's record in this area by Kuper, who argues that

> The performance of the United Nations in response to genocide is as negative as its performance on charges of political mass murder. There are the same evasions of responsibility and protection of offending governments and the same overriding concern for state interests and preoccupation with ideological and regional alliances. (Kuper, 1985, p. 160)

In the mid-1990s, however, the UN established *ad hoc* war crimes tribunals for Yugoslavia and Rwanda. Both were mandated to investigate accusations of genocidal activity and to indict individuals who may have a case to answer. However, there has been little support for the suggestion that a permanent War Crimes Tribunal could be established to introduce a more consistent international response to the atrocities committed during inter-state and intra-state violence.

The International Criminal Tribunal for the former Yugoslavia (ICTY), which could become the model for future *ad hoc* initiatives, was created in February 1993 by Security Council Resolution 808. This established an independent body with the power to prosecute four types of crime: grave breaches of the 1949 Geneva Conventions, violations of the laws and customs of war, crimes against humanity, and acts of genocide. The acts of genocide that can be punished are genocide itself, conspiracy to commit genocide, direct and public incitement to commit genocide, attempt to commit genocide, and complicity in genocide.

Two other suggestions have concentrated on the need to amend the state-centric bias of international norms. The first concerns the right of national self-determination. The present position in international law is that there is such a right, but that it is restricted in its applicability. Thus 'nations' have a right of self-determination if they are an oppressed group ruled by a colonial or racist power, but once independence is achieved the principle of sovereignty and territorial integrity becomes more important. So Nigeria had a right to self-determination when it was part of the British Empire, but the Ibo people in this newly independent state have no right of independence from Nigeria. The inconsistencies in this approach have led to suggestions that the international community needs to develop clear criteria to allow it to judge self-determination claims in a fairer manner. Halperin *et al.* (1990) believe that five factors are especially important: the conduct of the ruling group, the choice of the people, the conduct of the self-determination movement, the potential for violent consequences, and the historical background (does a group have a history of independence?).

The other suggestion is meant to reduce the need for 'external self-determination' and concerns the role of autonomy as a conflict resolution mechanism. Supporters point out that it offers a middle path between the conflict, promoting options of secession and forced integration. Hannum, who has written an influential study of this idea, points out that it 'recognises the right of minority and indigenous communities to exercise meaningful internal self-determination and control over their own affairs in a manner that is not inconsistent with the ultimate sovereignty . . . of the state' (Hannum, 1990, p. 473). Evidence from places like the South Tyrol (German speaking area of Italy) and the Aland Islands (Swedish population living in Finland) suggests that when minorities are offered such internal self-determination, ethnic conflict declines.

Ethnic conflicts are notoriously difficult to resolve. This is due to a number of factors that include the asymmetries introduced where the conflicts are between a state and a minority group, the non-negotiable nature of identity and security needs, and the difficulties of achieving a settlement through geographical separation based on recognized boundaries – which is how inter-state conflicts are often ended Yet, despite the inherent problems in attempting ethnic conflict resolution, it may be that the lack of success may also be due to the inadequacies of the methods used.

Much of the academic literature on conflict resolution is rather suspicious of what is called 'traditional' or 'track-1' diplomacy.

Critics claim that it is too rigid and unimaginative to be a consistently effective mechanism. It is based too much on techniques based on power and leverage – 'mediation with muscle'. It tends to promote 'win–lose' thinking, where each party will make concessions from its initial bargaining positions in order to reach a mutually acceptable agreement. Also, entering into official negotiations can have high entry and exit costs for the parties and such approaches also have to operate within existing frameworks of legitimacy. This can hinder constructive interventions in conflicts where one party (usually the state) does not want to confer recognition on a party that is challenging its authority. So the British government finds it difficult to talk directly to the IRA in Northern Ireland; and Israel, until recently, even had a law which made it illegal for any of its citizens to talk to the PLO (Palestine Liberation Organization).

In some circumstances, unofficial, 'track-2' approaches, undertaken by private individuals or groups, may be more successful. Such initiatives often focus on interests rather than positions. They have low entry and exit costs. Their informal and private nature may encourage the parties to be more relaxed and forthcoming and because they are not official initiatives they cannot confer formal legitimacy on any group. The role played by private Norwegian facilitators in the Israeli–Palestinian conflict and the activities of the US-based Carter Center has raised the profile of this sort of intervention in ethnic conflict. The Carter Center was created in 1982 by former US president Jimmy Carter as a non-partisan and non-profit-making policy institute based in Atlanta, Georgia. This serves as the headquarters for the 25-member International Negotiation Network, a group of experts and retired senior political figures from around the world who have provided assistance to the parties in several protracted ethnic conflicts. For example, in recent years the Network has organized meetings in Cairo and Tunis for leaders of the five Great Lakes states in Africa and has run workshops in Estonia that have facilitated dialogue between the ethnic groups there. In 1991 President Carter was invited by the protagonists in Liberia to assist their peace process. The Carter Center also helped to broker a four month ceasefire in Bosnia in early 1995.

With respect to unofficial approaches, the work of Burton (1990) has been the most influential. He has offered both a theory and a technique of ethnic conflict resolution. The theory calls for a major shift in the way we think about the resolution and prevention of conflict away from interventions based on power towards analysis based on universal human needs. From this perspective, protracted ethnic conflicts are not really about sovereignty, which is a 'win–lose' issue. Conflict is regarded as a symptom of a deeper problem, which is that one or more of the parties are not allowed to have their human needs fulfilled. Since basic human needs do not exist in a 'win–lose' situation – in recognizing my identity you do not have to renounce your identity – this approach to conflict resolution creates the possibility of 'win–win' outcomes. The technique which allows these insights to be introduced into a conflict is called the problem-solving workshop, where academic facilitators attempt to get the parties to engage in joint analysis of the problems they face.

Of course, there are problems with these ideas. Critics argue that the human needs approach may underestimate the role of cultural influences in conflict and point out that Burton produces little empirical evidence to support the reductionist claim that protracted conflict is caused by the denial of human needs. From a more traditionalist perspective, Zartman (1989) has emphasized the importance of leverage, and therefore of power, in the mediation process. Even some of those influenced by Burton have not fully embraced his call for a dramatic shift in thinking about this problem. Kelman (1992) has argued that Burton's ideas may be more appropriate for the 'pre-negotiation' phase of a conflict where they may increase the chances of a final settlement in the formal phase of negotiations, but cannot replace this stage. One of the most interesting new concepts in the theory of conflict resolution, which develops this 'stages of conflict resolution' approach, has emerged from the work of Fisher and Keashley (1991). Using the Cyprus case as an example, they have called both for a 'healthy eclecticism' towards conflict resolution within what they have called the 'contingency model'. This argues that as conflicts go through a series of stages, intervention strategies should be developed that are appropriate to each of these stages.

We have noted how the passing of the Cold War made it easier to resolve some ethnic conflicts and, in several states, cease-fires were arranged between the parties and new constitutional arrangements were introduced. The existence of a growing number of multi-ethnic societies coming out of conflict has stimulated research into what has been termed 'post-conflict peacebuilding' by Boutros-Ghali

(1992). What he means, of course, is post-*violent*-conflict peace-building. There is a mild form of post-conflict peacebuilding which concentrates on the reconstruction of war-torn societies. Here the emphasis is on economic reconstruction, the promotion of mutual understanding and the development of new constitutional struc-tures. On the other hand there is a more radical form that concentrates on conflict transformation through grass-roots social movements and the deconstruction of conflicting identities (Rupe-singhe, 1995). Important tests of peacebuilding approaches are occurring in a wide range of communal conflicts, including Israel/ Palestine, Northern Ireland, South Africa, Angola and Lebanon.

At the other end of the conflict cycle, there is also a growing interest in the prevention of ethnic conflict. Boutros-Ghali (1992) makes a number of suggestions under this heading. They include: confidence-building measures, including arms control (see Chapter 6); fact-finding; early warning; preventive deployment, such as the dispatch of UNPROFOR personnel to Macedonia; and the creation of demilitarized zones. The problem here is not the lack of ideas or information, but the unwillingness of states to use the available measures. So Boutros-Ghali suggests that the solution has to be long term. It will involve 'creating a climate of opinion, or ethos' within the international community in which the norm will be for states to accept UN involvement (1995, para. 28).

Nationalism, Ethnic Conflict and Contemporary World Politics

The fault-line between the state and the nation is likely to be a basic feature of world politics for the foreseeable future since many states are never going to be able to eradicate the ethnic challenge to their legitimacy and not all nations are going to be able to obtain their own state. So Mayall has pointed out that

> First, the primacy of the national ideal amongst contemporary political principles has modified the traditional conception of an international society but has not replaced it. Second, there is no immediate prospect of transcending the national idea, either as the principle of legitimation or as the basis of political organisa-tion for the modern state. (Mayall, 1990, p. 145)

Yet although the fact of ethnic difference and the ideology of
nationalism will present a major challenge to the territorial integrity, or even the survival, of certain states, they cannot be seen as a
fundamental challenge to the sovereign state system as a whole. The
state is important to the nation. It is a sign of self-worth and allows
a nation to have a stronger role in protecting its interests. Nationalists believe that only a state of one's own provides an opportunity
for the full expression of a distinct culture. Indeed, we should note
that the consequence of recent ethnic conflicts has been the creation
of more not fewer sovereign states. Twenty-two new sovereign
states have been established because of the break-up of the Soviet
Union, Yugoslavia and Czechoslovakia, though none of them are
really nation-states either. In fact it is difficult to think of any group
that is more tightly wedded to territory than ethnic and national
groups. So, although many commentators have referred to the crisis
of the nation-state, nationalists appear to be unimpressed by such
claims.

A state-centric bias is unlikely to facilitate constructive responses
to the ethnic issue, for several reasons. The anarchic nature of interstate politics breeds a sense of insecurity which tends to make
governments suspicious of minorities. Furthermore, the sovereign
state system means that international responses to particular ethnic
conflicts and national self-determination claims will be filtered
through the self-centred interests of states. This can lead to hypocrisy and inconsistencies. Serbia, for example, supported the right of
the Croatian and Bosnian Serbs to self-determination at the same
time as they were denying it to the Albanian majority in Kosovo.
Turkey invaded Cyprus in 1974 to uphold the right of Turkish
Cypriots to self-determination, but have denied such a right to their
Kurdish minority. Also, since most states feel threatened by ethnic
groups, they have a mutual interest in not extending them too many
rights. The temptation in inter-state politics, therefore, is to support
the status quo. What interests do Western states have in raising the
issue of Tibet with China or Russian policy towards Chechnya?

It is, therefore, interesting to note that all of the methods of
managing the ethnic challenge mentioned in the previous section
require some modification of the state-centric view of world politics.
The development of legal norms will involve a more intrusive role
for international organizations and will strengthen the notion that
the international legitimacy of states should be made conditional on

their human rights record. The idea of the international protection of minorities also challenges the norm that it is only states and individuals that are the main subjects and objects of international law. Effective conflict resolution may also involve a move away from the realist approach to the world society approach favoured by the 'Burton school', which recognizes the significance of non-state actors and of human needs analysis.

For more than a century, there has been the 'liberal expectancy' that ethnicity would not survive for very long, and Marxists expected nationalism to decline as communism spread (Moynihan, 1993). For a generation after the Second World War, the most obvious example of the 'liberal expectancy' was the nation-building idea. Today, the prophets of ethnic decline tend to emphasize globalization. From this perspective the blinkered parochialism of ethnic identity seems an unsatisfactory and inappropriate response to a world of multinational corporations, satellite television and the Internet. Hobsbawm (1990), for example, has argued strongly that although nationalism is clearly still prominent, it is now outdated. It has become a reactionary and negative force.

There are several possible responses to these claims. The first is to ask what are the alternatives to nationalism in contemporary world society? No convincing candidates present themselves at present, with the possible exception of strong religious attachment, though there has been speculation that the world may be moving to a situation where 'civilizations' rather than nations will be the main focus of identity. Another response is to point out that the effects of globalization are not spread equally throughout world society. There will be winners and losers. Waters points out that 'globalization is, in general, a differentiating, as well as an homogenizing process' (1995, p. 136). Where the divisions between those who do and those who do not benefit coincide with cultural differences, ethnic particularism may be reinforced and mobilization on the basis of nationalism may appear to be a rational option in the contest for resources.

A final response is to point out that globalization is not neutral. It is, in fact, closely linked to a specific world view that is 'Western'. It involves the diffusion of a certain culture (Hollywood, Disneyland, McDonald's, MTV), a certain form of economic organization (capitalist), and a European conception of human rights (individualistic rather than collective). Such globalization can threaten groups whose culture does not fit in with the dominant values and may, in fact, promote rather than reduce ethnic tensions.

Belgium presents an interesting case study of the contradictory nature of globalization. Here is a state which is at the heart of the integration process in the European Union. Indeed, it is difficult to think of any other society where the impact of globalization has been so significant. Yet Belgium is a state which has split into two separate linguistic communities (three, if we include the small German-speaking community), and where Brussels, the 'capital' of the European Union, sits uneasily across the communal divide.

As long as the sovereign state is the principle unit of organization in world politics the key determinant of the extent of ethnic conflict will be the policies adopted by individual states. Welsh is correct to point out that 'for the foreseeable future, individual states with ethnic problems will have no alternative but to grope towards political accommodation' (1993, p. 79). There is, however, a considerable literature to guide states on good governance in multi-ethnic societies (Horowitz, 1985; Lijphart, 1977; McGarry and O'Leary, 1993). Yet this emphasis on good government within states does not mean that there is no role for world society, and some of the most important contributions that the international community can make have been explored in this chapter.

We are living in a paradoxical world. Increased globalization is undermining the legitimacy of the nation-state, but one of the major consequences of globalization is an increasing identification with an ethnic community which may lead – though this is not inevitable – to the development of even more groups seeking national self-determination. To complicate matters even further, the internationalization of ethnic conflict is part of the process of globalization. The complex nature of identity means that we should avoid over-simplistic analysis. Perhaps, in the short run, all we can hope for is that self-determination will be informed by a desire not for separation but for autonomy within a broader, pluralist community. In other words that it will be civic nationalism rather than ethno-nationalism. We are witnessing this to some extent in Western Europe, where groups like the Scots and the Catalans, inspired by the vision of a 'Europe of the regions', now seem to prefer the idea of autonomy within the European Union.

One major task for the international community should be to make less exclusive and more pluralist choice an attractive option

for individuals belonging to ethnic groups. This will involve promoting good governance in multi-ethnic societies and developing
mechanisms and institutions that can enable the international
community to respond more constructively and more efficiently
to ethnic conflict. The failure to stop the genocide in Rwanda is just
one example that demonstrates how urgent this need is.

Guide to Further Reading

For a general study of ethnic conflict, see Horowitz (1985). A more up-to-
date analysis is Ignatieff (1993). The expanding literature on ethnicity and
nationalism includes several general studies of ethnic conflict and world
politics, such as Brown (1993); Gotlieb (1993); Gurr and Harff (1994);
Moynihan (1993); and Ryan (1995).

For analyses of national self-determination, see Ronen (1979) and
Halperin *et al.* (1990). A comparative study of secession is found in
Heraclides (1991) and the idea of autonomy is studied by Hannum
(1990). The most comprehensive account of the international protection
of minorities is Thornberry (1990). The problem of genocide is explored in
Kuper (1985) and Fein (1992). The Burton school approach to ethnic
conflict resolution can be found in Burton (1990); Azar (1990); and Rothman (1992). Also of interest are Montville (1990); Rupesinghe (1995); and
Zartman (1989).

9

Islamic Fundamentalism and Political Islam

Since the demise of the Soviet Union, it has become fashionable to warn of a new Cold War arising from 'the resurgence of parochial identities based on ethnic and religious allegiances' (Juergensmeyer, 1993, p. 2). Religion, in particular, is seen to pose a serious threat to international stability (Huntington, 1993), with the role being played by Islamic fundamentalism in the Western-dominated international system representing one of the major sources of danger. Although most of the world's 1.1 billion Muslims, who adhere to Islam, live outside the Middle East and North Africa (MENA), the politicization of Islam and the rise of Islamic fundamentalism are more readily identified with the Middle East than any other region.

Islam, however, in both its political and religious guises, is not a monolithic force and does not speak with one voice. Political Islam is shorthand for the diverse set of competing political opinions held within the Muslim community. Although Muslims are also split doctrinally between those adhering to the majority Sunni sect and the 10 per cent minority of Shiis, it is increasingly possible to find political groups who straddle the two main religious sects. Moreover, while political Islam is said to be a 'new invention' (Ayubi, 1991, p. 3), many of the radical Islamic groups have a long history of confrontation with the state, going back in some cases to the beginning of the twentieth century (Zubaida, 1989). But these groups are becoming increasingly important because they have come to pose a most significant challenge to the Arab state, subverting the status quo in the MENA region, offering an alternative world view to Western liberalism and claiming to provide a superior system of government to that offered by the liberal democratic states in the West.

Although Islamic fundamentalism and political Islam are often considered synonymous terms, they need to be distinguished. In this chapter, the former term is used to encapsulate the emotional, spiritual and political response of Muslims to an acute and continuing social, economic and political crisis that has gripped the Middle East. The nature of this crisis will be examined later. Many individuals, ideologies, political groups and countries have been blamed for the crisis. But for reasons that will become clear, Western countries and their commercial flagships are singled out for sustained criticism and attack. This response is as much a result of the fear of wholesale 'Westernization' of Islamic cultures as it is a reaction to the decades of direct intervention by the West in this region. Moreover, contrary to Western expectations, Iran's Islamist leader, Ayatollah Khomeini, who personified Islamic fundamentalism for the West, managed to strike a chord with many Muslims, particularly with his critique of the role of Western powers in the Muslim world. His anti-Western rhetoric, using terms like 'arrogant' and 'satanic' when referring to the United States, has gained much currency amongst Arab Islamists.

The term 'political Islam' is associated here with the goal and related political programme designed to establish a world-wide Islamic order. This goal has been pursued on two related levels: one challenging the status quo within Muslim countries and the other representing an increasingly transnational network of contacts aimed at establishing a 'pax-Islamica' (literally, Islamic peace) across the Arab and Muslim world.

The Diverse World of Islam

This Muslim world is in fact a dynamic but non-integrated, rapidly changing and evolving group of mainly Third World states and globally scattered communities (about one-third of all Muslims are minorities in the countries in which they live). The intricacies of this complex and diverse world of states and communities can best be illustrated through an examination of the geographical, political, economic and cultural features of the states ostensibly held together by pan-Islamism. It then becomes clear, as Al-Bazzaz, an Arab historian and former Iraqi prime minister, has warned, that although pan-Islamism 'aims to form a comprehensive political organization which all Muslims must obey' (1982, p. 88), it is unrealistic in practice to expect the formation of a union between a range of countries that can be as different as Iraq and Iran, for example.

The Muslim world is spread across Europe, Africa and Asia, with sizeable communities in the Americas, India and China. But the Middle East and South East Asia form the heartlands of this faith, with Saudi Arabia providing the birthplace of Islam, and Indonesia representing the most populous Muslim country (with around 90 per cent of its 188 million people being Muslim). The political geography of the faith, however, has experienced some significant changes in recent years. The emergence of a Muslim-dominated Bosnia in former Yugoslavia and the regeneration of Islam in Albania in Southern Europe has ended Turkey's position as Europe's only Muslim state. The presence of these states is already being felt in inter-state and inter-communal relations within the region, much of it discouragingly negative to date.

With the collapse of the Soviet Union, six Muslim republics came into existence in the Caucasus and Central Asia. These states, however, are not Muslim in the classic sense of the word, with Islam forming the dominant cultural influence. Culturally and linguistically these states have been permeated by Slavic influences. They are much more in tune with secularist Turkey than with the traditional Islamic forces in the Arab world. Nevertheless, their emergence does represent an expansion in the political geography of the Muslim world and a quantitative growth in the number of independent Muslim states operating in the international system as well as in the international organizations that have been established by Islamic countries. The birth of these six new states and the addition of their 70 million people to the Muslim world will begin to have an impact on the direction and policies pursued by the established Muslim states and they will influence the orientation and ethos of previously Arab-dominated international Muslim organizations such as the 54-member Islamic Conference Organization (ICO). Indeed the recent expansion of the Muslim world has almost exclusively taken place outside the Arab world with the exception of the establishment of the Palestine Liberation Organization's (PLO) control over a part of the Israeli-occupied Palestinian territories.

The expansion of the Muslim world beyond the Middle East is already creating new opportunities for cooperation among the non-Arab Muslim actors in this region. In the early 1990s, for example, Iran, Pakistan and Turkey, the founding members of the Economic Cooperation Organization (ECO), incorporated Afghanistan and all of the independent Muslim republics of the former Soviet Union into this organization, making it the largest regional organization in Asia. It represents over 300 million people and embraces huge natural resources, ranging from water and agricultural land to hydrocarbons, gold, lead, zinc, coal, copper, and uranium.

Political diversity

The popular image of Islamic fundamentalism in the West generates a very distorted impression of the varied and complex pattern of political organization in the Muslim world. Of course, some leaders do identify themselves as believers and actively incorporate the tenets of Islam into their policies. In the pro-Western monarchies of Morocco, Jordan and Saudi Arabia, for example, the family histories of their kings are closely woven into those of the Prophet Mohammed and his tribe. In Iran, the spiritual leader of the republic is a senior Shia cleric whose black turban is supposed to indicate a direct line of descent from the Prophet's family, and in Afghanistan the president enjoys the fruits of his office because he possesses the credentials to be an important Muslim leader. But there are other very different modes of political organization found in the Muslim world which are captured in the following typology:

- traditional Monarchical Muslim states (for example, Morocco, Jordan, Saudi Arabia)
- modernist Muslim states (for example, Malaysia, Indonesia and Turkey)
- revolutionary Muslim states (for example, Afghanistan, Iran, Sudan)
- secular Muslim states (for example, Algeria, Egypt, Tunisia)

This categorization reflects the fact that Muslim people are governed by very varied and competing political systems. The variation is sufficiently great for relations between Muslim states to be adversely affected. Nowhere is this problem more evident than in the Middle East, where radical secular and Islamist regimes co-exist with the traditional monarchies in a very uneasy and sometimes hostile set of relationships.

Economic diversity

It is not only in the political arena that Muslim states differ. They diverge economically as well. At one end of the scale, newly-industrializing Muslim countries like Tunisia, Morocco, Turkey, Malaysia, Indonesia, and possibly Pakistan, form part of the Third World challenge to Western domination of the capitalist world economy. Oil-endowed Muslim states constitute another area of potential prosperity within the Muslim world. The Middle Eastern oil states (along with Indonesia and Brunei) have been joined in recent years by potentially big players such as Azerbaijan, Kazakhstan, Turkmenistan and Uzbekistan. Many of these new states have the potential to emerge as new economic 'tiger' states and they already see themselves as the leading regional economies of the twenty-first century. But the ambition of these states to catapult themselves to prominence as key hydrocarbon providers in the next century threatens to bring them into a devastating competition with the established Middle Eastern hydrocarbon exporters, all of which are Muslim states.

At the other end of the economic scale lie a number of 'survivor' states with stagnant economies. More than a dozen Muslim states in Asia and Africa possess neither the natural resources nor the necessary human skills to prosper in the existing international economic environment. Pervasive poverty persists, even though many of these states have introduced the economic liberalization policies advocated by Western economists.

Despite the enormous economic differences experienced by the various Muslim states, all are part of the same international capitalist division of labour. Muslim states exist and function, albeit at different economic levels, within the same international economic system. There is no separate Muslim economic or political division of labour. Indeed, to the dismay of many Islamists, there are few sources of common interest drawing these states together: religion and history appear to provide the only threads available to bind Muslims into a single and very tenuous Islamic world order.

Different Perspectives on Islamic Fundamentalism

Islamic fundamentalism has been evaluated from three very different perspectives. First, as already mentioned, it can be seen as a response to the crisis confronting the nation-state in the Middle East. The crisis is associated with social deprivation, persistent poverty, corruption, nepotism, dependence on the West for security and defence as well as economic assistance, loss of political legitimacy, and a decline in the rule of law. It has been accentuated by the general political instability arising from unaccountable and unresponsive political systems together with persistent uncertainty surrounding the nature of political succession within Muslim states. These problems have been compounded in recent years by rapid population growth, urbanization, and environmental degradation. Fundamentalism, therefore, can be said to be an extremist response to a wide-ranging and commonly perceived crisis (Dekmejian, 1995). It is seen to constitute a form of cultural nationalism, reflecting a passing and badly misunderstood form of populism that poses little danger to the West (Husain, 1995).

A second perspective, championed by Samuel Huntington (1993), links the rise of Islamic fundamentalism to a 'clash of civilizations', with 'dar al-Islam' (the abode of Islam) on one side and the Judaeo-Christian civilization on the other. A conflict between civilizations is seen to be replacing the former Cold War ideological battles. According to Huntington, the 'central axis of world politics', by the twenty-first century, 'will be the interaction of Western power and culture with the power and culture of non-Western societies' (Huntington, 1995, p. 6). For Huntington, the end of the Cold War opened the way to a 'Confucian–Islamic' military and political connection designed to promote cooperation among non-Western civilizations against the dominance of the Western world (1993, p. 45).

Finally, fundamentalism has been linked to political Islam, which is identified as a new and 'authentic' force for positive change, encapsulated in the slogan 'Islam is the solution'. This is the perspective adopted by Muslims who wish to see Islam rather than secularism prevail in the Middle East and eventually throughout the Muslim world. The slogan is heard in countries where Islamists are engaged in violent attempts to overthrow existing regimes (Algeria and Egypt in particular), as well as in countries where Islamic groups have been able to advance their cause by operating within the existing political system (Sidahmed and Ehteshami, 1996). Legitimate political mechanisms have been used, very successfully in some cases, to promote Islamism in the Middle East. In December 1995, the Refah (Welfare) Party in secular Turkey won 21.3 per cent of the popular vote in the parliamentary elections giving the party 158 seats in the 550-member National Assembly; Jordan's Muslim Brotherhood won 22 of the 80 seats in the House of Representatives elections in 1989 and 16 seats in the 1993 elections, and it also secured membership in the cabinet; the Al-Islah (Reform) Party in Yemen won 62 seats of the 301 contested seats in the parliamentary elections of April 1993; the Lebanon's Hezbollah (Party of God) movement has had several MPs in the Lebanese parliament since the early 1990s; and the Kuwaiti Islamists have become an influential political bloc in the National Assembly, reestablished after the small sheikhdom's liberation from Iraqi occupation in 1991.

By contrast, in Iran, the Islamist country *par excellence*, an opposing trend can be observed, with the clerics' presence in the parliament in steady decline since the formation of the Islamic Republic's first parliament in 1980. In that year there were 137 clerics in the parliament; by the fifth set of elections in 1996, their numbers were down to 50 in the 270-seat Majlis or parliament. At the other extreme, in secularist Algeria, when the Islamic Salvation Front won a majority of the popular vote in the national assembly elections of 1991, the military annulled the election. This military intervention was the prelude to a bloody civil war between the ruling secular regime and the country's Islamist groups. The resulting stand-off between the regime and the Islamists precipitated a state of crisis that persisted despite the presidential election of 1995 which was designed to encourage a return to civil order.

Reassessing Islamic Fundamentalism

By the mid-1990s, analysts in the West started to reassess Islamic fundamentalism and political Islam. On the one hand, attention was drawn to the failure of political Islam to bring about any fundamental or lasting changes within the Muslim world. Roy suggested that 'the influence of Islamism is more superficial than it seems'

(1994, p. 26). It was argued, moreover, that the tide of militancy had crested, that the extremists were on the defensive, and that Islamists' power might even be on the wane. Certainly the prospects of an Islamic confrontation with the West was seen as unlikely and talk of a Muslim threat to the West as exaggerated. Confrontation between Islam and the West, it was suggested, was only a 'myth', which had been 'used to legitimize, to mislead, to silence, to mobilize' (Halliday, 1995, p. 6). Because the myth had been taken seriously, however, the Islamic threat had been largely misunderstood and there had been a failure to recognize that the challenge posed by the Islamists 'need not always result in a threat to regional stability or Western interests' (Esposito, 1992, p. 211).

A reaction to Westernization?

Other commentators in the 1990s, however, began to acknowledge that the rise of political Islam was part of a much more wide-ranging challenge to the attempt by liberal governments in the West during the twentieth century to establish an international order constituted by democratic nation states. A new set of issues, including nationalism, ethnic autonomy, and the right to a distinctive cultural identity, had been moved on to the international agenda after the Cold War and these new issues presented a challenge to the legitimacy of the liberal international order favoured by the West. At the same time, the new agenda made it necessary to view political Islam in a new light and from a more international perspective (Sick, 1992). Islamic unity, for example, could be seen to represent an alternative model to the one employed by the West which had led to a colonial division of the Muslim Middle East into separate states. This colonial division, moreover, could now be seen to be the source of the tension that has arisen in recent years for Muslims over the distinction between individual rights and collective duties, as well as over the conflict between the responsibility of citizens to their Islamic faith and to their country of origin.

By attempting to undermine the legitimacy of established states, therefore, Islamists have necessarily been challenging the foundations of the existing state-based international system laid down initially by the West. But it is not just the nature of the state and the structure of the international system that has been thrown into question by the Islamists. They have also attacked the validity of concepts such as democracy and human rights which the West have exhorted the rest of the world to adopt. Islamists in the MENA region (with tacit support from the more illiberal Middle Eastern rulers) have opposed what they regard as Western-imposed doctrines of democratic rule and universal human rights and they have actively developed their own Islamic Bill of Rights, adopted by the ICO in 1990, and based on Islamic law. The Islamists find the 'humanist' agenda, favoured by the West, unacceptable because it challenges their philosophical approach to state–society relations, where sovereignty lies not with the people, but with the deity – with Allah. Western democratic principles, that rely on individualism, run counter to this philosophical position. So, as a consequence, the emergence of human rights as an important component of the 'New World Order' has led to a deterioration in Western–Muslim relations. The tensions arising from the differences between Western and Muslim countries have been exploited, of course, by the Islamists, who have interpreted the UN's support for the Declaration of Human Rights as part of a continuing Western conspiracy to undermine Muslim values and traditions.

At the same time, there has also been a considerable internal debate among Islamists about the relationship between Islam and government. It is argued by some that Islam possesses an unambiguous view of the Islamic state. This view derives from Islamic law (Sharia) which makes it quite clear that imported concepts such as democracy (understood here as a secular form of government) must be outlawed. But there are Islamists who have adopted a more functional assessment of democracy, arguing that there is no incompatibility between Islam and a plural political system and even claiming that 'Islam and democracy are mutually reinforcing' elements of the Islamic political system (Al-Akim, 1993, p. 87). Rachid Ghannouchi, the Tunisian Islamist leader, has gone further and developed a somewhat unorthodox argument in answer to the question 'Can any Muslim community afford to hesitate in participating in the establishment of a secular democratic system if it is unable to establish an Islamic democratic one?' The answer, he says, is no, because it is 'the religious duty of the Muslims, as individuals and communities, to contribute to the efforts to establish such a system' (Ghannouchi, 1993, p. 56). From this perspective, then, the Western democratic system is regarded as a stepping-stone towards the establishment of a fully-fledged Islamic political system. Without any end to the struggle between the Islamic and secular forms of state in sight, however, the debate over the compatibility of Islam with democratic government seems likely to continue (Deegan, 1993; Ehteshami, 1995). Moreover, a survey of the debate suggests that democratic developments in the Middle East are no longer possible without embracing an Islamic dimension.

There are other international issues that have caused Islamists concern. The population conference in Cairo in 1994 and the Beijing women's conference in 1995 were both seen to raise issues of vital importance to the Muslim world. For many militant Islamists, these United Nations-sponsored conferences illustrate a trend in the new international order that threatens cultural diversity. The Islamic way of life, in particular, is seen to be under attack from international forces controlled by the West. But this reaction has not been universal within the Muslim world. Iran, for example, one of the key Islamist states, participated fully in both conferences. Indeed, the Iranian delegation in Cairo surprised most international observers by voicing its support for a series of UN-recommended population control measures, with the sole exception of the right to unconditional abortion. Nevertheless, there remains a wide and apparently unbridgeable gap separating Muslim and Western views on women in society. Muslims interpret women's rights in the context of religious edicts and traditional norms and practices. For them, feminism is an alien and dangerous set of ideas. Women, for the Islamists, have a special and important place in Muslim societies. However, the essentially patriarchal interpretation of gender relations in Islam which leans, for example, towards segregation of the sexes in public places, remains the dominant view in Muslim societies, and is enthusiastically endorsed by the Islamists.

Deep-seated cultural convictions make it difficult for secular governments to transform Muslim societies and, by the same token, these convictions help to reinforce the position of the Islamists. But the weaknesses of many Muslim states have been exacerbated by economic mismanagement and the social dislocation brought about by externally imposed structural adjustment strategies. These strategies have required Muslim states to withdraw from the public sphere and in doing so they have created a political space that the Islamists have been quick to exploit and occupy. The Islamists now frequently provide the vital social and welfare services previously offered by the state to vulnerable members of society. This move brings into question the state's social contract with the people and has thereby enabled the Islamists to erode further the legitimacy of many Muslim states. This has been facilitated by the large number of international organizations in the MENA (over 170) which have increasingly come to fill the political 'space' traditionally occupied by the state (see Table 9.1).

Fighting for the Muslim World

The ideal that the Islamists are aspiring to has been aptly summarized by Nasr, a Muslim intellectual. Islamists, he argues, aim 'to create a nomocratic society where men and women can live according to Allah's Will as contained in the Sharia and according to those virtues which have been manifested most fully in the exemplary life of the Prophet who is a model for both individual human life and rule over the Islamic community' (Nasr, 1993, p. 63). However, Islamists have not hesitated to use violence throughout the Muslim world and further afield in their endeavour to undermine regimes in Muslim countries that fail to subscribe to this ideal. In the 1990s, for instance, the Islamists have been responsible for assassinations, bombings and other acts of political violence in locations as far apart as Central Asia, the Philippines and North Africa. The residents of towns and cities in the Muslim

TABLE 9.1 *Main Islamist organizations in the Arab world*

Eastern Arab world	No.	The Levant	No.	North Africa	No.
Iraq	13	Lebanon	29	Egypt	40
Saudi Arabia	7	Jordan	15	Algeria	12
Kuwait	4	Syria	12	Morocco	8
Yemen	2	Palestine	6	Tunisia	6
Bahrain	1			Sudan	6
Qatar	1			Libya	6
UAE	1				

Source: Dekmejian (1995).

world, in Algiers (Algeria), Amman (Jordan), Ankara and Istanbul (Turkey), Manama (Bahrain), Cairo (Egypt), Kabul (Afghanistan), Dushanbe (Tajikistan), and Riyadh (Saudi Arabia) have all been subjected to violent Islamist attacks.

To secure their goal, the Islamists have also targeted Western countries by attempting to deny them access to markets and strategic resources such as hydrocarbons, perpetrating acts of terror against non-Muslims and extending operations beyond the boundary of their own state. There have been attacks on Egyptian and American officials in Pakistan and on American military personnel in Saudi Arabia. Western hostages were regularly taken in Lebanon in the 1980s and in Kashmir during the 1990s. Violence has also been extended to Western cities. London, Paris, Hamburg, Frankfurt as well as New York were subjected to Islamist terrorist attacks during the 1980s and 1990s.

Political violence of this nature will continue, particularly if Western states maintain their confrontational stance in the Middle East. Nevertheless, while known to be highly unpopular with the Islamists, Western security planners continue to assume that interventions like the one to secure Kuwait in 1991 will recur (Fuller and Lesser, 1995). Such actions will unquestionably prove counterproductive, however, because they will further encourage the Islamists to foster the very instability that the West is trying to discourage. At the same time, the Islamist strategy is also likely to prove self-defeating. They aim to discourage Western aid, capital and technical expertise from being sent to pro-Western rulers of Muslim states. If successful, the strategy would undermine these regimes but simultaneously protect the Muslim heartlands from Western influence. In practice, however, the tactics associated with this strategy are all too likely to encourage more Western intervention.

Putting Islamic Fundamentalism on the International Agenda

Although political Islam has been in evidence for most of this century, it was only in the late 1970s that it acquired international notoriety. Prior to this, secular leaders like President Anwar Sadat of Egypt had been willing to use the Islamists to counter the growing influence of leftists in their countries. But with the Islamic revolution in Iran and the Islamic resistance that emerged (with considerable Western assistance) to oppose the Soviet occupation of Afghanistan, Islamists successfully established an international profile for themselves and began to play a much more active role domestically and internationally. Paradoxically, by insisting that Islamic fundamentalism poses a threat to the 'Western way of life', liberals and conservatives in the West have helped to enhance this profile.

Some Western analysts have suggested that, for the American policy community, Islamic fundamentalism has now replaced communism as the main threat to the country's security (Johnson and Sampson, 1994). It has certainly been a subject for discussion in both international and regional fora for some time. The North Atlantic Treaty Organization, the European Union and the Western European Union all expressed interest in the 'anti-terrorism' summit held in Egypt in 1996. This summit provided the first occasion when Western and Middle Eastern leaders chose to make a public stand against the 'rejectionist' Islamists, so-called because their main strategy appears to be based on a policy of rejecting and actively opposing the post-Cold War Arab–Israeli peace process which has produced several agreements between Israel and its Muslim neighbours, including Azerbaijan, Jordan, Oman, the PLO, Qatar, Tunisia, Turkey, Turkmenistan and Uzbekistan. Islamists, who blame the United States for Israel's policies in the Middle East, were particularly dismayed when this process resulted in Israel establishing diplomatic relations with Jordan and closer ties with the PLO (Choudhury, 1993).

But the West's growing preoccupation with the presence of Islamist forces in the Middle East since the end of the Cold War has also been viewed as a knee-jerk reaction to the demise of the Soviet threat and the need to create a new source of danger in the international system, with the 'Green Peril' presented by Islamic fundamentalism emerging as a convenient substitute for the 'red menace' of communism. NATO has already taken steps to counter the impact of Islamic fundamentalism. As already indicated, however, this development is likely to prove counterproductive because the interest expressed by NATO's military leaders in 'Islamic-related instabilities' in the MENA region provides proof for the Islamists that they are confronting a major threat to the Islamic way

of life and it confirms their belief that there is a need for a strategy
to counter this threat (Barber and Gray, 1995).

Beyond the Cold War

Since the end of the Cold War, it has become increasingly evident
that there are many instances where religious and ethnic groups
have succeeded in precipitating a shift in the balance of power with
the state. As a result, states are often unable to control these groups
and this has led to growing tensions between diverse religious and
ethnic communities with, as a consequence, higher levels of domestic and international instability. At the same time, however, the
global alliances associated with the Cold War that helped to
maintain domestic and international stability in the past have also
been called into question, and states are now often being left to fend
for themselves.

But there are other cases, such as the Arab–Israeli peace process,
where international solutions are being sought to end conflicts that
had been fanned for so long by the Cold War. The Arab–Israeli
peace process, started in Madrid in 1991, has already had a
significant impact on the fortunes of the Islamists. They were
marginalized from the start of the process and disconcerted when
positive outcomes began to emerge. But, by the same token, set-
backs to the process acted as a stimulus to the Islamists. To secure
the long-term success of such a peace settlement, moreover, Arab
governments will have to suppress the Islamists and this would
inevitably generate a major backlash. So, even if a settlement
between Israel and the Arab states is secured, it will be unlikely
to lead to the demise of the Islamists.

Further afield, the end of the Cold War produced outcomes that
reinforced the Islamist view of the world and helped to create a
sense of siege amongst Muslims world-wide. There is growing
support for the Islamist contention that, in the absence of Cold
War divisions, anti-Muslim alliances between former enemies are
being forged. An anti-Muslim alliance between the West and Slavic
Russia has been identified. Western ambivalence towards Russian
policy in the Muslim-dominated territories of Chechnya and
Tajikistan, as well as the Serb policies in Bosnia have been cited

as examples of such complicity. The Malaysian Prime Minister has argued, for example, that

> 'Tens of thousands of Muslims in Bosnia-Herzegovina have been raped, starved, tortured and massacred by the Serbs. . . The Bosnian Serbs openly declared that they were carrying out 'ethnic cleansing' in order to prevent the setting up of a Muslim nation in Europe. . . Yet at no time have the massacres and terrorism by the Christian Serbs been described as Christian terrorism. Instead, European forces willingly handed over safe havens for the Muslims to the Serbs who subsequently massacred thousands of young Muslim men'. (Mohamad, 1996, p. 10)

Although the putative Slavic–Western alliance can be considered an essentially European anti-Muslim front, the Indian and Chinese treatment of their large Muslim minorities at the heart of Asia reinforces the Islamist belief that this trend is a global phenomenon. The burning of mosques in India by Hindus and New Delhi's use of force to suppress Muslim opposition groups in Kashmir since the early 1990s are cited as further evidence of this anti-Islamic trend.

The wave of democratization following the end of the Cold War, in conjunction with the inability of Middle Eastern regimes to rely on Cold War ideology to support the suppression of Islamist political movements, has given Islamists the political space needed to agitate in favour of reform and even the removal of regimes. After years of corruption and neglect in many Middle Eastern states, the Islamists are now in a better position than ever before to seek redress from the state for the underprivileged. Simultaneously, however, Islamists have also rejected demands for population control and the institution of human rights, which they associate with Western attempts to stifle Islam. From a Western liberal perspective, therefore, the Islamist position is full of contradictions. But this assessment simply reflects the cultural divide that separates Western liberals from the Islamists.

Curbing Fundamentalism

Attempts to curb Islamic fundamentalism are more evident in regional fora, such as the Arab League and the European Union, than at the global level. The anti-terrorist 'Code of Conduct' (for which Algeria and Egypt were leading sponsors) adopted at the Casablanca Islamic Conference Organization summit in December 1994 is one example of a regional response. The measures adopted were designed to prevent sponsorship of Islamist organizations by other Muslim countries. The Arab Ministers of Interior conference in Tunis in January 1995 also adopted multilateral measures to respond to the challenge of political Islam and the expanding trans-border cooperation between Islamist movements. Measures included agreement to exchange data and intelligence on the Islamist movements and to allow each other's security forces access to information on rejectionist groups which were seen to threaten the status quo. These measures were reinforced in June 1996 by the 20 Arab heads who attended the state summit in Cairo. Support was given to new proposals to coordinate action to stamp out terrorism and political violence (code words for Islamist activity).

Arab and non-Arab states are also taking action against the Islamists at a sub-regional level. For instance, the five Gulf Co-operation Council partners of the tiny island of Bahrain agreed to support the Al-Khalifa regime during the political crisis in 1994–5 precipitated in large part by the Islamist opposition movement. Saudi Arabia is said to have gone as far as providing Bahrain with counter-insurgency expertise. Similarly, at several high-level meetings in 1995 and 1996, Central Asian leaders were keen to show their collective resolve to counter any Islamist challenges in Central Asia. Some, like Uzbekistan and Kazakhstan, have been quite happy to assist the Tajiki government's efforts to keep its Islamists at bay. Turkey, NATO's only Muslim member which, until 1996, had had a secular regime in power since the end of the First World War, is also keen to participate in efforts aimed at containing the Islamist threat in the Muslim regions to its east and south. Ankara's willingness to participate in assisting both the Turkic republics of the former Soviet Union and the secular Arab regimes in their endeavours against Islamist movements is indicative of Turkey's grave concerns. Ironically, Turkey's efforts to contain Islamism on its periphery are being undermined by the political successes of their own country's Islamist party (the Refah), whose leader emerged as Turkey's first Islamist Prime Minister in 1996.

Russia, still the main player in Central Asia, has tended to act unilaterally to suppress the Islamists of Tajikistan, with tacit Western support, but has been unwilling to take on Afghanistan's Islamists – the chief suppliers of their Tajik counterparts – for fear of Western opposition and, perhaps more important, concern that another open-ended military disaster, following the ten-year occupation of Afghanistan by the Soviet Union, might follow its intervention in that country.

It has become more apparent since the end of the Cold War that in order for multilateral measures to work, regimes need to cooperate much more with outside forces, and show a greater degree of political flexibility in their dealings with each other. Although Western support for its besieged allies in the Muslim world has helped to bolster the resolve of these states to confront their Islamist organizations with force, the costs incurred have been high.

The strategic calculations of NATO, the Russian-dominated Commonwealth of Independent States, as well as the Eurasian-oriented Organization for Security and Cooperation in Europe (which now includes ex-Soviet countries in the heart of Asia, like Kazakhstan and Kyrgyzstan), all take account of the danger posed by Islamic fundamentalism. But no independent or overarching machinery for countering the Islamists' influence and activities has yet come into being. Nonetheless, increasing direct and indirect pressure on MENA countries, like Iran and Sudan, that are suspected of aiding the Islamists, has become more evident in the 1990s. Iran has been subjected to severe American political and economic pressure in response to its alleged disruptive foreign policy and support for Islamist terrorists. Sudan has also been threatened with political and economic sanctions orchestrated by the United Nations if it fails to sever its links with radical Arab Islamist movements.

Whether these *ad hoc* regional and international reactions to the Islamists in the Middle East will lead to a more institutionalized response remains uncertain. It will depend perhaps as much on the determination of the states under siege as on the future strategies of the Islamists themselves. But it has been argued that co-optation and accommodation would be a more effective way of eradicating the Islamist threat, forcing the Islamists to restore peaceful political dialogue. Others insist that the Islamist threat will only be removed by force. But at the moment, because the Islamists and the Arab states hold mutually hostile images of each other, only by an inversion of these images will there be any possibility of more constructive engagement.

Contemporary World Politics: Globalization v. Fundamentalism

From one perspective, it may appear that the contemporary world is more open and pluralistic than ever before and that the boundaries between states are rapidly being dissolved in the process. But the rise of Islamic fundamentalism draws attention to a much less benign image of the world. It is necessary to take account of the fact that the world is increasingly being divided along political, economic and technological lines. Nation-states are being confronted, from above, by the all-powerful global forces of capitalism that are generating, particularly in the Third World, economic and social dislocation and crisis. At the same time, from below, states are facing a violent challenge from minorities who see themselves to be disenfranchised and neglected. The Muslim world has been very much affected by these developments, and the rise of Islamic fundamentalism is an integral aspect of the changes that are taking place as a consequence.

From the Islamist perspective, the globalization of capital is having particularly pernicious effects on Muslim societies. Market forces are seen to cause widespread cultural dislocation. Capitalist production accelerates rural to urban migration. It bombards and eventually fractures the socially and economically supportive extended family units that are so vital to the renewal of Muslim cultural values. Capitalist expansion is seen to bring with it Western models of organization and management that promote divisive forms of economic competition in trade, investment and production among the Muslim states. These same economic forces are also seen to push the Muslim states into separate regional organizations. Overall, then, capitalism is considered to dissipate the economic potential and resources of the Muslim community of states by inhibiting or even preventing collective action. By contrast, as Beeley notes, 'connections between Muslim countries are attractive' because they cut across the established economic links (1993, p. 304).

Despite operating within an integrated international economy, a widening economic gap is seen by the Islamists to be opening up between the West and the Muslim world. It is clear to the Islamists that the Arabs (the Muslim heartland) have become, on the one hand, net consumers of Western products, Western production techniques and Western labour–capital relations, while, on the other hand, they have also become the suppliers of cheap labour for international producers and the source of relatively cheap strategic inputs (for example, hydrocarbons) for international consumers. To make matters worse, by copying production techniques from the West in the late twentieth century, the Arab states have exposed themselves to the decentralizing forces of modern technology, thereby running the risk of undermining the state's grip on society and weakening its control of the economy.

Becoming an appendage of the Western economic system has been made worse, moreover, by the failure of the Muslim world to establish self-sufficiency in food. The problem has been compounded by rapid population growth in the Middle Eastern sector of the Muslim world. The reliance on Western food producers has raised fears that the 'food weapon' might be used against the Muslims in any future political disputes with Western countries.

Political Islam is not alone in believing that the globe is experiencing a 'process of world-wide Westernization' (Latouche, 1996, p. 72). Guided by its 'civilizing mission' and emboldened by its moral and political victory over Soviet Communism, the West, it is argued, has become ever more determined to transculturalize capitalism. The aim is not only to globalize capitalism as an economic mode of production, but also to export a related set of values. Transculturalization, therefore, involves planting a culture which is deeply rooted in Western Europe and the United States into alien, non-Western soil. The end result, many commentators have observed, will be a global homogenization of culture under Western economic hegemony (Featherstone, 1990) – the 'Coca Cola' cultural syndrome.

The logic of global capitalism involves capturing new markets and profiting from the efficient production and exchange of goods and services world-wide. For radical and liberal Muslims alike, however, the globalization of capitalism is seen to be the cause of a cultural dislocation of such magnitude that salvation can only be found by retreating behind the protective walls provided by the all-encompassing faith of Islam. But because Islam represents a whole way of life and is part of the very fabric of Muslim societies, it is unsurprising that attempts by Islamists to preserve their faith against the vagaries of international capitalism have brought them into violent confrontation with the foot soldiers of capitalism. Nevertheless, the Islamist response to globalization and cultural homogenization needs to be seen in terms of a desire to return to and to promote their own cultural roots. And faced with the apparently inexorable deepening of globalization, it is unsurprising that some groups of Islamists have demonstrated a willingness to fight for their indigenous culture.

It is also unsurprising that it is in the Middle East that Islamic fundamentalism has been most in evidence. In Asia, Muslim societies have enjoyed the fruits of the region's economic success. Indeed, buoyed up by this success, Western culture and values have been frequently denigrated and, in contrast to the the forward-looking world of Asia, seen to characterize a decadent world in terminal decline. By contrast, in MENA, there has been a wide-spread inability to overcome the endemic crisis prevalent in society, or to diminish the reliance on the West. Political Islam may not offer a cure for the ills associated with the threat of Westernization, but it is being received by the mass of the people with enthusiasm. Moreover, since the end of the Cold War, political Islam has managed to identify both the necessary political space and ammunition in order to fight, with messianic vigour, the 'enemies of Islam' – real or imagined, at home and abroad. As a consequence, Islamic fundamentalism has become an issue, more complex than is often recognized, which students of world politics cannot afford to ignore.

Guide to Further Reading

The literature on Islamic fundamentalism and political Islam is large and growing. It can be divided into three types though there are overlaps between these categories. A first type looks at this issue as a source of tension in regional and international affairs, and includes Esposito (1992); Fuller and Lesser (1995); Halliday (1995) and Husain (1995). In a second category, where authors conduct detailed studies of movements and their interactions with each other and with states, the following can be recommended: Ayubi (1991); Donohue and Esposito (1982); Dekmejian (1995); Guazzone (1995); Roy (1994); Sick (1992); Sidahmed and Ehteshami (1996) and Zubaida (1989). A third category of work analyzes fundamentalism from a comparative perspective and treats it as a global problem. The most useful sources here include Featherstone, ed. (1990); Johnson and Sampson (1994); Juergensmeyer (1993).

10

Migration and Refugees

SITA BALI

International migration is inextricably connected to a wide range of issues and dilemmas that confront governments and peoples across the globe today. Increasing racism and neo-Nazi violence in Germany, 'ethnic cleansing' in former Yugoslavia and police brutality towards blacks in Los Angeles, are all recent examples of problems that are linked to migration in one way or another. Migration, however, is as old as humanity itself, and has played a crucial role in shaping the world throughout history. But while it has been a constant feature of human history, the causes, characteristics, patterns and directions of migration have never remained constant; they have always influenced and been influenced by changing economic, social and political conditions within and between states. The aim of this chapter is to chart the major developments in international migration and to examine their implications.

Migration as an International Issue

International migration involves the movement of people across state boundaries. In contrast to internal or intra-state migratory movements, international migrants leave the jurisdiction of one state and become subject to that of another. The migration can be either involuntary or voluntary depending on the underlying motivation of the migrant. Involuntary migration takes place as a consequence of natural disaster, war, civil war, ethnic, religious or political persecution, situations where people are forced to flee their homes and countries. Involuntary migration, however, can also be coerced as with slavery, when people are compelled by force to leave their homes and are taken abroad for the purpose of exploitation. Although now illegal, slavery remains a world-wide and flourishing business. Millions of people, especially women and children operate as slaves within their own societies, but there is also a huge traffic in slaves across state boundaries. For example, there are estimated to be 20,000 Burmese prostitutes in Thailand at any one time, some sold as slaves and others taken under false pretences (*The Economist*, 21 September 1996).

The motivation underlying voluntary migration also takes different forms and can be divided into three sub-categories. The first encompasses permanent settlers such as the migrants who populated the United States or constituted the Asian and Afro-Caribbean minorities in Britain. The second sub-category identifies temporary settlers who account for the bulk of voluntary migrants. This category includes people who move to acquire education, promote business, or encourage tourism. In addition, many temporary migrants take up a specific job, such as the workers admitted to the Gulf States to service the oil-powered economic boom. Finally there is illegal migration which can be temporary or permanent, but in either case is unauthorized by the receiving state.

Once a migration pattern has been established, it can extend to embrace additional categories of migrants. For instance, Sikhs migrated voluntarily from the Punjab to Britain, but have been followed by Sikhs suffering political persecution at the hands of the Indian government because of their support for the Khalistan independence movement. Thus a stream of voluntary migrants can be joined by a stream of involuntary migrants. This intermingling of categories has led more and more states to refuse to discriminate between different types of migration.

The two main issues that arise from migration in the contemporary era are the regulation and control of international migration, on the one hand, and the policies for dealing with ethnic migrant minorities, on the other.

States, by virtue of their sovereignty, claim absolute authority to decide who is able to enter or leave their territorial jurisdiction. Although democratic states accept that citizens have an unconditional right to exit from the state, they invariably impose restrictions and conditions on the right of entry for foreigners. These restrictions are based on a variety of factors that include the demand for labour within the economy, considerations of public welfare, and the preservation of the nature and integrity of society and its particular culture and way of life. However, most states officially support the international regime set up to deal with refugees in accordance with the Universal Declaration of Human Rights (1948) and the Convention Relating to the Status of Refugees (1951). Their response to involuntary or forced migration must, as a consequence, be consistent with these commitments. So categorization of international migration still has some relevance, even though the treatment of migrants by states is becoming increasingly undifferentiated.

In the long term, the most obvious effect of international migration is the creation of ethnic minorities in host countries. The existence of these communities has a substantial impact on social stability, economic prosperity and the internal politics of receiving states as well as on their relationship with the countries from where these communities originate. Thus the establishment of the Indian community in Britain has had an impact on the nature of British society, economy and politics as well as on Britain's relationship with India.

International migration has become more prominent on the international agenda in recent years both because of its increasing scale and because of its growing impact on world politics. Several factors account for these developments. First, the number of states in the international system has steadily increased since the end of the First World War. As the number of international boundaries containing the new states has increased, so too has the volume of international migrants. Second, there has also been a rapid increase in the world's population, and it continues to grow. The growth of population has led to over-exploitation of regional resources leading on occasions to catastrophic famine and population movement. Third, the revolution in communications and transportation has made people aware of conditions and opportunities in other parts of the world, as well as making travel to those areas easier. Finally, the turmoil and uncertainty of a turbulent and unstable world plays an important role in motivating people to search abroad for a better life (Teitelbaum, 1980, p. 21). However, care must be taken not to exaggerate the magnitude and importance of international migration as only a very small percentage of the world's population moves across borders. It is only in extremely rare cases that as much as 10 per cent of the population of a state emigrates.

People on the Move

Migration is global in scope. There is no part of the world unaffected by migration, although the nature and intensity of its impact may vary from region to region, and over time.

Colonialism provided the initial impetus for modern migration and it stimulated the movement of Europeans to Africa, Asia, South and North America, Australia and New Zealand. This initial pattern was then extended by the industrialization of Europe. The European demand for industrial labour first gave rise to internal migration from rural to urban areas, but it soon led to the mass international migration of Europeans to North America, with the British in the forefront. The United States became a country of immigrants who were indirectly responsible for the displacement and extermination of the indigenous population. Thirty million people arrived between 1861 and 1920. The immigrants came mainly from Britain, Germany, Ireland, Italy and Eastern Europe (mostly Jews). Canada also saw a large influx of immigrants in this period.

North America continued to be a favourite destination for migrants in the twentieth century, with the arrival of approximately 24 million people to the United States between 1920 and 1987 (Castles and Miller, 1993, p. 51). Asian immigration to North America had begun in the early years of this century, but restrictions on racial grounds were soon put into place, and these lasted until after the Second World War. Immigrants to North America after 1945 continued to be predominantly European, but when racial restrictions were finally eased in the late 1960s, substantial migration began from South East Asia and the Indian sub-continent, as well as from Latin America.

In Europe, the colonial era was marked not only by mass emigration to the New World and the colonies, but also by significant intra-European migration. Britain drew in vast quantities of labour to feed her rapidly growing industrial sector. They came primarily from Ireland, particularly after the potato famines, but also included Jews fleeing the pogroms in the Russian pale. German industrialization was supported by workers from Poland

and Italy, and French industry attracted workers from neighbouring countries. While French immigration to the New World was
extremely limited, there was a significant movement of settlers to
Algeria after its conquest in 1830. The long post-war economic
boom saw Europe, particularly Northern Europe, draw in workers
from peripheral countries of the Mediterranean and Southern
Europe, as well as immigrants from former colonies, while transat-
lantic emigration also continued. Some countries saw the development of guest-worker systems, such as that which brought large
numbers of Turks to Germany. France and Britain experienced
substantial migrations, from North Africa in the case of the former,
and the Caribbean, ex-colonies in Africa such as Nigeria and the
Indian sub-continent, in the case of the latter.

   Like the United States, Australia was a recipient of mass migration and settlement by Europeans (with the British dominating),
again at the expense of the indigenous population. But in contrast
to the United States and other parts of the European empires, there
was no movement of slaves or indentured labour to Australia. On
the contrary, the government's White Australia policy, in place until
relatively recently, ensured that the source of Australian immigrants
was exclusively Europe, stretching to include large numbers of
Southern Europeans after 1945. It was only with the victory of
the Labour government in 1971 that entry criteria were changed
ending the discriminatory policy and promoting a substantial
migration from South East Asia and the Indian sub-continent. By
the mid-1990s, Asian migration was the largest component of
migration to Australia. Immigration levels in Australia have reflected the world economic climate, being considerably lower in
recessions and improving in periods of recovery.

   In conjunction with the mass movement of European labour and
the creation of a global economy, there was also the forced
migration of an estimated 15 million slaves from the West African
coast to the Americas (Castles and Miller, 1993, p. 48). This trade
was replaced by the movement of indentured labour from India and
China after the abolition of slavery in 1834. The use of indentured
labour became even more widespread than slavery, encompassing
over 40 countries, between 12 and 37 million indentured labourers,
and lasting until 1941 (Potts, 1990, pp. 63–104). The long-term
political effects of some of these movements are only now, nearly a
century on, beginning to make themselves felt.

New Patterns of Migration

The mid-1970s marked the end of the post-war economic boom in most of the advanced industrialized countries. This change in the economic climate and the more long-term structural economic adjustment it heralded had a substantial impact on migration patterns. More recent international migratory trends have been marked by a severe reduction in permanent settler migration opportunities. Permanent migrants can only find a destination in the traditional countries of immigration (USA, Canada, Australia), and potential migrants must now either be sponsored by family members already settled in the host country or possess skills and qualifications needed by the host country. The main areas of origin of immigrants to these countries lie in Asia and South America, not Europe. As the demand for labour in industrialized European countries has declined, legal permanent settler migration has also almost ceased except for family reunification. New areas have drawn in labour, and some of the largest migrations of workers in this period have been from Asia and the Middle East to the oil producing states of the Persian Gulf. Israel has seen a dramatic increase in the number of Jews arriving from Eastern Europe and the former Soviet Union. With the collapse of the Soviet bloc, there has been an influx of ethnic Germans and others into Germany, and a movement of Gypsies, Romanians and Albanians into Hungary and Western Europe. The countries of Southern Europe and the Mediterranean, traditionally countries of emigration, have become countries of immigration with movements of people from Eastern Europe, Turkey and North Africa affecting them. Some of the newly industrialized countries in Asia are becoming attractive to workers from other Asian countries like China and Indonesia.

A refugee crisis

Also in the 1970s, a world-wide refugee crisis developed. This period saw the migration of hundreds of thousands fleeing Vietnam, Cambodia and Laos to escape repression and civil war. Conflict in Lebanon created yet another dimension to the already existing Palestinian refugee problem in the Middle East. The Soviet invasion of Afghanistan in December 1979 gave rise to a refugee flow in the millions from that country to Pakistan and Iran. Conditions in

Sudan, Uganda, Zaire and South Africa also created refugee movements, as did the repression of military dictatorships in Chile and Argentina. More recently, ethnic conflict in Sri Lanka and Rwanda, the collapse of the Soviet bloc and the disintegration of Yugoslavia have swelled refugee numbers. It has been estimated that the total number of refugees in the world was 8.2 million in 1980, had risen to 15 million by 1990, and was approximately 20 million by the end of 1992 (Castles and Miller, 1993, p. 84). It must be noted that the majority of refugees seek asylum in neighbouring countries, and that the impact of refugee movements is felt by Third World countries much more than it is by the developed world. Of the 15 million refugees in 1990, nine million were dispersed throughout Asia and the Middle East, about five million in Africa, and nearly one million in Latin America (Castles and Miller, 1993, p. 87).

New complexity

Contemporary international migration is more complex than migrations of the past because receiving countries are faced with various types of migration simultaneously. Thus immigration to Australia today is not only of the permanent settler kind, but will include refugees as well as seasonal migrations of labour from New Zealand. The migration of permanent settlers may turn into a stream of refugees if political conditions in the home state deteriorate. This differentiation of migration makes the task of governments devising policy regarding migration all the more complicated. Another change in migration in recent times is that increasing numbers of women are becoming migrants. Traditionally migration was a predominantly male phenomenon, with women only migrating to join their men, in a process of family reunification. More recently, however, women from a range of countries have begun to migrate as workers and refugees in their own right. Sri Lankan and Filipino women who take up employment as domestic workers in the Gulf countries are perhaps the most obvious manifestation of this trend. This increasing feminization of migration also raises new issues for states' migration policies (Castles and Miller, 1993, p. 8).

   In most host countries, and certainly in democracies, it has become clear that once migration takes place, for whatever reasons, and whether intended to be permanent or temporary, it almost inevitably results in at least some immigrants becoming citizens of the host country, and creating a cultural, linguistic, religious and possibly a racially distinct minority within the state. Further, immigration can affect political and social conditions, and even, in rare instances, fundamentally alter the nature of society in receiving countries, many years after the actual movement of people has ceased. An illustration of this can be seen in Fiji, where indenture migration created an Indian immigrant community over seventy years ago. In 1987 Fiji was racked by ethnic conflict when an election brought an Indian dominated political party to power, and gave Fiji its first Indian Prime Minister. He was overthrown in a coup by the largely Fijian army led by Colonel Rambuka.

The Pros and Cons of Migration

For a host state, the main economic concerns raised by international migration relate to the regulation of its flow, taking into consideration competing economic imperatives such as requiring more labour and avoiding increased unemployment rates. Home states need to strike a balance between economic reliance on the remittances from overseas workers and a concern about the loss of trained and qualified persons. Countries receiving migrants also need to maintain social stability and cohesion in the face of the multi-culturalism produced by migration. States must also ensure that they meet their obligations under international treaties and protect the interests of those who are fleeing persecution. Restrictions placed upon the entry of immigrants will also have an impact on relations with the home state of the migrants. So migration impinges directly upon a state's economic, social and foreign policy. A comprehensive analysis of migration needs to incorporate the views of countries sending and receiving migrants.

The economic dimension

Economic or labour migration is affected by two structural factors. The first relates to 'wage zones' or 'wage differentials' because differential levels of wages and social benefits and thus standards of living can have a major impact on migration between countries. The second factor relates to the demand for labour and the levels of unemployment. The combination of divergent wage and unemployment levels in different countries creates a powerful impetus for migration.

For a sending country, labour migration can relieve the problem of unemployment. But the extent of the relief depends on the proportion of the labour force that is able to emigrate. In countries like Algeria, Tunisia, Morocco and Mexico, where 10 per cent of the labour force have emigrated, the impact is certainly noticeable. However, given the large and rapidly expanding populations in most sending countries, labour migration would have to be much larger than is conceivable, given current economic and political realities, for states exporting labour to experience any substantial benefits. In most cases, migrant labour forms a small proportion of the sending country's work-force, even though it may constitute a substantial addition to the work-force in the receiving country.

Migration also reduces the pressure on facilities and consumption in the sending country. It lowers demand on schools, hospitals, transport and communication facilities. Labour migration can also relieve the tax-payer of the costs of social welfare. But, once again, it is the proportion of the work-force engaged in migration that is important. Current labour migration has a very limited effect in this context. Emigration is also believed to lead to a boost in exports for the sending country, as emigrants settled abroad tend to purchase goods from the home country. A visit to Southall in London, the hub of the Punjabi community in Britain, with its plethora of shops selling a variety of Indian goods, makes this point.

The remittances sent home by emigrants are the single most important consequence of labour migration. These rose from $40 billion in 1982 to $61 billion in 1989 (Collinson, 1995, p. 40). For several developing countries these remittances are equivalent to a third or more of earnings from exports and serve to make up the deficit in the balance of payments. The importance of these factors to a Third World economy (as most of the sending countries are) cannot be overestimated. Remittances improve the standard of living of the receiving families, and can lead to productive investment, and better social facilities like education and health-care. However remittances may be spent on non-essential 'luxury' goods, leading to inflation and the widening of societal inequality. Furthermore, remittances signify dependence, and their curtailment when migrants are forced home due to unfavourable economic circumstances in their host countries or due to war (as occurred in Kuwait in 1990), can have a detrimental effect on the economy of the sending country.

The governments of sending countries used to prefer the migration of unskilled or semi-skilled labour because they were worried about the impact on the domestic economy of the departure of trained, educated and skilled workers. The emigration of Third World professionals like doctors and engineers is often depicted as a 'brain drain'. However, the educated sector of the population in many sending countries is now too large to be fully employed and governments encourage members of their educated middle classes to emigrate. Some countries now regard the emigration of educated personnel as 'brain overflow' rather than brain drain. It is recognized that the domestic economy does not have the capacity to absorb all the graduates and professionals produced by their education systems. Governments of sending countries are increasingly coming to appreciate the net gain of having their nationals employed abroad, acquiring skills and technologies, accumulating capital and sometimes influence in industrialized and prosperous countries. The importance of these effects for sending countries encourages their governments to use every diplomatic means available to them to ensure continued emigration for those of their nationals who wish to seek their fortunes abroad.

The main economic imperative for permitting immigration is a shortage of labour. However this is not a sufficient condition. States like Japan faced with labour shortages still resist importing labour because of concerns about the impact of large numbers of foreigners on their highly prized cultural homogeneity. Industries have to find other ways to deal with labour shortages, for example by adopting more capital-intensive and less labour-intensive technology, by incorporating new participants such as women into the labour market, or by moving outside the country to areas where labour is cheaper.

Nevertheless, in purely economic terms, imported labour can contribute to the prosperity of a host nation, if economic growth has been impeded by the lack of human capital. Migrant labour can increase national productivity. It is no coincidence that large numbers of foreign workers were admitted to states during periods of rapid economic growth, such as that experienced by Europe after 1945. But although in some European countries imported labour came to make up approximately 9 per cent of the work-force, this does not begin to compare with the Gulf States where imported labour forms an overwhelming majority of the work-force: 70 per cent in Kuwait, 80 per cent in Quatar, and 85 per cent in the United Arab Emirates.

In recent years, increasing numbers of immigrants are highly skilled technical or managerial professionals. This development reflects the ever more globalized nature of the world economy and the importance of large international companies. But this increase does not appear to be of great concern to receiving countries, as this type of migration is easy to regulate, fills gaps in the skills of the indigenous work-force, is generally temporary and is perceived to be beneficial.

But there are economic reasons advanced for restricting migration although there are various counter-arguments. Immigrant workers, it is asserted, displace local people in employment because they are prepared to work for lower wages. However studies in the United States suggest that this is not always the case. Immigrants often do jobs rejected by locals because of their unpleasant nature or low remuneration. Moreover, immigrants can often enhance the economies of their host countries by starting up businesses and creating employment. Nevertheless, critics of immigration assert that it overstretches housing and other welfare benefits in a receiving country. But, advocates claim, immigrant labour provides taxation revenue and at least part of the migrant's income is spent within the host economy. Critics, in turn, counter by arguing that importation of labour can delay structural change in developed economies by slowing down the move towards more capital-intensive forms of production (Collinson, 1993, pp. 19–20).

The capitalist world economy, distinguished by the liberal Bretton Woods regime, permits and indeed encourages free movement of capital, goods and services. However, there has been a shift away from liberal principles in the context of labour. There is universal agreement that the free flow of people, however beneficial for the world economy, should not be permitted. Restrictions on immigration became universal in the first decades of this century and today every country has restrictions, making immigration the only exception to liberal notions of free movement for all factors of production. This is because receiving countries see immigration not only in economic terms, but in terms of its wider effect upon their societies.

The social dimension

Admitting immigrant labour has long-lasting social effects on receiving countries. It can turn homogeneous societies into multi-cultural ones by the introduction of ethnically different people. Receiving societies are now having to evolve various ways of dealing with immigrants. These range from the acceptance of cultural diversity, with rapid naturalization of immigrants by granting full economic, social and political rights and the formation of flourishing ethnic communities; to active discouragement of multi-culturalism by the denial of rights and the location of immigrants on the fringes of society. Most countries fall somewhere between these two extremes.

The traditional countries attracting migrants, Australia, Canada and the United States, are still the most open. Immigrants are quickly granted citizenship guaranteeing the security of their status and the permanence of their stay. Multi-culturalism is accepted and even encouraged. Government help to preserve the language and culture of immigrant communities is the norm in Canada and Australia. It was not always so; all these countries have histories of excluding immigrants on purely racial grounds. But since the early 1970s, racially non-discriminatory policies have been in place. Some European countries like Sweden have also followed similar policies, while others like Britain and France have granted citizen-ship and full rights only to immigrants from former colonies. Germany, Belgium and Switzerland have operated 'guest-worker' policies which only granted temporary admission to workers, and no rights to citizenship or permanent settlement. These differences should not be exaggerated. Countries like Britain and France amended their rules to put citizens of former colonies on a par with all other foreigners when they began to restrict immigration in the late 1960s, and many guest-workers were granted wider rights including settlement in Germany.

The Gulf states, with their authoritarian regimes and excessive reliance on an imported work-force, have followed extremely harsh policies with regard to the status and rights granted to immigrant workers. The latter have to seek government permission before taking up a job, cannot change jobs without further approval, cannot form trades unions or hold public meetings, cannot usually own land, houses or businesses, are not granted the same social service facilities as citizens, cannot bring their families into the country unless their salaries are above a level specified by the state (which is high enough to exclude unskilled and semi-skilled workers), and cannot become citizens of the state. By placing such severe restrictions on the freedom of immigrant workers, and creating wide disparities between the indigenous population and immigrant labour, the Gulf states have been able to minimize both settlement and the social impact of the huge imported labour force in their countries.

Migrants raise social concerns because they potentially threaten to undermine the popularity and strength of the nation-state. At the moment nation-states remain the dominant unit of social organization across the globe. Their members are seen to share a common history, language, religion and culture that binds them into a cohesive integrated unit with a shared sense of nationhood. As citizens of one state, moving to live and work in another, migrants clearly challenge traditional notions about membership of a state, the meaning of nationality and citizenship, and the rights and duties of citizens towards their state and vice versa. The fact that very few states fit the idealized picture of the homogenous nation state, and that most states are cultural and social products of earlier movements of peoples, fails to register on the popular consciousness.

Societies are also seen to have a limited 'threshold of toleration' for immigration and, if crossed, the flow of migrants will begin to undermine the social and political cohesion of the receiving country. The threshold is affected by economic, social and cultural circumstances in the receiving society as well as by the nature of the immigrants themselves, but it remains difficult to determine. In 1996, for example, facing an increasing level of Hispanic immigration, the United States Congress voted in favour of the English Language Empowerment Act, which declared English to be the official language of the United States. Anti-immigrant feeling and xenophobia also increases in times of recession and high unemployment and then abates in times of economic boom. Toleration levels are likely to be lower in countries without a tradition of immigration, and higher in those that have. Immigrants that are similar to the host population are also easier to accommodate and tolerate than if they are racially and culturally distinct. Often unrecognized is the fact that the attitudes and responses of governments can themselves affect levels of toleration in societies.

The political dimension

Immigration is also perceived to have an impact on a nation's security. Immigrant communities tend to maintain a strong connection with their home countries, and turbulence or instability in those societies can find expression within the immigrant community as well, thereby bringing external problems into host societies. Instability in Algeria, for example, extends to the Algerian community in France and to the wider French polity. This factor sometimes has to be taken into account in foreign policy decision-making by the host state. The stance of the Muslim communities in various European states, for example, affected the policies of those states during the Gulf War (Collinson, 1993, pp. 15–16).

Immigrant communities often indulge in political activities, with considerable implications for home and host countries, when they try for instance to influence events directly in their home country. This can involve economic, political or military instruments, and may be used to promote or undermine their home government. Immigrant communities can also provide financial and military assistance to rebel groups, as the Irish Americans have done for the Irish Republican Army (IRA). They also try to influence events in the home country by marshalling international public opinion through publicity campaigns, for example, aimed at the international community and at particular international organizations. The activities of Palestinian emigrants have certainly been successful in encouraging United Nations countries to embarrass Israel in that forum and elsewhere. Immigrant communities try to use their host government to influence events in their home country. Success depends on their own strength and the susceptibility of the host's political system. Jewish lobbying in the United States has long been recognized as an important factor in maintaining America's pro-Israel stance. The Greek community in the United States helped to get Congress to embargo military assistance to Turkey, after the Turkish invasion of Cyprus. But an immigrant community can also be used by the government of the home country to pursue its own aims. The relationship between successive Israeli governments and American Jews illustrates this point. Host governments too will try to use their ethnic minority communities to achieve their own goals, particularly those in relation to events in the country of origin of that community, with Mafia leaders, for example, assisting the Allied invasion of Sicily during the Second World War.

Political activity by migrant groups can often become a source of conflict between the home government and host government. For instance, when the activities of a migrant community harm its home government, then the host government will be pressured to restrain the migrants. But, if the migrants are operating within the law, there may be little the host government can do. Relations between previously friendly countries can be strained as a consequence. US governments have been embarrassed by the activities of Irish Americans in assisting the IRA, and the activities of British Sikhs have brought tensions into generally amicable Anglo-Indian relations.

The impact of large refugee flows has serious implications for sending and receiving countries, who are often neighbours. When a government becomes the unwilling host to a large refugee population, it is likely to take steps to ensure that the stay of the refugees is temporary. The movement of Afghans from their country to Pakistan in the 1980s, and Palestinians to a variety of Arab states after 1948, are examples of such situations. In both cases, the refugee influx played a decisive role in impelling the receiving governments to try to bring about a change of government in the sending state by arming the refugees.

Immigrant or ethnic minority communities, formed by labour or refugee migration, can play a significant independent political role in world politics. Their continued political involvement in states in which they no longer live, and whose rules they are not subject to, present a serious challenge to the sovereignty of that state. By the same token they challenge the ability of host states to exercise independent control over the direction of their own foreign and domestic policy.

Putting Migration and Refugees on the International Agenda

Until recently, migration was not seen as a central political issue by most governments, who usually let the various government departments like Employment and Immigration deal with it. It was only in the 1980s, as the effects of past migrations began to be felt both domestically and internationally, and as immigration pressures on developed states increased, that migration rose on the international political agenda and became of increasing concern to students of world politics.

In the 1980s, many industrialized countries were in severe recession. As always, with a deterioration in the economic climate resulting in high levels of unemployment and social instability, attention started to focus on immigration. By this time, labour migration to most advanced countries had virtually ceased but, nevertheless, immigrant communities became the target of animosity from right-wing groups who blamed them for the high levels of unemployment and decline in general living standards. This period saw the rise of Le Pen in France, neo-Nazis in Germany and Austria, and a renewal of extreme right activity in Britain. Many immigrant communities, now in their second generation, responded with new confidence to this threat.

The rising tide of extremist opinion and associated violence focused the attention of governments on immigration. Many responded by hardening their stance, adopting, in modified form, the anti-immigrant agenda of the extreme right. The acceleration in immigration pressures, they claimed, had to be resisted, if only for the sake of better race relations and to integrate the established immigrant communities. Governments failed to realize that by taking a strongly anti-immigrant stance – reinterpreting their obligations towards refugees ever more strictly, legislating to deport immigrants found guilty of serious crimes and denying subsistence to asylum seekers – the message sent to society at large pandered to the worst instincts of the extreme right, and undermined the social stability that they sought.

As labour migration was reduced, asylum applications rose. Conditions that cause people to flee their homelands in search of a better life persisted and conflict continued to create refugee flows. But now, more of these refugees than ever before could seek asylum in Europe and America rather than in neighbouring countries. The collapse of the Soviet bloc and the conflict in former Yugoslavia led to refugee flows into Europe, making it the second largest source of refugees after Africa. Asylum applications to OECD countries rose from 116,000 in 1981 to 541,000 in 1991 (Castles and Miller, 1993, p. 84), reaching a peak of around 700,000 in 1992 before falling back to 550,000 in 1993 and to 330,000 in 1994 (Collinson, 1995, pp. 19–20). Compared with a total refugee population of approximately 20 million, these numbers may seem small, but their importance lies in the impact they had on European policy.

A further element that brought attention to migration, although far less easy to document by its very nature, was the rise in unauthorized migration in Europe. This development brought home the inability of the state to implement fully any immigration policy or to police its borders. While this problem has long been acknowledged in the United States, where approximately a quarter of a million South Americans cross the Mexican–United States border illegally each year, it had not been so widespread in Europe. With the opening up of the Eastern bloc, the war in former Yugoslavia, and the ever tightening restrictions on immigration into Europe, illegal migration, particularly into the Southern European states, has increased.

Another factor helping to bring migration to the fore on the international political agenda was the progress being made on European integration. Started after the Second World War, by 1987 the process had begun to dismantle internal boundaries and to create a single market with freedom of movement across internal borders. It was impossible to ignore the immigration policies of the various states involved, and raised the question of strengthening controls on borders with countries external to the Union, and the need to develop uniform policies for dealing with all types of international migration. This harmonization of immigration policy is based on an inter-governmental approach, and has led to the creation of an *ad hoc* Ministerial Group on Immigration in 1986, and a continuing focus by European governments on immigration issues.

The loss of asylum

While the Universal Declaration on Human Rights grants everyone the right to exit from any country including their own, this right was and is denied by many states. 'Closing off free emigration is probably an essential policy for any regime that relies heavily on coercion' (Dowty, 1987, p. 60). A survey of countries that have had or continue to have total or limited restrictions on the right to exit shows that they have included all the erstwhile communist states across the globe; Angola, Mozambique, Afghanistan, Laos, Mongolia, North Korea, Vietnam, Cuba, and China, as well as other coercive regimes like Iraq, Cameroon, Togo, Tanzania, Iran, Burma, Libya, Sudan and Syria. With the collapse of the Soviet bloc, and the unification of Germany, the restrictions on the right to exit in all East European countries and in many of the former republics of the Soviet Union were lifted. The less prosperous countries of Eastern Europe, Romania and Albania in particular, became a source of large numbers of immigrants for the first time leading to a substantial increase in East to West movements. Ethnic Germans, from all parts of the former Soviet bloc, took advantage of German law that extends the right of return to them, and began to move to Germany. The war in Yugoslavia also contributed to the numbers trying to move from East to West. This influx put European countries under great pressure, at a time when their attitudes to asylum were hardening.

The collapse of Communism has had a more deep-seated impact on Western governments' attitudes towards refugees. During the Cold War, when the Soviet Union and its allies restricted emigration, the West's willingness to offer asylum and refuge to those who did manage to escape the 'evil empire', was a weapon, albeit a small one, in its armoury. It reinforced the belief that communist repression was worth resisting, and that those escaping such repression were worth assisting. In the period 1952–80, a refugee was defined in the United States by the McCarran-Walter Act (1952) as a person fleeing Communist persecution (Teitelbaum, 1980, p. 24). With the removal of the threat which had dominated Western thinking for nearly half a century, and the lack of any equivalent substitute, the commitment of Western countries to the whole notion of asylum collapsed. Asylum depended upon the continued existence of a common enemy confronted simultaneously by the refugee and the West.

Institutional Responses to Migration and Refugees

International institutional responses to deal with refugees have been in place since 1951 when countries signed up to the Convention Relating to the Status of Refugees. This Convention, designed to deal with large numbers of displaced persons in Europe at the end of the Second World War, obliges states to extend asylum and protection to those facing persecution, on grounds of religion, race, nationality or political opinion. Further, implicit in the meaning of refugee lies an assumption that the person concerned is worthy of being assisted and ought to be assisted, and if necessary protected from the cause of flight (Goodwin-Gill, 1983, p. 1). A fugitive from justice, trying to escape a criminal prosecution, does not fall into this category. In practice, the convention commits states to ensure that no refugee is sent back to any country where they are likely to face danger to life or liberty. Also relevant is the Universal Declaration of Human Rights (1948), which states in Article 14 that everyone has the right to seek and enjoy asylum from persecution, in other countries.

Initial international efforts to deal with the problem of refugees began with the League of Nations, which defined refugees as those who were (i) outside their country of origin and (ii) without the protection of the government of that state (Goodwin-Gill, 1983, p. 2). These were the criteria used to identify and assist Russians fleeing from the Soviet Union and later those fleeing Nazi persecution in Germany. Today, the office of the United Nations High Commissioner for Refugees (UNHCR) is the primary United Nations agency concerned with refugees, and the norms it follows are based on the 1948 Declaration and the 1951 Convention, as well as on customs and practices used in practical situations.

It must be noted that none of these agreements or practices actually guarantees anyone the right to asylum, only the right to seek it. This is because in practice there is total acceptance in the international community of the right of every sovereign state to decide for itself who should be allowed entry to its territory. Thus, the question of whether someone is a refugee and should be treated as such by a state is an issue to be decided by the government and the courts of the country in which refuge is sought. Nevertheless, these instruments form an important part of the international consensus on the treatment of refugees, and they lay down an important universal principle that most countries have come to endorse, namely that people with a well-founded fear of persecution have a right to exit from their own country, have international status and cannot be returned to their country of origin.

For a refugee to be recognized as such is a political decision, and depends to some extent on the relationship between the sending and receiving countries. For instance, in the 1980s the United States government refused refugee status to Salvadoreans fleeing civil war because not to have done so would have acknowledged that a friendly government was indulging in human rights abuse. Nicaraguans, on the other hand, were readily identified as refugees because of American opposition to the Sandanista regime. Thus, states have considerable leeway in deciding whether or not people qualify for refugee status. The advanced industrial governments have come to ever stricter interpretations to enable them to minimize the number of people (mostly from Third World countries) eligible to enter their states. Some, like the British government, have enacted laws, like the Carriers Liability Act (which imposes a fine of £2,000 per person who arrives in the UK without proper documents on the airlines that carry them here), which undermine the internationally established principle that 'everyone has the right to seek and enjoy asylum'.

European Union countries, faced with increasing applications for asylum, have made moves towards a common set of policies for dealing with asylum seekers. For instance, when Germany, the country with the most unrestrictive asylum laws, tightened its policies in 1993, other European states followed suit, so that a decline in asylum applications to Germany would not result in a corresponding rise elsewhere. Further, the EU agreed at the Dublin Convention that asylum seekers could only apply for asylum to the EU country first entered, and that asylum seekers arriving from safe third countries should be returned to those countries. Many of the measures taken by European governments are designed to discourage asylum seekers and include visa restrictions and carrier liability policies like the one adopted by the British government. While a common European policy is still some distance away, its emerging form makes clear that it is unlikely to offer much hope to those suffering persecution. There is a danger that in the rush to protect themselves against unwanted immigration, states are creating a 'fortress Europe', failing to protect legitimate refugees and placing in jeopardy the existing albeit minimal international consensus.

No universal regime for the treatment of voluntary migrants exists, and states retain full powers to determine who shall enter their territory. In the absence of any universally agreed norm regarding immigration, all countries have set up their own restrictions, which they redefine as and when necessary, depending on their economic and social needs. However, European Union members have embarked on what promises to be a fairly long-drawn-out process to create common immigration policies. Some have moved faster than others and in 1985 the Schengen agreement, between Germany, France, and the Benelux countries, established a common set of rules for entry to these countries. They were later joined by Italy, Spain, and Portugal, and the agreement came into effect in March 1995. It put in place a common list of countries whose nationals require visas to visit 'Schengen' states and a common set of policies on visa restrictions. But there is still a long way to go before a comprehensive European immigration policy emerges.

Migration and Contemporary World Politics

Migration casts light upon both the nature of the state and inter-state relations in contemporary world politics. The traditional concept of a nation-state, consisting of a population unified by history, culture, language and religion, no longer stands up to scrutiny. Democracies are increasingly multi-cultural, and to maintain their democratic status these states are having to learn to deal with cultural differences and to evolve policies that are inclusive and non-discriminatory. Ethnically distinct minorities within these states have heightened the awareness of the need to reconsider our understanding of fundamental concepts like citizenship. Citizens can no longer be identified by common historical, ethnic, cultural or religious ties. The inhabitants of the state must be identified and protected by laws that stress the rights of citizens.

The inability of states to maintain complete control of entry to their territory, or to prevent the formation of immigrant communities with extra-territorial connections and affiliations, points to an erosion of sovereignty. States are no longer able to exert control over their own destinies. The growth of non-indigenous ethnic minorities is helping to blur all distinctions between domestic and international boundaries. Migration also highlights the importance of economic issues in contemporary world politics, because of the close association between economic pressures and the motivations for and responses to migration. Improved travel and communication not only facilitates global cultural exchange but also promotes international migration. Thus migration contributes to, illuminates and reinforces the interdependent nature of world politics.

The ability of immigrant communities to act as independent actors on the world stage undermines the traditional state-centred analysis of world politics. To understand contemporary world politics, we need to recognize the role played by non-state, non-governmental, even non-institutionalized actors, amongst which we must number politically active immigrant groups. Migration also casts light on the divided nature of the world in which we live, illuminating the vast gulf in living conditions between the developed, stable countries of the North and the unstable and under-developed South. It serves to reinforce the view that the turbulence created by Southern poverty and political uncertainty is not a phenomenon from which the North can easily insulate itself. It provides a forceful argument for constructive and supportive Northern assistance to the South.

Guide to Further Reading

The literature on migration is wide-ranging and interdisciplinary, reflecting the nature of the phenomenon itself. Explicitly political treatments of migration are still thin on the ground, but include Castles and Miller (1993), Collinson (1993, 1995) and Hammar (1985) on Europe. Sheffer's (1986) edited volume on diaspora political activity is unique and insightful. Gordenker (1987), Goodwin-Gill (1983) and Zolberg, Suhrke and Aguayo (1989) treat refugee issues comprehensively, while Dowty (1987) lucidly examines the political uses and implications of restrictions on emigration. Two edited volumes that present a useful interdisciplinary survey of migration issues are Jackson (1969) and Kritz, Keely and Tomasci (1981). Potts (1990) provides a succinct study of the indenture system and Castles and Kosack (1985) an analysis of European guest-worker systems, while Cohen (1987) analyzes the role of immigrant labour in the world economy. Journals like *International Migration Review, Population and Development Review* and the migration bulletins published by the OECD are also useful.

11

Environment and Natural Resources

JOHN VOGLER

Governments have been concluding agreements on matters relating to the conservation of the physical environment for over a century. International action to preserve 'birds useful to agriculture', for example, can be traced back to 1868 (Caldwell, 1990, pp. 17–18). A large number of international fisheries commissions were set up in the first half of the twentieth century and current international marine pollution law dates back to the 1950s. However, environmental issues were most definitely not considered to be part of the mainstream of world politics. Environmental politics were so 'low' on the international agenda as to be virtually invisible. In the most important textbook of the Cold War era, Hans J. Morgenthau's *Politics Among Nations* (1967), the only mention of the physical environment was as one element of national power (alongside decisive factors such as national character). Natural resources were, in Morgenthau's words, 'another relatively stable factor' (1967, p. 109). The environment, then, was simply regarded as the unchanging context of international politics, and environmental issues the preserve of technical negotiations about fish stocks, wildlife preservation and the design of oil tankers.

By contrast, it would be difficult today to write a textbook on world politics that did not contain a chapter on, or at least extensive reference to, environmental issues. The change – a rapid growth in the significance of environmental issues – started to occur in the 1960s. It grew from a public awareness of environmental degradation, the damage being done by pesticides to the countryside, the polluted state of rivers and beaches, and the finite limits of a natural world confronted by the ever more voracious demands of developing industrial civilization. Concern was reflected in the emergence of pressure groups (mainly in the developed West) such as Friends of the Earth and Greenpeace and a distinctive brand of 'green' activism and political thought. Governments responded, not always very effectively, by creating ministries of the environment and by passing legislation for the protection of habitats and endangered species and for the regulation of the discharge of effluents and the preservation of air quality. In Britain, the latter was well advanced and the 'pea soup' smogs of the 1950s had already been eliminated through the Clean Air Acts. Similarly, the US conservation movement had long been active, but the late 1960s and the early 1970s saw environmental concerns moving rapidly up the 'political agenda'.

International Awareness: From Stockholm to Rio

Pollution, whether atmospheric or marine, knows no boundaries. Neither do many endangered species. Birds or fish can travel great distances through many national jurisdictions or through none (the high seas and Antarctica). The destruction of endangered species also has an international dimension because of the significance of trade in animal products such as ivory. The first formal recognition of the international dimension of the new 'green' awareness occurred in 1972 with the calling of the United Nations Conference on the Human Environment at Stockholm, to which 113 states sent representatives, though the Soviet bloc refused to participate on the grounds that the German Democratic Republic had not been invited. The Conference drew up 26 Principles calling upon states to cooperate in the protection and improvement of the physical environment through the prevention of pollution, the fostering of education and the institution of rational planning. June 5 was chosen as World Environment Day and 109 specific recommendations for international action were made including a 10-year moratorium on commercial whaling. At the same time the United Nations Environment Programme (UNEP) was created.

Reports of the Conference make it clear that many of the essential dilemmas of subsequent international environmental politics were already emerging (see *UN Yearbook 1972*, pp. 318–23). Several state representatives highlighted the role of capitalism, apartheid and nuclear proliferation in environmental degradation. The Americans and their allies responded by deploring the raising of such 'political' issues and asserting the sanctity of free trade and the GATT system. Most important were the fundamental divisions of opinion about development and the environment and about the allocation of responsibility. Could continued economic growth and industrialization be channelled to allow the preservation of the natural environment, or were there, as a famous report of the period argued, *Limits to Growth* (Meadows *et al.*, 1972)? Was the main problem unbridled population growth in the less developed countries (something that continues to be an extraordinarily sensitive and controversial subject in international gatherings), or was there a clear duty on the developed countries, which had both created and benefited from the environmental 'mess', to pay for clearing it up ?

In the following twenty years, leading up to the 1992 Rio 'Earth Summit', interest in environmental issues among developed world publics waxed and waned. Occasionally, it reached peaks of intensity stimulated by disasters such as the lethal radioactive discharge that blew across Europe from the crippled Soviet reactor at Chernobyl in 1986, the 1989 Exxon Valdez oil spill, or the dramatic discovery of the Antarctic 'ozone hole' in the mid-1980s. At other times, concern with economic recession seemed to exert a contrary pull. Nonetheless, the scientific effort to comprehend the mechanics of global environmental change gathered pace as did the policy response in terms of the development of international environmental law. In 1987, the World Commission on Environment and Development, headed by the then Prime Minister of Norway, Gro Haarlem Brundtland, published *Our Common Future*, providing an influential warning and call to action. Most significantly, it coined the phrase 'sustainable development' – an attempt to reconcile the conflict between growth and environmental conservation that had dogged international discussion since Stockholm. Some would say that this was merely a highly political attempt to 'square the circle', but it provided a major cue for the subsequent Rio 'Earth Summit' attended by most heads of government and an additional cast of thousands.

Before Rio, there had already been some landmark international agreements, notably the 1985 Vienna Convention and 1987 Montreal Protocol on restoring the stratospheric ozone layer through action to ban ozone-depleting chemical substances. At Rio, which was preceded by several years of intense preparatory negotiations, the participants agreed not only a declaration of principles, but also Agenda 21. This was a vast document of 40 chapters and hundreds of pages itemizing recommendations for environmental good practice in almost every conceivable area. Painstakingly negotiated, Agenda 21 was remarkable not only for its scale but also for its reach which explicitly extended below the level of government action to communities and local authorities. Its recommendations continue to be discussed and monitored by the UN's Commission on Sustainable Development (CSD).

Elsewhere at Rio, however, there was no agreement on an issue which had given rise to increasing alarm – the systematic and accelerating destruction of tropical rainforests, but a convention was signed (over American objections) on the maintenance of biodiversity. The other Rio outcome was the drawing up of a Framework Convention on Climate Change (FCCC). This was significant in that it marked the beginnings of a systematic international attempt to grapple with the problem of 'global warming' . With the recession of fears of nuclear war, many of those who have studied the scientific evidence consider that this represents the gravest threat to the long-term survival of human civilization. The FCCC was subsequently developed through the first Conference of the Parties at Berlin (1995) which set itself the daunting task of developing control measures to protect the planet from some of the serious climatic consequences that will, it is predicted, occur during the twenty-first century if nothing is done. Thus environmental questions have become part of the regular agenda of world politics, a process nicely described in a book by a British Foreign Office participant as *The Greening of Machiavelli* (Brenton, 1994).

The Rising Profile of Environmental Issues

The sources of environmental change and degradation are various, interconnected and sometimes highly controversial. The simplest cases involve emissions of particular chemicals or pollutants (such as pesticides, heavy metals, sewage) which are readily identified and can be avoided or regulated without excessive costs. Much more difficult to cope with are the inevitable environmental consequences of 'normal' human activities, of economic growth and industrialization and associated population growth and pressure upon resources.

The scale of the problem

Environmental damage may be localized with the effects of pollution incidents confined to a particular area. It may be regional with transboundary phenomena, such as 'acid rain' deposition spanning national frontiers, or it may occur on a truly global scale as with stratospheric ozone layer depletion. A very significant trend in the interval between the Stockholm and Rio conferences was a broadening awareness of the scope of environmental problems. In the 1970s, the dominant concern was with issues such as long-range transboundary air pollution or the pressing need to 'save' the Mediterranean from being abused as a sewer. The solution to such problems required intensive international cooperation because the sources of pollution were frequently located far away from their impact. A well-known case is provided by the emissions of British coal-burning power stations which, without expensive 'scrubbing' equipment, emitted sulphur dioxide which was then carried eastward by the prevailing winds and deposited on German and Scandinavian forests as highly toxic 'acid rain'. Effluents in the North Sea which are deposited by the prevailing currents many miles away from their source provide another example.

By the end of the 1970s, indications of degradation on a global scale began to emerge. The most important case was provided by a new scientific understanding of the destructive impact of certain man-made chemicals, Chlorofluorocarbons (CFCs) and Halons, on the earth's stratospheric ozone layer. Such supposedly benign and inert gases had been manufactured since the 1930s and used for a variety of purposes in refrigerators, air conditioners, fire extinguishers, most famously as propellants in aerosol cans, and for the production of the polystyrene boxes in which burgers were sold. Although there was then no indisputable evidence that the ozone layer was being harmed, US environmental groups pressed Congress to legislate a 1977 ban on the use of CFCs. They made the point that risks should not be taken with the health of the ozone layer because of its fundamental significance in protecting human beings, animals and plants from the harmful effects of UV/B radiation from the sun. This was known to increase the risk of skin cancer and to cause other genetic mutations. By the mid-1980s, dramatic evidence was found that very serious damage had in fact already occurred to the stratospheric ozone layer and the first systematic attempts to organize a solution to a global environmental problem were made – the Vienna Convention 1985 and Montreal Protocol 1987.

The most comprehensive of global environmental issues is 'global warming' and associated climate change. Unlike the scientific understanding of ozone depletion, hypotheses concerning global warming have long been propounded. To be precise we are dealing here with the 'enhanced greenhouse effect'. The 'greenhouse effect' refers to the way in which the temperature of the earth is maintained by certain gaseous components of the atmosphere – carbon dioxide, methane, nitrous oxide (to which may be added the CFCs). The presence of these gases in the atmosphere ensures that the warmth from solar radiation is retained at the earth's surface – hence the 'greenhouse' analogy. Without this effect, life on earth as we know it would be impossible.

However, what has occurred since the industrial revolution is a gradually increasing concentration of greenhouse gases – notably carbon dioxide resulting from the burning of fossil fuels (but also methane from agriculture). This, according to the majority of scientific opinion, leads to an enhanced greenhouse effect where, instead of the maintenance of a stable temperature, there is a slow but inexorable increase. There is evidence that this has been occurring (the 1980s was the hottest decade on record), but there is still a range of uncertainty and some dispute as to the likely future magnitude of change and, most crucially, as to the consequences in the twenty-first century. An understanding of these rests upon predictions made by climate modelling which cannot provide exact answers. The world-wide consensus amongst climate modellers has been presented in the assessments of the Intergovernmental Panel on Climate Change (IPCC). One global impact is likely to be a rise in mean sea levels through a process of thermal expansion and the melting of the polar ice caps. Another is greater climatic turbulence and shifts in the climate of various regions of the world – although there is, as yet, little precision in the prediction of such effects.

When considering these phenomena it is now commonplace to speak of Global Environmental Change (GEC) or in US usage simply 'global change'. This is because, in dealing with greenhouse gas concentrations and the 'drivers' of the world's climate, we are confronted with a single, yet extraordinarily complex, global system. Awareness of this has been one of the defining characteristics of environmental debates since the 1980s. To give one example, Antarctica, once regarded as a frozen wilderness of no great significance, is now seen to be intimately connected to global change in a number of ways. The drilling of its ice cores provides the best record of atmospheric chemical concentrations in previous centuries; it is an integral part of the climate system in terms of its role in establishing thermal gradients; and it provides an enormous store of ice which once melted would increase sea levels.

It is no exaggeration to say that what occurs in Antarctica is related to, for example, increasing desertification in sub-Saharan Africa. There are also global connections between the destruction of tropical rainforests, the emissions of carbon dioxide from industrialized areas and long-range shifts in agriculture (where temperate zones will become arid) and rising sea levels. Forests are 'sinks' for carbon dioxide (as are the oceans) and they have normally helped to maintain 'the carbon balance' by absorbing carbon dioxide through photosynthesis. Their destruction and the burning of felled trees is therefore doubly disruptive to that balance. It is also worth noting that the remaining tropical forests also contain the greatest store of unresearched and untapped bio-diversity. The loss of this bio-diversity threatens future progress in medicine and agriculture. There is no need to labour the point. Skolnikoff sums it up nicely when he writes that global climate change is the 'apotheosis of the idea that everything is connected to everything else' (1993, p. 183).

Evaluating the threat

Those who seek to ameliorate or to retard global environmental change face real problems of urgency, intensity and visibility. Some environmental issues exhibit all three characteristics. Examples would include 'disasters' when supertankers spill oil, volcanoes erupt or when environmental damage occurs in the context of military action. Saddam Hussein's release of oil into the Persian Gulf and the subsequent torching of the Kuwaiti oil wells as a last desperate response to military defeat in 1991 provides a dramatic instance. It is much easier for issues to appear on political agendas and for national and international action to be concerted if environmental effects are tangible and immediate. Unfortunately the effects of polluting activities may not always be known until it is too late to prevent damage or there may be endless scientific uncertainty which serves as an excuse for political inaction.

It is for this reason that the 'precautionary principle' has become so significant in environmental debates. This states that it is prudent to assume the worst in dealing with potential hazards and not to wait until there is full scientific consensus. Stratospheric ozone depletion provides a perfect example of how an issue moved from the level of scientific uncertainty and public ignorance to one of high visibility and urgency which, in turn, impelled the chemical industry and governments to take concerted action. Underpinning this process through the 1970s and 1980s was growing scientific certainty as to the nature of the problem and the effects of CFCs that had previously been considered benign. It took some time, however, for any sense of urgency to be instilled into governments.

In the United States, there were bizarre suggestions from the Secretary of the Interior that the solution was to be found not through regulating industry in order to restore the ozone layer, but in the wearing of sunglasses and hats. A *New York Times* cartoon appeared depicting a flock of sheep protecting themselves from genetic mutations by following the Secretary's advice! Eventually US policy was reversed – and it was not without significance that President Reagan himself suffered from a skin cancer at this time. The event that gave real impetus to the ozone negotiations and established a sense of urgency, however, was the discovery in mid-1985 of what had only been inadequately predicted – a very large 'hole' in the stratospheric ozone layer over the Antarctic. This thinning of the ozone layer was of much greater severity than had been expected. In fact, data from a US Nimbus satellite had previously been rejected as spurious because they were so far beyond the expected values. It took a British Antarctic Survey balloon to confirm the alarming magnitude of the damage that had already been done to the ozone layer.

The problem with other global change phenomena is that they are much more insidious and uncertain even though, in the longer run, they may potentially pose an even greater threat than ozone layer depletion. The full impact of increasing concentrations of greenhouse gases in the atmosphere will only be visited on the earth towards the end of the twenty-first century – current IPCC predictions offer a range of scenarios. The best estimate is for a mean temperature increase of two degrees centigrade between 1990 and 2100 with an associated sea-level rise of 50 centimetres. Higher estimates are for a 3.5 degree temperature rise and a 95 centimetre sea-level rise (Houghton *et al.*, 1996, pp. 5–6) These figures may seem small and they depend upon what can be achieved in restraining climate change in the next decades. However, even small increases can have radical effects upon agricultural production, diseases and the habitability of land. They are also sufficient to inundate many low-lying areas including not only the small island states of the Pacific but also some of the major world cities which are built at sea level. This has already alarmed some of the most immediately vulnerable like the Association of Small Island States (AOSIS) who have been very active in international negotiations on climate change. The 1995 Berlin meeting demonstrated some of the different perspectives on interest and threat in world environmental politics. The Group of 77 – a UN-based grouping of 'developing' states – found itself divided on the issue. The oil producing states, unlike other members, refused to accept international restrictions on the use of fossil fuels. One can only speculate as to the kind of private disagreements that must have occurred between say, Bangladesh, with its miserably poor population located at sea level, and oil-rich Saudi Arabia.

For many countries the threat, although potentially catastrophic, is hardly urgent or immediate. Thus, in the climate change negotiations, Japan, Canada, the United States, Australia and New Zealand, concerned about the effects upon their economic performance, have opposed stringent measures to control greenhouse gas emissions. The European Union has taken a more proactive stance to which the US government had by the mid-1990s become more sympathetic.

A reluctance to be involved with making immediate economic and political sacrifices in order to confront an uncertain long-range threat is understandable. Politicians notoriously tend to discuss issues within a time frame that does not extend very much further than the next elections. Corporate executives are often longer-sighted, having an horizon that is bounded by the life-cycle of a product, a process, or an investment. Thus for example, discussions under the Montreal Protocol about the point at which HCFCs (the relatively less damaging substitutes for CFCs) will be phased out tend to converge around a date 25 years hence, when the current generation of air conditioners will have reached the end of their useful life.

In dealing with long-range threats, one critical determinant will be the extent, to use economists' language, to which we discount the future. Are we concerned enough about what will happen to our great-grandchildren to induce us to make inconvenient changes in present consumption patterns or lifestyles? Very much to the point in discussions of sustainable development is the difference between the way in which the affluent and the poor discount the future. For the poor who worry about whether they will be able to survive tomorrow, contemplating the impact of their actions upon conditions one hundred or even thirty years hence, must seem an irrelevant luxury. Cutting down and burning trees or other non-sustainable activities may seem the only way to ensure immediate survival regardless of the long-run damage inflicted upon the biosphere.

The problem of lack of immediacy is compounded by uncertainty. It cannot be over-stressed that at present potential climate change is still hypothetical, although confirmatory evidence is becoming available. Even less clear and dependent upon complex modelling are the precise impacts of temperature changes. As has often been said, the fateful irony is that by the time we acquire absolutely certain evidence that the enhanced greenhouse effect hypothesis is correct, temperature rise will have become irreversible and there will be no possibility of taking effective remedial action to prevent its more disastrous impacts. High levels of scientific uncertainty and public scepticism militate against political action and there are always those who will argue that no action is needed unless – as in the case of stratospheric ozone – there is tangible evidence and an obvious threat to life.

This has been counteracted by extensive organization of international scientific cooperation on environmental matters since Stockholm. At the centre is the IPCC itself, which has institutionalized a process whereby governments are continuously warned as to the nature and gravity of the threat on the basis of a general scientific consensus which is difficult for sceptics to challenge. However, generating the political momentum to make the required economic sacrifices in terms, for example, of energy taxes to limit carbon dioxide emissions, remains exceedingly difficult. In Britain, the attempt to double the VAT on domestic fuel in the early 1990s (ostensibly to assist in meeting Rio commitments) proved so unpopular as to be politically unsustainable. While high-profile events such as Chernobyl, the ozone hole or Rio itself may increase the short-run saliency of environmental issues, tax and economic welfare questions tend to dominate the domestic political agenda. Environmentalists often hope, therefore, for a run of hot summers in the United States which would put some urgency and immediacy back into the discussion of global environmental change.

Defining the Problem

At the most profound level the imperative of sustaining the physical environment has to be reconciled with a range of other human aspirations, most notably those relating to economic growth. Ever since the industrial revolution, key indicators of production – resource use, emissions of carbon dioxide, and so on – have shown an exponential growth pattern that accelerates rather than maintains a steady linear increase. The increase in the human population provides the most awesome illustration. In 1700, world population was 615 million, in 1800, 900 million, and by 1900, it had reached 1.625 billion. By 1965, despite two world wars, population had more than doubled to 3.33 billion, by the mid-1990s it was 5.37 billion, and it is projected to rise to 8.89 billion by the year 2030 (World Bank, 1992, p. 196).

Most people continue to exist in relative poverty and have legitimate aspirations to achieve the living standards of affluent 'developed' sections of the world's population. In absolute terms, levels of human development have improved since the 1960s; but in relative terms, there have been sharp increases in inequality. Thus, the share of world income for the richest 20 per cent of world population has risen in the last thirty years from 70 to 85 per cent (UNDP, 1994, p. 35; see also Chapter 5). At the same time, however, the contribution of this richest 20 per cent to environmental degradation, as measured for instance in carbon dioxide emissions per capita, is incomparably greater. Yet the consequences of environmental change are likely to be visited first and with the greatest severity upon the poor. It is they, for example, who are forced to migrate through increasing desertification or who live in the midst of unregulated and life-threatening pollution of air and water. Bangladesh provides a telling example. Its people are already subject to the impact of climatic instability and would be amongst the first casualties of predicted sea-level rises. Nor does Bangladesh have the resources to cope with change in the ways that some other low-lying countries like the Netherlands do. Yet Bangladesh is hardly responsible for the problem – producing a mere 0.3 per cent of global greenhouse gas emissions but threatened with the loss of 17 per cent of its land area (UNDP, 1994, p. 36).

It is important to grasp the point that the 'problem' here is not really environmental but socio-economic. From the very first international discussions of the environmental crisis, at Stockholm, it has been impossible to separate environmental issues from questions of development and North–South inequality. At issue is the question of whether Brundtland's objective of 'sustainable development' can be achieved. Will the attempts by less developed countries to engage fully in the global trade and production system mean that they are bound to follow the growth trajectory of the current industrialized countries? Will not the attainment of levels of consumption for the majority of earth's population that even approach those of the currently developed countries in terms of resource exploitation, inevitably mean the collapse of the physical environment and the realization of the worst fears of those who study climate change? There is no clear consensus on this most contentious of questions. Optimists argue that there are 'win–win' solutions and that new technologies and a more prudent and efficient use of resources can, if implemented in time, produce a sustainable future that satisfies development aspirations (Meadows *et al.*,1992).

The Role of International Cooperation

As was most evident at Rio, the world political system now provides a forum in which such questions are frequently aired. The UN has established the Commission on Sustainable Development and holds special General Assembly sessions and conferences. Multilateral institutions like the World Bank and the World Trade Organization (WTO) now have sustainable development as a permanent feature on their respective agendas. The conventional wisdom, both amongst practitioners and most academics involved with the international politics of the environment, is that however hypocritical and self-interested governments may be, their involvement in finding solutions to the problem of sustainable development is indispensable.

The argument proceeds as follows. Because there is no overarching political authority at the global level and the authority to regulate lies with 185 sovereign states, the solutions to transboundary and global environmental problems have to be sought through inter-state cooperation. This is particularly so in the global commons – the oceans, Antarctica, outer space and the atmosphere (Vogler, 1995). Their defining feature is that they do not come under any national jurisdiction but are nevertheless critical to human welfare. Without some form of regulation there is an inevitable short-term temptation for users to exploit common resources bringing about their long-term degradation and collapse. The fate of the great whales, virtually wiped out by the voracious whaling fleets of the late nineteenth century and early twentieth century, provides a graphic illustration, and it is worth noting that the whaling industry itself (with a few isolated exceptions) soon followed its prey into extinction.

The problem has been most famously described by Hardin (1968) as the 'tragedy of the commons'. International cooperation is needed to prevent such tragedies, to ensure, for example, that common fish stocks are not overexploited. There will need to be agreed 'sustainable' catch limits and some form of policing to prevent cheating by fishermen. The principle is the same for the protection of the atmosphere. When it was agreed that the restoration of the ozone layer required a universal ban on the production and use of CFCs, it became important to ensure that no countries or industries could profit from the responsible behaviour of others by continuing to produce cheap CFC-based products when others have been forced to adopt more expensive alternatives. Just as the solution to domestic problems of pollution has been found through central government regulation and enforcement – for example the British Clean Air Acts – global and transboundary problems can be solved, it is argued, in an equivalent way by producing a form of 'governance' through international cooperation.

In this sense the problem of 'cooperation under anarchy' is the same one that is encountered in other issue areas – developing arms control measures or managing international trade and monetary relations. In fact they are all related anyway, not just in terms of the common problem of cooperation but in very substantive ways. Environmental change in relation to, say, forests cannot be isolated from the trade and monetary systems which set the context within which trees are either logged to extinction or sustained. A major difficulty is that the UN and other bodies continue to treat the problems separately and even schizophrenically. For instance the WTO has only just begun to consider environmental issues, though still in a very limited way, within its new Committee on Trade and the Environment.

Radical alternatives

Although most International Relations scholars (Young, 1989; Haas, Keohane and Levy, 1994) conceptualize the problem in terms of the imperative of international cooperation, other activists and writers disagree, arguing that this approach offers a narrow and ultimately fruitless representation of the issue of global environmental change. An insight into a radically different conceptualization can be gained from the following commentary on Rio in *The Ecologist*.

> Unwilling to question the desirability of economic growth, the market economy or the development process itself, (the Rio Summit) never had a chance of addressing the real problems of 'environment and development'. Its secretariat provided delegates with materials for a convention on biodiversity but not on free trade; on forests but not on logging; on climate but not on automobiles. Agenda 21 – the Summit's action plan – featured clauses on 'enabling the poor to achieve sustainable livelihoods' but none on enabling the rich to do so; a section on women but none on men. By such deliberate evasion of the central issues which economic expansion poses for human societies, UNCED condemned itself to irrelevance even before the first preparatory meeting got under way. (1993, pp. 1–2)

For more radical commentators such as Saurin (1996) and Sachs (1993), international cooperation between states can never really address the problems of environmental degradation. Indeed the states system itself, intimately connected with corporate capitalism and imbued with authoritarian 'managerialist' conceptions, is very much part of the problem. Thus the problem is not one of promoting international cooperation but of generating resistance and self-reliance at local levels in what Ekins (1992) calls 'grass roots movements for global change'.

Getting on the International Agenda

The exact way in which particular issues appear and disappear in the public consciousness and become significant for governments continues to puzzle and intrigue political scientists. Certainly, as we have seen, environmental issues have moved rather dramatically on to the international political agenda but their salience appears to have a cyclical character, rising to a peak in the period 1988–92, but then falling away.

Certain critical events have clearly helped to stimulate public awareness and political responses. At the same time there has been persistent pressure from transnational scientific and expert communities on particular issues which have kept them alive and influenced the policies of governments. A well-known case of such influence by what he terms an 'epistemic community' has been provided by Haas (1990) in his study of the development of the Mediterranean pollution abatement regime. Similar influence can be traced in the evolution of the regime for stratospheric ozone.

No discussion of environmental politics would be complete without mention of a vast range of non-governmental organizations (NGOs) that have made environmental issues peculiarly their own. Greenpeace and other campaigning NGOs 'cut their teeth' by generating public protest against whaling and have gone on to deal with radioactive and oil pollution and the whole range of global commons issues, often taking direct action in order to generate public interest. More 'establishment' groups like the World Wildlife Fund or the International Institute for Environment and Development routinely advise governments, and NGOs are now granted observer rights at UN conferences and some of their members even appear within national delegations. The 'Global Forum' at Rio demonstrated the full range and diversity of NGOs and some have even begun to talk of the rise, alongside the states system, of a 'global civil society'.

The rise of environmental NGOs in the period under consideration is clearly part of a deeper trend in the political systems of Western societies – although there are now very many NGOs located in the South who do not always agree with their developed world counterparts. This appears to have involved increasing public disillusionment with orthodox party politics – as evidenced by low voting turnouts and opinion surveys. Instead the politically active have tended to pursue 'single issue politics' through the application of a variety of external (and sometimes, and most effectively internal) pressures on governments. A recent study credits NGOs with being agents of change and social learning in a variety of environmental policy areas and 'key actors in moving societies away from current trends in environmental degradation and towards sustainable economies' (Princen and Finger, 1994, p. 11). Citizens are concerned but unorganized and governments are wedded to the status quo. The role of independent NGOs is to act as a transmission belt between states and international institutions and local communities.

There is little doubt that NGOs have made a very major impact upon world environmental politics and that their public campaigning has virtually created a number of issues – for example, the early public opposition to ozone-depleting chemicals, the moratorium on whaling, and the need for a more environmentally stringent regime in Antarctica. In comparison with many state governments, well-financed NGOs deploy far greater research resources and can therefore enjoy a serious position of influence if invited to advise. However, a note of caution is in order. In the final analysis they will always lack legitimacy alongside an elected government and they, like other actors, will have their own organizational interests to pursue and will not, on occasion, be above misrepresenting scientific evidence (as Greenpeace was honest enough to admit in the case of the Brent Spar oil platform). Their role is pre-eminently to create and publicize issues and it is here that they have played their most significant role in recent environmental politics.

Environmental Issues after the Cold War

The end of the Cold War coincided with the rise of environmental issues in the period before Rio. Was there a connection? It might be argued that a slackening of Cold War tension gave the political 'space' for environmental issues to assume a greater prominence. Indeed, Thomas conjoins the end of the Cold War with the influence of NGOs:

> the current diplomatic profile of environmental issues derives largely from the activities of NGOs who took advantage of the political space provided by the fortuitous ending of the Cold War. (Thomas, 1992, p. 14)

Politicians, including President Clinton, have argued that the common threat of environmental destruction has replaced the threat of mutual nuclear annihilation that characterized superpower relations during the Cold War. There have also been suggestions that redundant military establishments should be given a new role as protectors of the environment. Consideration of the environment as a national security issue is one aspect of the wider debate on the re-definition of security that will be discussed in the final section of this chapter. In the aftermath of the Cold War some activists attempted, often in a rather grandiose way, to suggest that the problems of GEC were so daunting that only the kind of sustained mobilization of resources that had sustained the Cold War confrontation would be adequate. Hence, national security and environmental security were uneasily yoked together in an attempt both to generate extra attention and funds for environmental projects and, on occasion, to provide new missions for military establishments facing an uncertain future.

During the Cold War some environmental and global commons issues had provided one of the few areas on which the superpowers *could* agree – for example, the Long Range Transboundary Air Pollution Convention of 1979 and its Helsinki and Sofia Protocols of 1985 and 1988. Another important example is provided by the Antarctic Treaty, signed in 1959 in the depths of the first Cold War. This placed territorial claims in abeyance and initiated a regime that demilitarized Antarctica and committed participants to peaceful scientific research. Since then the scope of the Antarctic Treaty System has greatly expanded to include a wide range of provisions protecting the environment of this last great wilderness on earth.

Although Cold War concerns sometimes interfered with environmental negotiations (as in the Soviet bloc's refusal to participate in the Stockholm Conference) the key disagreements were not East–West but North–South. This arose from the nature of the issues at stake: population, development and the responsibility for funding environmentally sound policies.

Managing Environmental Problems

International cooperation to 'manage' environmental and global commons problems does not enjoy universal approval but it remains the dominant approach. There may be no world government to regulate and enforce but there are forms of international *governance* that can fulfil similar functions. These forms of governance can be described as *regimes*. This is an all-encompassing term that includes the principles, norms, rules and decision-making procedures that serve to coordinate international action.

Thus, if we were to speak of the marine pollution regime we would include shared understandings on the dangers of certain forms of pollution (oil, radioactive material, sewage, and so on) and on the legitimacy of controlling the activities of governments, shipowners and operators, industrial plant, and so forth. There would be general norms of behaviour concerning what could and could not be thrown into the oceans and very specific sets of rules deriving from the various legal conventions and protocols like the 1972 London convention on dumping, the 1973/8 Convention for the Prevention of Pollution from Ships (often known as MARPOL) and specific regional rules for the Mediterranean and North Sea. These are supported by 'guidelines' for good environmental behaviour developed by UNEP. UNEP itself and the International Maritime Organization (IMO) are also key parts of the regime because they organize the monitoring of compliance, the conduct of research and the taking of collective decisions about how the regime will develop. A major problem with such regimes is that they tend to be partial – in the sense that they are designed to deal with certain sources of pollution from ships or through industrial dumping, but not well developed when it comes to regulating the major land-based sources of marine degradation.

At the heart of international environmental regimes are multilateral treaties – usually referred to as conventions. These constitute sets of binding legal rules and they may be regional or global in scope. A survey undertaken at the beginning of the 1990s listed 124 such 'multilateral legal instruments' (Sand, 1992). The European Union participates in 31 major multilateral environmental agreements, many of which (like the 1979 Convention on Long Range Transboundary Air Pollution) have a number of separate protocols. As we have seen in the case of the MARPOL or the ozone regime, these conventions and protocols contain the agreed principles, norms and rules for managing a wide diversity of environmental problems, from the preservation of African Elephants (1973 Convention on Trade in Endangered Species [CITES]) to the restraint of climate change (1992 Framework Convention on Climate Change [FCCC]).

One problem with the development of international environmental law is that the growth of scientific understanding often outpaces the more cumbrous procedures of negotiation and ratification of international conventions. When negotiators identify a problem they may wish to commence remedial action but they may not be fully aware of its extent or the precise measures that will be required. To meet this problem the ozone negotiations started with a 'framework' Convention (Vienna 1985) and then proceeded to draw up detailed control measures in the Montreal Protocol 1987 and subsequent London and Copenhagen agreements – which reflected a growing scientific and political consensus on the dimensions and causes of stratospheric ozone depletion.

The Framework Convention on Climate Change (1992) has followed a similar pattern. Its parties recognize that a serious problem exists and that the developed countries have a particular responsibility to curb the sources of greenhouse gases and to preserve 'sinks'. They failed however to establish a binding target for reductions in carbon dioxide emissions. Thus the operative Article 4 in the FCCC merely states that the parties will attempt to reduce their emissions to 1990 levels by 2000. Following the Berlin meeting of 1995 efforts have been made to negotiate a more binding agreement (similar to the Montreal Protocol) that will actually commit the developed world countries to make reductions.

Another approach to the problem of negotiating binding rules that reflect current scientific understanding is the growth of what lawyers term 'soft law' – that is to say guidelines for good environmental behaviour which do not have the full force of international treaty law but can as a consequence be produced and revised much more speedily. UNEP has pioneered a mass of 'soft law' in, for example, its Regional Seas Programme. The whole of Agenda 21 (agreed at Rio in 1992), which provides guidelines on almost every environmental topic imaginable at every level – see, for instance, the special role of women and the responsibilities of local authorities – constitutes an exercise in 'soft law' making.

There are a number of international organizations like the World Meteorological Organization (WMO) or the International Council for the Exploration of the Seas (ICES) whose primary remit has always been research relevant to environmental questions. They, together with UNEP, have since Stockholm actively sponsored the development of environmental regimes. UNEP has also been involved in monitoring compliance with international rules (in the ozone regime) and it has been described as having a 'catalytic and coordinating' role (Imber, 1993). This is certainly needed in the UN system where not always successful attempts have been made to persuade all its component parts, from the World Bank to the Food and Agriculture Organization (FAO), to take environmental issues seriously. At the apex of the system the new Commission on Sustainable Development attempts to continue the work of Rio and receives periodic reports from members and from the EU and other organizations on how they have responded to Agenda 21. Sometimes existing organizations like IMO are closely involved with the running of environmental regimes, but a recent trend has been to avoid the creation of dedicated organizations and to rely instead on a small secretariat and a regular 'Conference of the Parties' to develop and review the implementation of multilateral agreements. This path has been followed in the development of the FCCC.

The ultimate and much disputed question is whether such management efforts have been effective in arresting environmental degradation and whether they stand any chance of coping with the new agenda of GEC issues. For radical commentators the answer, almost by definition, is a resounding no. Even those who hope for effective international cooperation make the point that it is very difficult in a world of sovereign states not only to persuade governments to agree to environmentally sound policies which may be contrary to their short-run economic interests, but also to enforce those to which they have agreed. The record is extremely patchy. There have been disasters such as the near extinction of the great whales before the 1985 International Whaling Commission moratorium and the world-wide collapse of fish stocks in the 1990s, where international regulation has been fragmented and inadequate. On the other hand, there are regimes where rules have been adequate and well respected and where threatened environments have been preserved. With some reservations, Antarctica and Mediterranean pollution control could be placed in this category. The air pollution regime in Europe has also proved to be a success. The ozone regime has attracted most attention because it addressed a dramatic global problem. The indications here are good because strong measures have been taken to eliminate CFCs. Even though the ozone layer will not return to its former health until some point beyond the middle of the twenty-first century, the signs are encouraging. In early 1996 readings were taken which showed a reduction in atmospheric concentrations of ozone-depleting chemicals. This is the first physical indication that the ozone regime is 'working'.

The problem of climate change is, of course, another matter. Attempts to preserve forests and to limit CO_2 emissions raise in stark form the inequalities between North and South and the difficulties of making 'sustainable development' anything more than a convenient political slogan. Climate change also highlights the fact that environmental issues are not essentially separate from other issues and cannot sensibly be compartmentalized in the UN system. It may be that the most effective action that can be taken to address climate change will involve the 'greening' of the trade and monetary regimes.

The Environment and Contemporary World Politics

Arguably the recent treatment of environmental issues reveals a shift in the subject matter of world politics or at least some reordering of the priority afforded to these issues. It also, at the same time, involves new participants. Diplomats at the United Nations in New York have been required to deal with environmental specialists and foreign offices have had to contend with subject matter, such as the content of Agenda 21, which was previously well beyond their remit. What this demonstrates is that the distinction between the high politics of 'state to state' diplomacy and the low politics of areas such as environmental protection is exceedingly blurred and has probably ceased to exist. Summit meetings between the leaders of the G7 nations now make declarations about forests and pollution alongside their more traditional preoccupations with interest rates and 'political' and security matters.

The erosion of the boundary between high and low politics is nowhere more evident than in considerations of the changing meaning of the concept of security. Traditionally, security was construed as 'national security' and involved the construction of military defences and alliances against potential external armed threats. Such thinking dominated the Cold War period. Yet, after the Cold War, the question may legitimately be asked, do such threats still constitute the essential security problem?

In response it can be argued that global environmental change and a complex of interrelated issues involving poverty, population growth and inequality constitute the new security problem and should be treated with the same urgency as national defence. After all, if the definition of security is absence of threat then some of the gravest, if not the gravest threats to the survival of societies are environmental. This idea has some attractions but it also has serious drawbacks. Environmental issues are very different from traditional security issues. There is usually no identifiable enemy and degradation is the result of 'business as usual'. In national defence the threats are usually evident and military measures can be taken to counter them – this is not the case with long-run environmental threats. Indeed the application of a militaristic approach could be extremely counterproductive in the interdependent world of environmental management. Daniel Deudney put it well when he said that if the Pentagon had been put in charge of the Montreal Protocol negotiations they 'would still be stock-piling CFCs to use as bargaining chips'! (1990, p. 467).

Even if we reject the attempt to re-define, or more correctly, to expand the traditional concept of security, there is still a sense in which environmental issues are entangled with the old preoccupations of international relations. Environmental degradation is not just the consequence of war as in Laos and Cambodia in the 1960s, or more recently in the Gulf, but it is increasingly likely to be among the causes as well. As natural resources are destroyed, conflict between those who depend upon them is likely to become sharper, while desertification and ecological collapse will produce social and economic disruption and population movements, the consequences of which are likely to pose security threats of the most traditional kind.

The discussion so far has centred upon the relationship between environmental issues and the international political system, primarily composed of sovereign state governments. We have noted that most of the academic writing about the environment and world politics focuses upon how states can be induced to cooperate in the solution of common problems. Yet it is also the case that environmental change is increasingly viewed as a truly global phenomenon which has given rise to forms of activism that transcend the nation-state. The role of non-governmental organizations has been particularly important in this area and, although they attempt to influence state policy, many of those involved in 'green' politics are increasingly irritated by the hypocrisies and delays of inter-state cooperation. In philosophical and practical terms they often regard the nation state as part of the problem and urge community action in response to world environmental problems in accord with the famous slogan 'think globally act locally'.

One of the most interesting questions about post-Cold War politics is whether this kind of activity, particularly when it is linked together across frontiers by such powerful tools as the Internet, presages the emergence of a global polity that may ultimately subvert the international political system. This is a question for the future, but events such as the Rio summit and much of the environmental politics of the 1980s and 1990s certainly demonstrate the co-existence and interaction between the inter-state system and a bewildering range of transnational and even, perhaps, global political action. This is not to say that, in environmental policy-making and the generation of scientific knowledge, state governments do not remain centre stage. The Framework Convention on Climate Change, for example, is an *international* treaty and the authoritative scientific body is significantly named the *Intergovernmental* Panel on Climate Change. Nonetheless, responsibility for the emergence of environmental issues on the international agenda certainly lies elsewhere.

A Guide to Further Reading

The increasing significance of environmental issues in world politics is demonstrated by the availability of good recent textbooks. Of these, Porter and Brown (1991) and Thomas (1992) stand out. An older but very extensive and influential treatment is to be found in Caldwell (1990). Hurrell and Kingsbury (1992) provide a significant set of essays on many aspects of the subject, to which may be added the recent collection in Vogler and Imber (1996) which provides some indication of the range of theoretical debate. For a liberal and institutional approach, Young (1989) is indispensable. An angry, radical and readable alternative is to be found in *The Ecologist* (1993), while the specifics of Rio and the various agreements are well covered in Grubb *et al.* (1993).

There is a vast technical literature on GEC problems but an accessible source is provided by the UNEP-sponsored Tolba, El-Kholy *et al.* (1992). Finally the journal *Environmental Politics,* published quarterly in London by Frank Cass, is always worth consulting.

12

Issues in World Politics Reviewed

BRIAN WHITE, RICHARD LITTLE AND MICHAEL SMITH

There must always be a sense of anticipation when a new century dawns. It is a moment when people tend to take stock, reassessing the past and looking forward to the future. But with the move into the twenty-first century, the level of expectation is inevitably heightened with the inauguration of a new millennium. The stock-taking must, as a consequence, occur on a grander scale, embracing not only the previous century but the last thousand years. Although nothing so ambitious has been attempted in this book, there is an assumption that there may have been a transformation in world politics at the end of the twentieth century. World history, however, does not necessarily oblige by ensuring that the transformation occurs at just that point in time when one century and, as it happens, one millennium, gives way to another.

We have assumed, in fact, that the transformation, if it did take place, began in 1989, when it was officially declared that the Cold War was over, and it was then consolidated, two years later, at the end of 1991, when the Soviet Union suffered its final demise. The importance of these events has already encouraged some historians to suggest that we need to reassess the past two centuries, viewing the nineteenth century as a long century, extending from the French Revolution to the start of the First World War, in contrast to the short twentieth century, which is considered to have started with the gunshots at Sarajevo in 1914 and ended in 1989 with the East Germans surging through the Brandenburg Gate on the Berlin Wall. From this perspective, then, war is seen to provide the defining characteristic of the twentieth century. The century opened with the First and Second World Wars, punctuated by what the historian E. H. Carr described as the 'twenty years crisis'. This first half of the short twentieth century then gave way to over forty years of Cold War. But now that it is over, this familiar metaphor is also being reassessed and it has been suggested that the Cold War era can more appropriately be described as the Third World War, because although the United States and the Soviet Union managed during this period to avoid a nuclear confrontation at the centre of the international system, more by good luck than by good management perhaps, it is equally apparent that they were directly or indirectly engaged in persistent hot war on the periphery of the international system, involving the death of millions of people across the globe.

The passage of time and the analysis of future historians will determine, no doubt, whether from a long-term perspective, war should be taken to be a defining characteristic of the twentieth century and whether 1989, with the benefit of hindsight, appears to be such a crucial juncture in world history. From our perspective, however, while it would be a mistake to ignore the significance of war in the twentieth century, it would also certainly be an error to focus exclusively on war. There are a wide range of issues that have played a very important role in the evolution of world politics during the course of the twentieth century and many of these issues will continue to be of significance in the twenty-first century. What we have done in this book is to isolate some of these issues and to examine, among other things, what general problems they represent; whether or not they have been affected by the ending of the Cold War; what factors have influenced their salience in world politics; how these issues have been managed at the level of world politics; and what an analysis of the issues tells us about the nature of contemporary world politics.

The Selection of Issues

The issues that have been investigated were chosen, of course, because we regard them as important and representative features of world politics today. Taken together, we think that they provide an interesting cross-section of what is happening in the international system at this time. But the issues do not add up to a comprehensive picture of world politics. So, for example, although we have focused on the development and impact of Islamic fundamentalism on contemporary world politics, as we noted in the first chapter, Muslims only represent 20 per cent of the world's population. The study of Islamic fundamentalism, therefore, does not begin to exhaust the impact of religion on world politics. The Catholic Church, for example, has always had a global role to play in world politics and it continues to do so, although its influence is being frequently challenged today by fundamental Christian groups which are making major inroads into areas like Latin America that were previously the preserve of the Catholic Church. At the same time, in Asia, Hindus, Confucians and Buddhists have begun to play an increasingly assertive role in world politics.

It should also be noted that fundamentalism is not an exclusive prerogative of Islam. Attention has been focused on Islamic fundamentalists in this book, however, not only because so much attention has been paid to them in the West but also because the assessments of Islam found in popular accounts are so often and so flagrantly distorted. Indeed, the West has always subscribed to highly distorted accounts of Islam. As a consequence, Islamists are very distrustful of the West and believe that policies pursued by the West have been designed to undermine the global influence of Islam from the Middle Ages onwards. But, as we have seen, it is certainly possible to argue that the images of the West adhered to by the Islamic fundamentalists are just as distorted and that there is a need for mutual reassessment. In focusing on Islamic fundamentalism, however, it is important not to overlook the impact of other religions on world politics and to keep in mind that the overall importance of religion has all too often been underestimated in the study of world politics.

A range of issues that are central to the study of world politics have simply not been touched on at all in this text. *Crime*, for example, has not been examined. Yet it is now an international issue of crucial importance, as exemplified most clearly by the drug trade. Trafficking in drugs is not, of course, a new international phenomenon. During the eighteenth century, for instance, opium represented the major source of revenue for the Moghul Empire in India, at least until the East India Company established a monopoly on its sale and production. The company was then able to use its monopoly to control the sale of opium to China in return for the supply of China tea for which there was an increasing demand in England.

By the end of the nineteenth century it is estimated that one out of every ten Chinese had become an opium addict. Ever since the end of the nineteenth century, however, there has been increasing concern about the use of drugs. In the 1860s, cocaine was first produced from the coca leaf, and then in 1898 heroin was manufactured from morphine, itself a derivative of opium. Both drugs proved to be highly addictive.

During the course of the twentieth century, the production and distribution of illicit drugs processed from natural plant products in conjunction with synthetically produced drugs, such as amphetamines, has escalated in an astonishing fashion. Figures produced by the United Nations suggest that the annual turnover now exceeds $500 billion. This illegal traffic is estimated to represent one-tenth of total international trade and both production and distribution is world-wide. The sale of drugs is now larger than the sale of either oil or food. The supply, of course, is primarily from the Third World, but the high return on the sale of drugs is a consequence of the demand from Europe and the United States which still represents the economic centre of the developed world. There are many ironies associated with the drug trade. Afghanistan, despite the influence of Islamic fundamentalists, is now the largest exporter of opium and heroin. No country, however, is completely free of the international consequences of the drug trade and it is an issue that requires much more attention than it has so far received in the study of world politics. The drug trade, moreover, is just one aspect of the much broader issue of international crime.

It is not difficult to identify other issues that have been left untouched in this text. International *sport*, for example, is an interesting feature of world politics with antecedents which can be traced back to ancient Greece where the first Olympic Games were held. As with crime, this is an issue that has tended to be ignored in traditional discussions of international relations. The issue of *gender* has also been overlooked, though there are passing references to it in Chapters 5, 9 and 10. In Chapter 9, for example, it is noted that Islamists were concerned about the international women's conference held in Beijing in 1995 because they feared that it opened up a threat to their interpretation of the Islamic cultural heritage. International *communications* is another area that is increasingly impinging upon world politics. The impact of the Internet and the world-wide web has opened up the possibility, for example, that globalization and localization may go hand in hand, giving rise to what has been called 'glocalization'

There are other significant areas of interest that have not been touched on directly in the book but which have been encompassed within the discussion of other issues. International *terrorism*, for example, has occupied an important position on the international agenda ever since the 1970s. Most attention has been focused on the use of terror by non-state actors that are endeavouring to put pressure on an established government by attacking civilians across international borders. International terrorism was epitomized by the incident at the Olympic Games in Munich in 1972 when a faction of the Palestinians infiltrated the Olympic Village and took Israeli athletes hostage and eventually killed them before being killed themselves. There was, of course, a very good reason for choosing to attack the Olympic Village. Terrorists not only aim to intimidate civilians but to do so in circumstances that will give their cause international publicity. There were echoes of this earlier incident when a bomb was planted in a public arena at the 1996 Olympics in Atlanta. The emergence of a world-wide media has undoubtedly made international terrorism an increasingly attractive option for terrorist groups. The role of the media in providing terrorists with what critics refer to as the 'oxygen of publicity' has often been condemned, largely because the strategy seems to be so successful. Although the death of civilians may have been a source of moral outrage, there is little doubt that the Palestinians managed to draw the attention of the world to their plight by successive acts of international terror in a way that had never been managed by diplomatic means. The attacks by the IRA on mainland cities in Britain have had a similar effect.

States too have been accused of engaging in terrorist acts. But such acts are generally disowned. So, although Britain and the United States have held the Libyans responsible for the bomb that destroyed the Pan Am flight 103 over Lockerbie in 1988, the Libyan government has never accepted responsibility. International terror-ism remains an important feature of world politics. The issue has not been tackled directly in this text, but it has been discussed in the context of Islamic fundamentalism where it is made clear that political Islamists have felt perfectly entitled to use violence to promote their goal of establishing a Muslim world order. The link between religion and terrorism is not confined, of course, to Islamic fundamentalism. In plural democratic societies, however, the link between religion and violence may seem to be a contradiction in terms. But the link is not new and there have always been fundamentalists who have been willing to resort to violence in order to promote their religious beliefs.

Links between Issues

As the connection between religion and terrorism illustrates, issues in world politics are, in fact, inextricably linked to each other and attention has frequently been drawn to this characteristic feature of world politics in earlier chapters. An important link can be observed, for example, between migration and development. Although, tragically, there are still people being sold into slavery, the vast majority of migrants in the contemporary world are motivated to move for economic gain. They leave their own country voluntarily and settle in another in order to improve their standard of living. But, as we have seen, migration not only assists the individual migrant and the receiving country; there are also many economic side payments associated with migration that accrue to the benefit of the sending country. There is, therefore, an important link between migration and economic development.

A more complex link can also be established between economic development, migration and ethnicity. There are, of course, many factors that account for the growth of ethnic tensions in contemporary world politics, but the problems associated with economic development are certainly an important element. In the case of the genocidal conflict that escalated between the Hutus and the Tutsis in Rwanda during 1994, for example, one source of the conflict related to the lack of economic development and the Hutu resentment of the economic advantages putatively enjoyed by the Tutsis. A direct consequence of this conflict was the migration of thousands of Hutus into refugee camps in neighbouring Zaire because, in the aftermath of the conflict, they feared Tutsi reprisals. There have been, in fact, many cases of enforced migration taking place because of national and ethnic conflict. At the time of the partition between India and Pakistan, in 1947, for example, between 12 and 14 million people moved across the frontier, because they believed that it was unsafe to remain in their homes, with Hindus moving out of Pakistan into India and Moslems moving out of India into Pakistan.

It would not be difficult to multiply these examples of issues that become interrelated at the level of world politics. All the issues discussed in the previous chapters can be shown to be interlinked together in one way or another to form a complex matrix of interrelated issues. But this does not diminish the usefulness of treating them separately in the first instance for analytical purposes. The task of the analyst is to identify the central features of any issue and then to explore how these features are affected by links with other related issues.

Practitioners proceed in a similar fashion. In the search for analytical clarity, therefore, it is important not to overlook that issues are interlinked. Analysts who fail to reveal how issues are interrelated inevitably produce a distorted picture of world politics. By the same token, if practioners fail to take account of these interrelationships, then they can often end up by implementing policies that are, even from their own perspective, counterproductive or self-defeating. To cite an example from an earlier chapter, states in the Middle East have been required by the World Bank to introduce structural adjustment strategies that have had the effect of eliminating state-sponsored welfare programmes. This development, however, has created a political opportunity that has been exploited by organizations sponsored by political Islamist groups. As a result of the structural adjustment programmes, therefore, and contrary to the intentions of the World Bank, political support for the Islamist groups has increased whereas support for the governments has diminished.

Governments are frequently well aware of the interlinkage between issues and they have developed a variety of strategies to cope with these linkages. In the United States, for example, it has been noted that there is a substantial gap between the rhetoric and practice surrounding immigration. The stated policy associated with immigration suggests that immigrants are subject to very severe restrictions. In practice, however, the policy is to maintain a half-open door. In this way, the government can use the stated policy to contend with the hostility to migration frequently expressed by the indigenous population, while using the actual policy to regulate the flow of immigrants dictated by the needs of the economy.

Issues and Contemporary World Politics

Although it was never intended in this book to offer a comprehensive assessment of the issues that emerge in world politics, it is hoped that the issues examined provide a representative picture of contemporary world politics. Having acknowledged that there are important issues that have not been investigated here and that, although they can be isolated for analytical purposes, in practice they are all interlinked, we will now go on to examine the picture of world politics that emerges from a survey of the issues that have been presented in this text.

It is appropriate to start with the state and statehood. Throughout the first half of the twentieth century it was very widely taken for granted that the state was, and would remain for the foreseeable future, the primary unit of organization in world politics. For many theorists and practitioners it was taken as a basic assumption that world politics was about the relations between states. The growth of nationalism in the nineteenth century, however, had also encouraged the belief that states should coincide with nations. This belief had a substantial impact on events throughout most of the twentieth century. Attempts were made after the First World War, for example, to carve up the Ottoman and Austro-Hungarian multinational empires into their constituent national units. Then in the era after the Second World War, the European colonial empires, established over the previous four hundred years, were also dissolved to form a host of new states. By the end of the Cold War, colonization was a thing of the past and the entire globe was ostensibly divided into independent states and it did not now seem out of place to identify these basic building blocks of world politics as nation-states. This was the term habitually used in textbooks on world politics.

But the label was and always had been a fiction, as subsequent events were to demonstrate. During the final decade of the twentieth century, at one end of the spectrum, the last but one of the Eurasian multinational empires collapsed, demonstrating the failure of the Soviet Union to weld the people on its territory into a nation or even a cohesive multinational unit. The start of the short twentieth century, therefore, was marked by the final collapse of two major multinational empires: the Ottoman and Austro-Hungarian empires – and it closed with the collapse of a third – the

Soviet Union. There has been much discussion subsequently about whether China, the last remaining Eurasian multinational empire, can survive in a post-imperial era.

At the other end of the spectrum, Czechoslovakia, ostensibly established as a nation-state after the First World War, divided into two new states, the Czech Republic and Slovakia, because of long-running ethnic tensions. Developments of this kind have raised the spectre of world politics in the future taking place in an arena made up of many hundreds of states. But as Chapter 2 makes clear, this is not the only possible outcome. Large tracts of Africa have been rendered ungovernable because of persistent violence between groups fighting for self-determination. A similar phenomenon occurred for a time following the collapse of Yugoslavia. During the last decade of the twentieth century, therefore, some credence was given to the assertion that the whole notion of statehood was coming under threat as a growing sector of the globe was falling prey to anarchy. The more apocalyptic version of this scenario suggested that this was not only a feature of the Third World, but was a significant characteristic of the developed world, with state authorities increasingly losing control of inner-city areas. But no one is suggesting that there is any virtue to living under conditions of civil war and so this development, far from undermining the relevance of statehood, has served to reinforce the importance of this dimension of world politics.

Attention, however, is also drawn in Chapter 2 to the argument that statehood started to be drained of much of its significance during the second half of the twentieth century. As the end of the century approached there were increasing references to the idea of the 'hollow' state emerging as the result of processes that were reducing the power and role of the state, either by design or by default. In part, this development was the consequence of the triumph of liberalism and the widespread belief that the state had become bloated during the Cold War era and needed to be 'down-sized'. Privatization, deregulation and structural adjustment pro-grammes are obvious examples of processes set in motion across the globe in the 1980s and 1990s that were intended to transfer power from the state to the market. But, paradoxically, some of the most vociferous advocates of these processes were simultaneously de-manding, certainly in Britain, that the sovereignty of the state – statehood – must be protected and they were vehemently opposed, as a consequence, to the establishment of a single European currency among other things. The role of the state, therefore, remains of crucial significance. Throughout subsequent chapters there are persistent references to the issue of statehood and the changing status of the state in contemporary world politics.

Nowhere is this more true than in the discussion of the world economy in Chapter 3. Ever since the 1970s, increasing attention has been paid to economic issues in the study of world politics. This represented a substantial shift in the discipline. In the years after the Second World War, there was a tendency to assume that economic issues fell within the arena of 'low politics'. Attention was concentrated on the study of the military and political implications of the confrontation between the United States and the Soviet Union. By the 1970s, however, there was a growing realization that the world economy had become much more politicized than had previously been acknowledged. In the early days of the Cold War, an economic division between East and West had mirrored the ideological split. During this period, the United States had been able to use its overwhelming economic strength to isolate the Soviet bloc and to ensure that the rest of the world was locked into the capitalist world economy. By the 1970s, however, the United States no longer had the economic muscle to regulate this global economy. As a consequence, there was increasing reference during this period to the fact that states were operating under conditions of economic interdependence. Of course, this was not a new phenomenon, but it is a phenomenon that is much more apparent when economies are on a downward spiral. Governments had been very conscious of economic interdependence during the 1920s and 1930s when they discovered that it was not possible to escape the effects of an economic depression that extended across the entire world economy.

The implications of economic interdependence had been left largely unexamined during the first 20 years of the Cold War because it was an era of extraordinary economic recovery. But, by the 1970s, and as a consequence of this recovery, it was impossible to ignore either the economic potential of Japan and the members of the European Economic Community or the fact that these countries had their own views on the nature of the mechanisms and rules that should regulate the world economy. From this point on, the world economy became more overtly political, although the

United States continued to dominate economic discussions not only because it still possessed the largest economy, but also because it was impossible to ignore the impact of issue linkage brought about by the continued reliance of every state in the West on the security guarantee provided by the United States.

During the 1970s and 1980s, the assumption still prevailed that it made sense to talk about the state as an economic unit. Since the start of the 1990s, however, particularly after the demise of the Soviet Union, this assumption has been seriously questioned. The idea of economic interdependence has begun to give way to the concept of globalization. In conjunction with the assumption that the state is being 'hollowed out' from the inside has emerged the idea that it is also losing the ability to hold the external economic environment at bay. The outer shell of the state is seen to be ever more porous. This development can be observed in the areas of investment, trade and finance. From the 1970s onwards, attention had been drawn to the ability of multinational corporations to engage in foreign direct investment, whereby these firms set up production operations outside of their home economies. But even in the 1970s, this development simply meant that companies that were clearly associated with the United States were extending their production abroad. Now this has become a global phenomenon and multinational corporations have become transnational organizations that not only operate in more than one country, but engage in a high volume of intra-firm trade which now constitutes more than three-quarters of all trade. A final illustration of the porous nature of the state's outer shell is growth in foreign exchange dealing. The volume is now so great that it is beyond the capacity of any state to defend its own currency if it comes under attack on the foreign exchange market. All of these developments support the conclusion that states are not even empty shells any longer. From the perspective of the world economy, there is apparently no longer a role for states to play.

Although the argument has sometimes been pushed this far, there are good reasons for pulling back. It is an illusion to imagine that economic markets operate in a political vacuum. Foreign trade, investment and exchange markets may appear to be completely unfettered, but in fact they operate within a complex framework of rules, established and supported by states. The same is true for trade and investment. It is simply not the case that states have, or even could, hand over all their power to markets. Nor is it true to suggest that states are now hollowed-out and very porous shells. The major industries of some states may have been privatized, but those states continue to support these industries in the global market. The state, it could be argued, has simply changed the traditional instruments which they have used to regulate the economy. In place of an increasingly permeable shell, they have established a porous but very much stronger steel mesh to protect their domestic economies.

An important illustration of the new ways of coping with interdependence in economic and other areas of state activity is provided in Chapter 4. Regions defined as geographical areas in which states have a 'common historical experience and sense of shared problems' provide an opportunity through what is called regionalism for states to cooperate together to solve common problems. At one extreme, European countries through the European Union have a highly developed sense of regionalism and have constructed over the last 50 years a close integrating network of relationships that extends across an ever widening range of issue areas. At the other end of a spectrum is a large number of regional agreements in many areas of the world that focus on a much smaller range of states and a limited number of issue areas.

While there are considerable variations, one of the most important developments in regionalism in the 1990s, with implications for the role of states and the structure of world politics, has been the growth of economic integration in a number of regions creating new powerful blocs. Apart from the European Union, other important examples include NAFTA and APEC. Paradoxically, such developments can also be interpreted as both strengthening and weakening states. On the one hand, governments regard these organizations as a way of improving their chances of securing national policy objectives particularly in the areas of wealth and welfare. Such blocs can also provide a means of extending and consolidating influence and a useful defence against the vagaries of global economic and financial systems. But, from a different perspective, regionalism can also be seen as providing a challenge at best and a threat at worst to states and statehood to the extent that key functions hitherto performed by states are being transferred to regional organizations. This apparent loss of independence or 'sovereignty' is itself a highly controversial issue which can be seen most clearly in contemporary political debates in Western Europe.

The universal ability of the Western economies to industrialize during the nineteenth century and the speed with which the European economies recovered after the Second World War encouraged economists to believe that it would be possible for the European colonies to achieve similar success once they had been given their independence. There was a widespread assumption, particularly in the United States, that the colonies had been systematically exploited and held back during the colonial era and that independence, in and of itself, would help the backward economies of the erstwhile colonies to take off. By the 1970s, however, it was clear that these hopes had been over-optimistic. And by the 1990s, the assessment had become even more pessimistic as it was acknowledged that poverty and hunger was as much a feature of the inner-cities in the so-called developed world as it was in the so-called underdeveloped world. The traditional assumption of modernization theorists that development was a linear process and that once an economy had taken off, standards of living would steadily improve across the board, is now seriously questioned. By the same token, the idea that the Third World would be given a helping hand by the developed world has proved to be sadly mistaken. Even the hope that wealth over time would 'trickle down' to the poor has proved false. On the contrary, as the figures given in Chapter 5 illustrate, income inequality increased during the second half of the twentieth century.

It would be simplistic to suggest, however, that the problems confronted by the Third World are simply the consequence of exploitation by the rich states. The economies of many of these developing countries have been generating higher rates of growth than those found in the developed world. But the anticipated benefits to be accrued from economic growth have failed to materialize because the population has been increasing at an even faster rate in these developing countries. It is also the case that wealth in some of these countries has been concentrated in the hands of too few people. There is a growing recognition, moreover, that it may not be helpful to think purely in terms of a North–South divide. Taking a broader perspective, it becomes possible to see that the problems confronted in the Third World have some obvious counterparts in the developed world. It has been noted, for example, that every First World state contains a Third World city in which unemployment, overcrowding, hunger, and disease are the norm. But by the same token, every Third World state contains a First World city characterized by international fashion, high technology, global communication and transnational corporations. It needs to be acknowledged that cities across the globe have common interests as well as common problems and this was very apparent when representatives of cities from all round the world came together at Istanbul in 1996 under the auspices of the UN Habitat 11 programme.

But, of course, there is also some truth to the idea of a North–South split. In particular, many of the poor in Third World countries live in rural conditions. Developmental economists have taken too little account of this fact. There is, therefore, growing attention being paid to the work of Muhammad Yunus. Trained in the United States, he soon found the economics he was teaching when he returned to South Asia in 1972 to be utterly irrelevant to the circumstances of his own country. There were terrible man-made famines in 1974 in the newly formed state of Bangladesh and, according to some estimates, as many as 1.5 million people died. The attempts by Western economists and institutions to alleviate the poverty in countries like Bangladesh were not working. Muhammad Yunus attempted to identify more effective remedies. In place of large-scale aid programmes, he concluded that attention should be focused on the people who were endeavouring to escape the poverty trap in which they found themselves. What they almost invariably lacked was the necessary capital, often very small amounts, to create their own small businesses. He set up the Grameen Bank ('rural bank' in Bengali) staffed, initially, by his own graduate students, with the objective of providing microloans to the destitute. The clients were mainly women and it was found that women were more careful about managing debt and ensuring that the entire family benefited from the loan. It is too early to be sure about the long-term consequences of this experiment. But Yunus has been consulted by the World Bank and his ideas have been seen to provide a model for relieving poverty in inner-city areas in the United States. What this experiment illustrates is that some development issues may be dealt with most effectively at the local level and this is a lesson that needs to be taken on board by those operating in the sphere of world politics.

If some issues can be dealt with effectively at local or regional levels, there are other issues that do need to be dealt with primarily at the level of world politics. The discussion of the spread and control of weapons in Chapter 6 provides a good illustration. During the Cold War most attention in the West was focused on weapons of mass destruction – nuclear weapons in particular – although the dangers of chemical and biological weapons were also widely recognized. Very little progress was made to eradicate these weapons during the Cold War. Indeed, the doctrine of deterrence did much to legitimate the decision to maintain the weapons. Throughout the Cold War the emphasis was on arms control rather than disarmament. The intention was not to eliminate these weapons of mass destruction but to make possession of them safer.

After the Cold War was over, it was argued by opponents of these weapons that a window of opportunity had opened up through which it might be possible to push some substantial disarmament measures. Ironically, however, with the Cold War over and the Communist threat eliminated, it proved impossible for proponents of disarmament to engender any sense of urgency about the need to eliminate weapons of mass destruction. Hopes for a new world order, where weapons of mass destruction would be eliminated, quickly faded. Analysts of a realist persuasion were unsurprised. Defence managers are necessarily concerned with an uncertain, indeed an unknown future. Under these circumstances it is impossible to escape the security dilemma which is seen by realists to represent a structural feature of the anarchic international system.

Even more depressing for advocates of disarmament have been developments in the area of conventional weapons. It is made very clear in Chapter 6 that whereas the sale of conventional weapons was justified during the Cold War era in terms of security considerations, arms sales are now justified on economic grounds and these sales remain a crucial element of world trade. Hopes that conflict on the periphery of the international system would diminish in the absence of the fuel provided by the ideological competition between the United States and the Soviet Union quickly faded. The pattern of conflict established during the Cold War, with an uneasy peace maintained at the centre of the system and persistent outbreaks of violence on the periphery, remains unchanged: states are as unwilling as ever to curb the arms industries that enable these conflicts to continue unabated.

Growing despair at the inability to transform the nature of world politics has also been very evident amongst advocates of peace-keeping measures. It was believed that, in the wake of the Cold War, it would be easier for the international community to take concerted action to stem violence within and between states. The vigorous response orchestrated by the United States after the invasion of Kuwait by Iraq in 1990 seemed to suggest that it really was possible for the international community under the auspices of the United Nations to stand up to international aggression. As Chapter 7 makes clear, the number of peacekeeping missions established by the United Nations mushroomed in the early 1990s. It began to seem possible that the United Nations could in fact start to police the international system. Such optimism, how-ever, proved to be misplaced and failed to take account of the very real constraints under which the United Nations operates. The United Nations is not a supranational organization with an auton-omous executive and independent sources of finance. It is an international organization made up of states that fund the organi-zation and need to reach a consensus before any major police actions can be undertaken. The response in 1990–1 to Saddam Hussein in Kuwait was only possible because the United States was prepared to take military action and, as a consequence, provide the very considerable diplomatic and economic support needed to establish a coalition of states that would legitimize the action. But it is not only a matter of cost. Peacekeeping missions can only take place if states are willing to provide the necessary personnel.

There is, in fact, no great incentive for wealthy states to expend resources on peacekeeping action unless their own interests are directly or indirectly involved. At a time when even the most wealthy states are finding it impossible to fund basic welfare programmes and are looking for ways to divest themselves of the responsibility, there is a very great reluctance to divert scarce resources to fund ventures in places which their electorate could not even locate on the map. As governments around the world engage in the task of hollowing out their own state, it is unlikely that they are going to provide the necessary resources to bolster the United Nations. Only when an event captures the attention of the public do governments feel pressed to take action and only then with great reluctance because they recognize that the commitment will persist long after the public's attention has waned.

Nevertheless, as is apparent from Chapter 8, there are occasions when images projected by the world's media of the misery caused by conflict has periodically galvanized public opinion. During the Cold War there was a widespread assumption that conflict anywhere around the world related to the ideological conflict between the superpowers. In the early days of the Cold War, there was widespread support in the West for the strategy of providing military support for the opponents of communism. The rationale for this support, however, was based on a distorted picture of world politics. It encouraged the image of leaders on the periphery as puppets on strings that were pulled from Moscow. The disastrous intervention by the United States into Vietnam in the 1960s complicated the task of responding to conflict on the global periphery. But there was always an assumption during the Cold War that the explanation of any conflict could be traced back to the ideological bipolar confrontation. Now that easy equation has been eliminated, but it has been replaced by an alternative and equally facile explanation. Conflicts are now seen to be the result of ethnic tensions that arise from primordial roots.

The conflict between Serbs, Croats and Bosnians in former Yugoslavia or between the Tutsis and Hutus in Rwanda, for example, are accounted for in terms of hostility that can be traced back to the beginning of time. There is nothing that can be done about such atavistic conflict, it is suggested, and so we are absolved of any responsibility to take any action. The reference to ethnicity, however, does not so much explain conflict, as explain it away. And it conveniently justifies the reluctance to make judgements about the conflict or to become involved. A closer investigation of the conflicts in former Yugoslavia and Rwanda, however, fail to support the idea that the sources of the conflict are primordial. The conflict between the Hutus and the Tutsis can be traced back to policies pursued by the West during the colonial era and the conflict in Yugoslavia was fostered, albeit inadvertently, by policies implemented during the Communist era. A better understanding of the conflict does not necessarily make it any easier to solve. But as Chapter 8 makes clear, it should persuade the international community to encourage a greater tolerance of pluralism when demands for self-determination are raised.

Securing a plural world, however, will not be easy. As the discussion of Islamic fundamentalism in Chapter 9 makes clear, there are very wide cultural divisions opening up in the contemporary international system. The Islamists have a vision of social order which is very much at odds with the vision projected in the West. When the Islamists took control in Iran in 1979, for example, although they made some concessions to the indigenous Jews, Catholics and Zoroastrians, these were not extended to other indigenous minority groups that have been systematically persecuted ever since. Similarly in Afghanistan, the Taliban militia which started as a movement of Islamic seminary students, eventually captured the capital Kabul in September 1996 and imposed a very strict Islamic order. As in Iran, it was women who were most affected. Schools for girls were closed, women were banned from most jobs, and females were not allowed to go shopping without being accompanied by a male. The identification of this regime with a faithful interpretation of the Koran, however, also served an important strategic goal because it justified the Taliban claim to transcend the ethnic divisions within the country. In practice, however, the Taliban had recruited very heavily from among the Pathan clans in the South and central regions of the country. The Taliban regime, however, not only opened up the potential for future ethnic confrontation, but also generated unease amongst the minority Shii community because of their strict interpretation of the Koran.

Yet, as is made clear in Chapter 9, the issue is more complex than the advocates of pluralism allow. Globalization is seen to be a product of Western capitalism which, far from tolerating cultural diversity, is having the effect of eroding cultural differences. But much worse, it is seen to be locking many sectors of the Third World into a subordinate economic position. Islamic societies, seeing the effect of globalization, have, perhaps inevitably, started to retreat and shelter behind the walls of a very strict interpretation of Islam. But this assessment of globalization can be questioned. It is an over-simplification to suggest that globalization can be equated with Westernization. As the economic tigers of East Asia have demonstrated, it is possible for non-Western cultures to flourish in the global economy. It is much more likely, as a consequence, that globalization will be associated with multiculturalism rather than Westernization.

Some support for this assessment can be found in the discussion of refugees and migration in Chapter 10. The evidence reveals very clearly that neither migrants nor refugees disperse in a random fashion. Very clear patterns emerge. Individuals move to where contacts have already been established. As a consequence, although the link may initially have been economic, with migrants moving to improve their standard of living, they may later be followed by refugees seeking political asylum. Strong links are maintained, therefore, between individuals in the receiving and sending states. Migrants not only bring their labour but also their culture. Of course, this is not a new phenomenon. It is a characteristic feature of world history. But it is one that does not square easily with the recent concept of the nation-state. The concept is, of course, a myth. But it is a powerful myth that many wish to defend.

The fear of imported culture has led defenders of the nation-state in the United States to worry about the 'decay of our civilization' rather than to celebrate the diversification of culture. But, in any event, the evidence suggests that such fears are wildly exaggerated. Although it is true that there are 329 languages spoken in the United States, out of a population of 230 million Americans, 198 million speak English. Only the 17 million Spanish speakers pose any threat to the dominance of English. Moreover, studies show that 90 per cent of the children of migrants speak English. But culture involves a great deal more than language and certainly in cities there is increasing evidence of cultural diversification. This is an important dimension of globalization. There is a tendency to focus on the homogenization of culture as the result of the ubiquitous signs for McDonald's and Coca-Cola. But this under-estimates the significance of multiculturalism fostered, at least in part, by migration.

The diversification and the homogenization of culture appear, in practice, to be two processes going on simultaneously in world politics. It is impossible to predict what the outcome of these competing forces will be in the twenty-first century. What will become increasingly apparent, however, is that human beings, whatever their cultural differences, are operating within a common global environment which is much more fragile than previous generations realized. The image of the earth swimming in space is now almost a cliche, but it remains an important dimension of globalization. Whatever the differences that separate human beings, it has become impossible to ignore the fact that the accumulation of apparently insignificant individual acts across the globe, like spraying a deodorant, can collectively have devastating effects. As the end of the Cold War drew to a close in the 1980s, for example, scientific evidence began to mount that the ozone layer in the earth's stratosphere, protecting the globe from the sun's ultraviolet light, was being slowly but surely destroyed. Despite attempts to alleviate the causes, the evidence by the mid-1990s indicated that the hole over the Antarctic, already three times the size of Continental North America, was larger than ever and expanding faster than ever. Even if full cooperation is secured across the globe, the ozone hole is not expected to close before the middle of the twenty-first century.

As is noted in Chapter 11, the environment was an issue that scarcely registered on the international agenda at the onset of the Cold War, but it is now a major source of concern. Nevertheless, states have proved reluctant to take decisive action. The reluctance stems in part from the fact that the scientific evidence about the nature and scale of many environmental problems remains controversial. But it is also a product of the conflicts of interest that continue to divide states despite the existence of common environmental problems. For example, Third World states are of the opinion that since there are substantial costs associated with the measures that will have to be put in place in order to protect the environment, these costs should primarily be borne by the developed states. The developed world, however, endeavours to justify policies that will allow it to escape from this responsibility. But in the long haul, failure to implement conservation measures now means that the real cost of these delays will be shouldered by future generations.

Conclusion

A survey of the chapters in this book fails to reveal a dominant picture or image of world politics. During the Cold War, there was a tendency to portray world politics in terms of two major fault lines, one running East–West and the other running North–South. Even during that era, this characterization was problematic and it has become even more so in the post-Cold War era. There is, of course, still some mileage in thinking of world politics in these terms. If there were no East–West division, then it becomes possible to think of Europe extending across Eurasia to the Pacific. In practice, the Europeans are unwilling to think in these terms, but there is no agreement about where the longitudinal line separating East from West lies. And the connotations of this line now embrace cultural factors as well as economic and security ones. No one doubts that the Czechs and the Poles are European. But some see it as problematic to identify the Turks or the Russians as European. As with the East–West division, although there still remains some substance to a metaphorical latitudinal line dividing the developed from the less developed states, attention is now frequently being drawn to the evidence of the 'South' in the 'North' and vice versa. So, all in all, world politics appears more complex since the end of the Cold War.

The survey also suggests that some kind of transformation is taking place at this juncture. But the changes are cumulative; many have coincided with the ending of the Cold War rather than having been brought about by the end of the Cold War. The Cold War has been thought of metaphorically in terms of an overlay, placed on the top of world politics, influencing state practice but also dominating the analyses of world politics throughout that era. Once removed, while there has been considerable readjustment in world politics it has also become easier to see clearly what has been going on beneath the overlay. Ethnicity, for example, was a feature of world politics throughout the Cold War. But, with the ending of the Cold War, it has become easier to observe this feature. By contrast, the greater salience of environmental issues was unrelated to the ending of the Cold War.

The tentative conclusion that can be reached at the end of this survey is that as the twentieth century closes, world politics has developed the potential to become truly globalized politics. The concept of globalization has become seriously overworked over the last few years and its use often conveys very little of significance. It provides a rhetorical flourish to suggest that we are living in momentous times. In attempting to justify the flourish, the rather dramatic idea is sometimes advanced that the nation-state is now a 'hollow' state and that we are witnessing the demise of this mode of political organization. More frequently the term suggests no more than that there is a lot of activity going on in the international arena, with British firms, for example, setting up factories in China to produce plastic bags that are then shipped back to Britain to be sold to supermarkets to hold our weekly shopping.

What has emerged from the analysis offered in this book, however, is that we are entering an era where citizens and states are having to come to terms with the fact that we are living in a global system where states remain the only viable mode of political organization. To a very large extent, the foundations for this view of world politics were laid down during the Cold War. During that era, the implications of what it means to live in a global system were fully assimilated for the first time. No one who thought about world politics could doubt that if a nuclear war escalated, it would have catastrophic consequences for the entire globe. But as the Cold War persisted, states developed a range of mechanisms for managing this global problem, embracing arms control measures to stabilize nuclear deterrence between the superpowers, to prevent horizontal proliferation, and to establish nuclear free zones. When the global implications of the environment became apparent, therefore, it is unsurprising that states quite quickly began to design measures to bring the problems under control. No doubt the measures to regulate nuclear weapons and conserve the environment have been inadequate, but it seems clear that the solutions to the problems associated with these and other issues are more likely to be solved by means of inter-state collaboration than by any other route.

Bibliography

Adams, N. (1993) *Worlds Apart: The North–South Divide and the International System*, London: Zed.

Agence France-Presse International News (1995) 'Russia Probes Alleged Cyprus Chechenya Arms Link', 12 January.

Al-Alkim, M. (1993) 'Islam and Democracy: Mutually Reinforcing or Incompatible?', in A. Tamini (ed.), *Power-Sharing Islam?*, London: Liberty for Muslim World, pp. 77–89.

Al-Bazzaz, A. (1982) 'Islam and Arab Nationalism', in J.J. Donahue & J.L. Esposito (eds), *Islam in Tradition: Muslim Perspectives*, Oxford: Oxford University Press, pp. 84–90.

Allen, T. and Thomas, A. (1992) *Poverty and Development in the 1990s*, Oxford: Oxford University Press.

Anderson, K. & Blackhurst, R. (eds) (1993) *Regional Integration and the Global Trading System*, London: Harvester-Wheatsheaf.

Annan, K. (1997) 'Peace Operations and the United Nations: Preparing for the Next Century', in M. Doyle and O. Otunnu (eds), *Peacemaking and Peacekeeping for the Next Century*, New York: International Peace Academy, forthcoming.

Arms Project of Human Rights Watch and Physicians for Human Rights (1993) *Land Mines: A Deadly Legacy.*

Ayubi, N.M. (1991) *Political Islam: Religion and Politics in the Arab World*, London: Routledge.

Azar, E. (1990) *The Management of Protracted Social Conflict*, Aldershot: Dartmouth.

Badaracco, J. (1991) *The Knowledge Link*, Boston, Mass.: Harvard Business School.

Bailey, C. 'Problems with a Chemical Weapons Ban', *Orbis: A Journal of World Affairs*, vol. 36 (2), pp. 239–51.

Balaam, D. and Veseth, M. (1996) *Introduction to International Political Economy*, New Jersey: Prentice-Hall.

Banks, M. (1984) 'The Evolution of International Relations Theory', in M. Banks (ed.), *Conflict in World Society*, Brighton: Wheatsheaf Books, pp. 3–21.

Barber, L. and Gray, B. (1995) 'Nato Turns Its Attention to the Turbulent Moslem South', *Financial Times*, 9 February, p. 6.

Barkin, J.S. and Cronin, B. (1994) 'The State and the Nation: Changing Norms and Rules of Sovereignty in International Relations', *International Organization*, vol. 48 (1), pp. 107–30.

Batt, J. (1991) *East Central Europe from Reform to Transformation*, London: RIIA/Pinter.

Beeley, B. (1993) 'Islam as a Global political Force', in A.G. McGrew and P.G. Lewis *et al.* (eds), *Global Politics*, Cambridge: Polity Press, pp. 293–311.

268

Bennett Jones, O. (1996) 'Calls for Landmines Ban Ignored', *The Guardian*, 4 May, p. 3.

Berdal, M. R. (1993) *Whither UN Peacekeeping?*, Adelphi Paper 281, London: IISS.

Berdal, M. R. (1995) 'Reforming the UN's Organisational Capacity for Peacekeeping', in R. Thakur and C. A. Thayer (eds), *A Crisis of Expectations: UN Peacekeeping in the 1990s*, Boulder CO: Westview, pp. 181–92.

Berridge, G. (1992) *International Politics. States, Power and Conflict since 1945*, 2nd edn, New York: Harvester Wheatsheaf.

Best, G. (1994) *War and Law Since 1945*, Oxford: Clarendon Press.

Bettati, M. (1991) 'Un droit d'ingérence?', *Revue Générale de Droit International Public*, no. 3, pp. 693–70.

Bettati, M. and Kouchner, B. (1987) *Le devoir d'ingerence. Peut-on les laisser mourir?*, Paris: Denoël, *passim*.

Black, R. M. and Pearson, G. S. (1993) 'Unequivocal Evidence', *Chemistry in Britain*, July, pp. 584–7.

Blaikie, P., Cannon, T., Davis, I. and Wisner, B. (1994) *At Risk: Natural Hazards, People's Vulnerability, and Disasters*, London: Routledge.

Booth, K. (1991) 'Introduction: The Interregnum: World Politics in Transition', in K. Booth (ed.) *New Thinking about Strategy and International Security*, London: Harper Collins, pp. 1–28.

Boutros-Ghali, B. (1992) *An Agenda for Peace*, New York: United Nations.

Boutros-Ghali, B. (1995) *Report of the Secretary-General on the Work of the Organization. Supplement to an Agenda for Peace*, UN Doc. A/50/60, 3 January.

Bowen, W. Q. and Dunn, D. H. (1996) *American Security Policy in the 1990s: Beyond Containment*, Aldershot: Dartmouth.

Brenton, T. (1994) *The Greening of Machiavelli: The Evolution of International Environmental Politics*, London: Earthscan/RIIA.

Broad, R. and Landi, C. M. (1996) 'Whither the North–South Gap?', *Third World Quarterly*, vol. 17 (1), pp. 7–17.

Brown, L. R. and Kane, H. (1995) *Full House: Reassessing the Earth's Population Carrying Capacity*, London: Earthscan.

Brown, M. (1993) *Ethnic Conflict and International Security*, New Jersey: Princeton University Press.

Brown, S. (1995) *New Forces, Old Forces and the Future of World Politics*, New York: Harper Collins.

Brown, S. (1996) *International Relations in a Changing Global System*, Boulder: Westview.

Bull, H. (1977) *The Anarchical Society: A Study of Order in World Politics*, London: Macmillan.

Burton, J. W. (1990) *Conflict: Resolution and Prevention*, Basingstoke: Macmillan.

Buzan, B. (1991) *People, States, and Fear: An Agenda for International Security Studies in the Post-Cold War Era*, London: Harvester-Wheatsheaf.

Buzan, B. (1995) 'Focus On: The Present as a Historic Turning Point', *Journal of Peace Research*, vol. 30 (4), pp. 385–98.

Buzan, B. and Rizvi, G. (1986) *South Asian Insecurity and the Great Powers*, London: Macmillan.

Cable, V. and Henderson, D. (eds) (1994) *Trade Blocks? The Future of Regional Integration*, London: RIIA.

Caldwell, L. K. (1990) *International Environmental Policy: Emergence and Dimensions*, 2nd edn, Durham and London: Duke University Press.

Camilleri, J. A. and Falk, J. (1992) *The End of Sovereignty? The Politics of a Shrinking and Fragmenting World*, Aldershot: Edward Elgar.

Campaign Against the Arms Trade (CAAT) (1996) *Campaign Against the Arms Trade News*, Issue 136, March, p. 6.

Cantori, L. and Spiegel, S. (1970) *The International Politics of Regions: A Comparative Approach*, New Jersey: Prentice-Hall.

Caporaso, J. (1996) 'The European Union and Forms of State: Westphalian, Regulatory or Post-Modern?', *Journal of Common Market Studies*, vol. 34 (1), pp. 29–52.

Carment, D. (1994) 'The Ethnic Dimension in World Politics: Theory, Policy and Early Warning', *Third World Quarterly*, vol. 15 (4), pp. 551–82.

Carpenter, T. G. (1992) 'A New Proliferation Policy', *The National Interest*, Summer, pp. 63–72.

Castles, S. and Kosack, G. (1985) *Immigrant Workers and the Class Structure in Western Europe*, 2nd edn, Oxford: Oxford University Press.

Castles, S. and Miller, M. (1993) *The Age of Migration: International Population Movements in the Modern World*, London: Macmillan.

Cavanagh, J., Wysham, D. and Arruda, M. (1994) *Beyond Bretton Woods: Alternatives to the Global Economic Order*, London: Pluto Press.

Central Statistical Office (1996) *Social Trends 26*, London: HMSO.

Chalmers, M. and Greene, O. (1995) *Taking Stock: The UN Register After Two Years*, Bradford Arms Register Studies Number 5, Bradford: Westview Press.

Chatterjee, P. and Finger, M. (1994) *The Earth Brokers*, London: Routledge.

Childers, E. and Urquhart, B. (1994), 'Renewing the United Nations System', *Development Dialogue*, vol. 1, Uppsala: Hammarskjöld Foundation.

Choudhury, G. W. (1993) *Islam and the Modern Muslim World*, Essex: Scorpion Publishing.

Ciechanski, J. (1997) 'Enforcement Measures under Chapter VII of the UN Charter: UN Practice after the Cold War', in M. Pugh (ed.), *The UN, Peace and Force*, London: Cass, pp. 82–104.

Clancy, T. (1994) *Debt of Honour*, London: HarperCollins.

Clark, J. (1991) *Democratizing Development: The Role of Voluntary Organizations*, London: Earthscan.

The Cocoyoc Declaration (1974) *Development Dialogue* (Uppsala), no. 2, pp. 88–96.

Cohen, R. (1987) *The New Helots: Migrants in the International Division of Labour*, Aldershot: Avebury Press.

Collinson, S. (1993) *Beyond Borders: Western European Migration Policy Towards the 21st Century*, London: RIIA & Wyndham Place Trust.

Collinson, S. (1995) *Migration, Visa and Asylum Policies in Europe*, Wilton Park Paper 107, London: HMSO.

Cox, R. (1986) 'State, Social Forces and World Orders: Beyond International Relations Theory', in R. Keohane (ed.), *Neorealism and Its Critics*, New York: Columbia University Press, pp. 204–54.

Cox, R. (1987) *Production, Power and World Order*, New York: Columbia University Press.

Cuny, F. C. (1983) *Disasters and Development*, New York: Oxford University Press.

Davis, Z. S. (1996) 'The Spread of Nuclear-Weapon-Free Zones: Building a New Nuclear Bargain', *Arms Control Today*, vol. 26 (1), February. pp. 15–19.

de Silva, K. M. and May, A. J. (eds) (1991) *The Internationalization of Ethnic Strife*, London: Pinter.

Dean, J. (1994) 'The Final Stage of Nuclear Arms Control', *The Washington Quarterly*, vol. 17 (4), pp. 31–52.

Deegan, H. (1993) *The Middle East and Problems of Democracy*, Buckingham: Open University Press.

Dekmejian, R. H. (1995) *Islam in Revolution: Fundamentalism in the Arab World*, New York: Syracuse University Press.

Del Rosso Jr., S. J. (1995) 'The Insecure State: Reflections on "the State" and "Security", in a Changing World', *Daedalus*, vol. 124 (2), pp. 175–208.

Deudney, D. (1990) 'The Case Against Linking Environmental Degradation and National Security', *Millennium*, vol. 19 (3), Winter, pp. 461–76.

Dicken, P. (1992) *Global Shift*, 2nd edn, London: Paul Chapman.

Dobbie, C. (1994) *A Concept for Post-Cold War Peacekeeping*, Oslo: Norwegian Institute for Defence Studies.

Donohue, J. J. and Esposito, J. L. (eds) (1982) *Islam in Transition: Muslim Perspectives*, Oxford: Oxford University Press.

Dowty, A. (1987) *Closed Borders*, New Haven and London: Yale University Press.

Dunning, J. (1993) *The Globalisation of Business*, London: Routledge.

Durch, W. (ed.) (1994) *The Evolution of United Nations Peacekeeping: Case Studies and Comparative Analysis*, Basingstoke: Macmillan.

Dyson, K. (1980) *The State Tradition in Western Europe*, Oxford: Martin Robertson.

Edwards, G. and Regelsberger, E. (eds) (1990) *Europe's Global Links: The European Community and Inter-Regional Cooperation*, London: Pinter.

Ehteshami, A. (1995) *After Khomeini: The Iranian Second Republic*, London: Routledge.

Ekins, P. (1992) *A New World Order: Grassroots Movements for Global Change*, London: Routledge.

Esposito, J. L. (1992) *The Islamic Threat: Myth or Reality?*, New York: Oxford University Press.

Falk, R. (1995) *On Human Governance. Toward a New Global Politics*, Cambridge: Polity Press.

Fawcett, L. and Hurrell, A. (eds) (1995) *Regionalism in World Politics: Regional Organisation and International Order*, Oxford: Oxford University Press.

Featherstone, M. (ed.) (1990) *Global Culture: Nationalism, Globalization, and Modernity*, London: Sage.

Fein, H. (ed.) (1992) *Genocide Watch*, New Haven: Yale University Press.

Feinberg, R. (1988) 'The Changing Relationship Between the World Bank and the International Monetary Fund', *International Organization*, vol. 42 (3), pp. 545–60.

Fetherston, A. B. (1994) *Towards a Theory of United Nations Peacekeeping*, London: Macmillan.

Fisas, V. (1995) *Blue Geopolitics. The United Nations Reform and the Future of the Blue Helmets*, London: Pluto Press.

Fischer, D. (1995–6) 'The Pelindaba Treaty: African Joins the Nuclear-Free World', *Arms Control Today*, vol. 25 (10), December/January, pp. 9–14.

Fisher, R. J. and Keashley, L. (1991) 'The Potential Complementarity of Mediation and Consultation Within a Contingency Model of Third Party Interventions', *Journal of Peace Research*, vol. 28 (1), pp. 29–42.

Forsberg, R. (ed.) (1994) *The Arms Production Dilemma: Contraction and Restraint in the World Combat Aircraft Industry*, Cambridge, Mass.: MIT Press.

Frieden, J. and D. Lake (eds) (1991) *International Political Economy*, London: Unwin Hyman.

Frost, M. (1991) 'What Ought to be Done about the Condition of States?', in C. Navari (ed.) *The Condition of States. A Study in International Political Theory*, Milton Keynes: Open University Press, pp. 183–96.

Fukuyama, F. (1989) 'The End of History', *The National Interest*, vol. 16, pp. 3–18.

Fuller, G. E. and Lesser, I. O. (1995) *A Sense of Siege: The Geopolitics of Islam and the West*, Boulder, CO: Westview.

Galtung, J. (1976) 'Three Approaches to Peace: Peacekeeping, Peacemaking, and Peacebuilding', *Peace, War and Defense: Essays in Peace Research*, Vol. II, Copenhagen: Christian Eljers, pp. 297–304.

Gamble, A. and Payne, T. (eds) (1996) *Regionalism and World Order*, London: Macmillan.

Gellner, E. (1983) *Nations and Nationalism*, Oxford: Blackwell.

Gellner, E. (1994) 'Nationalism and the International Order', in E. Gellner, *Encounters with Nationalism*, Oxford: Blackwell, pp. 20–33.

George, S. (1992) *The Debt Boomerang*, London: Pluto Press.

Ghannouchi, R. (1993) 'The Participation of Islamists in a Non-Islamic Government', in A. Tamimi (ed.), *Power-Sharing Islam?*, London: Liberty for Muslim World, pp. 51–63.

Gibb, R. and Michalak, W. (eds) (1994) *Continental Trading Blocs: The Growth of Regionalism in the World Economy*, Chichester: Wiley.

Gill, S. and Law, D. (1988) *The Global Political Economy*, London: Harvester Wheatsheaf.

Gilpin, R. (1987) *The Political Economy of International Relations*, Princeton N.J.: Princeton University Press.

Goodwin-Gill, G. (1983) *The Refugee in International Law*, Oxford: Oxford University Press/Clarendon.

Goose, S. D. and Smyth, S. (1994) 'Arming Genocide in Rwanda', *Foreign Affairs*, vol. 73 (5), September/October, pp. 86–96.

Gordenker, L. (1987) *Refugees in International Politics*, New York: Columbia University Press.

Gotlieb, G. (1993) *Nation Against the State: New Approaches to Ethnic Conflicts and the Decline of Sovereignty*, New York: Council on Foreign Relations.

Goulding, M. (1996) 'The Use of Force by the United Nations', *International Peacekeeping*, vol. 3 (1), pp. 1–18.

Gow, J. and Dandeker, C. (1995) 'Peace-Support Operations: The Problem of Legitimation', *The World Today*, vol. 51, pp. 171–4.

Greenwood, C. (1993) 'Is There a Right to Humanitarian Intervention?', *The World Today*, vol. 49, p. 35.

Grieco, J. (1988) 'Anarchy and the Limits of Co-operation: A Realist Critique of the Newest Liberal Institutionalism', *International Organisation*, vol. 42 (3), pp. 485–507.

Grubb, M. *et al.* (1993) *The Earth Summit Agreements: A Guide and Assessment*, London: RIIA/Earthscan.

Guazzone, L. (ed.) (1995) *The Islamist Dilemma: The Political Role of Islamist Movements in the Contemporary Arab World*, Reading, UK: Ithaca.

Gurr, T. R. (1993) *Minorities at Risk: A Global View of Ethnopolitical Conflict*, Washington: United States Institute of Peace.

Gurr, T. R. and Harff, B. (1994) *Ethnic Conflict in World Politics*, Boulder, CO: Westview Press.

Haas, P. M. (1990) *Saving the Mediterranean: The Politics of Environmental Cooperation*, New York: Columbia University Press.

Haas, P. M., Keohane, R. O. and Levy, M. (eds) (1994) *Institutions for the Earth. Sources of Effective Environmental Protection*, Cambridge, MA.: MIT Press.

Halliday, F. (1995) *Islam and the Myth of Confrontation: Religion and Politics in the Middle East*, London: I.B. Taurus.

Halperin, M. *et al.* (1990) *Self-Determination in the New World Order*, Carnegie Endowment for International Peace.

Hammar, T. (ed.) (1985) *European Immigration Policy: A Comparative Study*, Cambridge: Cambridge University Press.

Hancock, G. (1989) *Lords of Poverty*, London: Macmillan.

Hannum, H. (1990) *Autonomy, Sovereignty and Self-Determination*, Philadelphia: University of Pennsylvania Press.

Hardin, G. (1968) 'The Tragedy of the Commons', reprinted in G. Hardin and J. Baden (eds) (1977), *Managing the Commons*, San Francisco: W.H. Freeman & Co., pp. 16–30.

Harrison, P. (1983) *Inside the Inner City*, Harmondsworth: Penguin.

Harrison, P. (1987) *Inside the Third World*, Harmondsworth: Penguin.

Hartung, W. D. (1995) 'U.S. Conventional Arms Transfers: Promoting Stability or Fueling Conflict?', *Arms Control Today*, vol. 25 (9), November, pp. 9–13.

Helman, G. B. and Ratner, S. R. (1992–3) 'Saving Failed States', *Foreign Policy*, no. 89, pp. 3–20.

Heraclides, A. (1991) *The Self-Determination of Minorities in International Politics*, London: Frank Cass.

Hewitt, K. (1983) *Interpretations of Calamity from the Viewpoint of Human Ecology*, London: Allen & Unwin.

Hill, C. (ed.) (1983) *National Foreign Policies and European Political Cooperation*, London: Allen & Unwin.

Hill, C. (ed.) (1996) *The Actors in Europe's Foreign Policy*, London: Routledge.

Hinsley, F. H. (1966) *Sovereignty*, London: C.A. Watts & Co.

Hobsbawm, E. J. (1990) *Nations and Nationalism Since 1790*, Cambridge: Cambridge University Press.

Hobsbawm, E. (1995) *Age of Extremes: The Short Twentieth Century, 1914–1991*, London: Abacus.

Hocking, B. and Smith, M. (1995) *World Politics. An Introduction to International Relations*, 2nd edn, Hemel Hempstead: Prentice-Hall/Harvester Wheatsheaf.

Hoffmann, S. (1995–6) 'The Politics and Ethics of Military Intervention', *Survival*, vol. 37 (4), pp. 29–51.

Hogan M. J. (ed.) (1992) *The End of the Cold War: Its Meaning and Implications*, Cambridge: Cambridge University Press.

Horowitz, D. (1985) *Ethnic Groups in Conflict*, California: University of California Press.

Horsman, M. and Marshall, A. (1995) *After the Nation-State. Citizens, Tribalism and the New World Disorder*, London: HarperCollins.

Houghton, J. T. *et al.* (1996) *Climate Change 1995: The Science of Climate Change, Contribution of Working Group I to the Second Assessment Report of the Intergovernmental Panel on Climate Change*, Cambridge: Cambridge University Press.

Howard, M. (1989–90) 'The Springtime of Nations', *Foreign Affairs*, vol. 69 (1), pp. 17–32.

Howard, M. (1995) 'Ethnic Conflict and International Security', *Nations and Nationalism*, vol. 1 (3), November, pp. 285–96.

Human Rights Watch/Arms Project and Physicians for Human Rights (1993) *Landmines: A Deadly Legacy*, New York.

Hunger Project, The (1985) *Ending Hunger: An Idea Whose Time Has Come*, New York: Praeger.

Huntington, S. (1988) 'The U.S. – Decline or Renewal', reprinted in W. Stiles and T. Akaha (eds) (1991), *International Political Economy: A Reader*, New York: HarperCollins, pp. 481–98.

Huntington, S. P. (1993) 'The Clash of Civilizations', *Foreign Affairs*, vol. 71 (3), pp. 22–49.

Huntington, S. P. (1995) 'The Clash of Civilizations?', *Peaceworks*, no. 4, August, pp. 5–6.

Hurrell, A. (1992) 'Latin America in the New World Order: a regional bloc of the Americas?', *International Affairs*, vol. 68 (1), pp. 121–39.

Hurrell, A. (1995) 'Explaining the Resurgence of Regionalism in World Politics', *Review of International Studies*, vol. 21 (4), pp. 331–58.

Hurrell, A. and Kingsbury, B. (eds) (1992) *The International Politics of the Environment*, Oxford: Clarendon.

Husain, M. Z. (1995) *Global Islamic Politics*, New York: HarperCollins.

Hymer, S. (1972) 'The Multinational Corporation and the Law of Uneven Development', in J. Bhagwati (ed.), *Economics and World Order*, London: Collier-Macmillan, pp. 113–40.

ICPF (1994) *Uncommon Opportunities: An Agenda for Peace and Equitable Development*, London: Zed.

IFRC (1996) *World Disasters Report, 1996*, Oxford: Oxford University Press.

IFRC (1997) *World Disasters Report, 1997*, Oxford: Oxford University Press, forthcoming.

Ignatieff, M. (1993) *Blood and Belonging: Journeys into the New Nationalism*, London: Chatto & Windus.

Imber, M. (1993) 'Too Many Cooks? The Post Rio Reform of the UN', *International Affairs*, vol. 69 (1), pp. 150–66.

Jackson, B. (1990) *Poverty and the Planet*, London: Penguin.

Jackson, J. A. (1969) *Migration*, Cambridge: Cambridge University Press.

Jackson, R. H. (1990) *Quasi-States: Sovereignty, International Relations and the Third World*, Cambridge: Cambridge University Press.

Jackson, R. H. and James, A. (1993) 'The Character of Independent Statehood', in R. H. Jackson and A. James (eds), *States in a Changing World*, Oxford: Oxford University Press, pp. 3–25.

James, A. (1987) *Sovereign Statehood. The Basis of International Society*, London: Allen & Unwin.

James, A. (1990) *Peacekeeping in International Politics*, Basingstoke: IISS/Macmillan

James, A. (1994) 'The Problems of Internal Peacekeeping', *Diplomacy and Statecraft*, vol. 5 (1), pp. 21–46.

James, A. (1997) 'Humanitarian Aid Operations and Peacekeeping', in E. Belgrad and N. Nachmias (eds), *The Politics of International Humanitarian Operations*, Westport, CT: Praeger, ch. 4.

Jervis, R. (1978) 'Cooperation Under the Security Dilemma', *World Politics*, vol. 30 (2), January, pp. 167–214.

Johnson, D. and Sampson, C. (eds) (1994) *Religion, the Missing Dimension of Statecraft*, Oxford: Oxford University Press.

Juergensmeyer, M. (1993) *The New Cold War? Religious Nationalism Confronts the Secular State*, Berkeley: University of California Press.

Katzenstein, P. (1993) 'Regions in competition: comparative advantages of America, Europe, and Asia', in H. Haftendorn and C. Tuschhoff (eds), *America and Europe in an Era of Change*, Boulder, CO: Westview Press, pp. 105–26.

Kay, D. (1994) 'The IAEA: How Can it be Strengthened?', in M. Reiss and R. S. Litwak (eds), *Nuclear Proliferation After the Cold War*, Washington DC: Johns Hopkins University Press, pp. 309–33.

Kearns, I. (1996) 'Eastern Europe in Transition into the New Europe', in A. Gamble and T. Payne (eds), *Regionalism and World Order*, London: Macmillan, pp. 55–91.

Kegley, C. W. and Wittkopf, E. R. (1993) *World Politics: Trend and Transformation*, 4th edn, Basingstoke: Macmillan.

Kelman, H. C. (1992) 'Informal mediation by the Scholar/Practitioner', in J. Bercovitch and J. Z. Rubin (eds), *Mediation in International Relations*. Basingstoke: Macmillan, pp. 64–96.

Keohane, R. and J. Nye (1977) *Power and Interdependence*, Boston: Little, Brown & Co.

Keohane, R. O. and Anderson, L. (1995) 'The Promise of Institutionalist Theory', *International Security*, vol. 20 (1), pp. 39–51.

Khiddu-Makubuya, E. (1994) 'Violence and Conflict Resolution in Uganda', in K. Rupesinghe (ed.), *The Culture of Violence*, Tokyo: United Nations University Press, pp. 144–77.

Kinloch, S. P. (1997) 'Utopian or Pragmatic? A UN Permanent Volunteer Force', in M. Pugh (ed.), *The UN, Peace and Force*, London: Frank Cass, pp. 166–90.

Knudsen, T. B. (1997) 'Humanitarian Intervention Revisited: Post-Cold War Responses to Classical Problems', in M. Pugh (ed.), *The UN, Peace and Force*, London: Frank Cass, pp. 146–65.

Korten, D. C. (1990) *Getting to the 21st Century: Voluntary Action and the Global Agenda*, Connecticut: Kumarian Press.

Krasner, S. (1995) 'Power-Politics, Institutions and Transnational Relations', in T. Risse-Kappen (ed.), *Bringing Transnational Relations Back In*, Cambridge: Cambridge University Press, pp. 257–79.

Krasner, S. (1995–6) 'Compromising Westphalia', *International Security*, vol. 20 (3), pp. 115–51.

Kritz, K., Keeley, C. B. and Tomasci, S. M. (1981) *Global Trends in Migration: Theory and Research on International Population Movements*, New York: Center for Migration Studies.

Kuper, L. (1985) *The Prevention of Genocide*, New Haven: Yale University Press.

Latouche, S. (1996) *The Westernization of the World*, Cambridge: Polity.

Laurance, E. J. (1993) 'The UN Register of Conventional Arms: Rationales and Prospects for Compliance and Effectiveness', *The Washington Quarterly*, vol. 16 (2), pp. 163–72.

Leahy, P. (1995) 'The CCW Review Conference: An Opportunity for U.S. Leadership', *Arms Control Today*, vol. 25 (7), pp. 20–4.

Leyton-Brown, D. (1994) 'The Political Economy of North American Free Trade', in R. Stubbs and G. Underhill (1994), pp. 352–65.

Lijphart, A. (1977) *Democracy and Plural Societies*, New Haven: Yale University Press.

Luard, E. (1990) *The Globalization of Politics*, London: Macmillan.

Macrae, J. and Zwi, A. (1994) *War and Hunger: Rethinking International Responses to Complex Emergencies*, London: Zed Books/Save the Children, UK.

Mann, M. (1993) 'Nation-States in Europe and Other Continents: Diversifying, Developing, Not Dying', *Daedalus*, vol. 122 (3), pp. 115–40.

Markusen, A. and Yudken, J. (1992) *Dismantling the Cold War Economy*, New York: Basic Books.

Mayall, J. (1990) *Nationalism and International Society*, Cambridge: Cambridge University Press.

McGarry, J. and O'Leary, B. (1993) *The Politics of Ethnic Conflict Regulation*, London: Routledge.

Meadows, D. H. *et al.* (1972) *The Limits to Growth: A Report for the Club of Rome's Project on the Predicament of Mankind*, London: Pan.

Meadows, D. H. *et al.* (1992) *Beyond the Limits: Global Collapse or a Sustainable Future?*, London: Earthscan.

Meirsheimer, J. J. (1994–5) 'The False Promise of International Institutions', *International Security*, vol. 19 (3), pp. 5–49.

Midgeley, M. (1992) 'Can Science Save Its Soul?', *New Scientist*, 1st August, pp. 24–7.

Midlarsky, M. I. (ed.) (1992) *The Internationalisation of Communal Strife*, London: Routledge.

Miller, J. D. B. (1986) 'Sovereignty as a Source of Vitality for the State', *Review of International Studies*, vol. 12 (2), pp. 79–89.

Miller, L. H. (1994) *Global Order. Values and Power in International Politics*, Boulder, CO: Westview Press.

Minear, L. and Weiss, T. (1995) *Mercy Under Fire: War and the Global Humanitarian Comunity*, Boulder, CO: Westview.

Mohamad, M. (1996) 'Islam – the Misunderstood Religion', Speech presented at the Oxford Centre for Islamic Studies, 11 April, pp. 1–16.

Montville, J. (ed.) (1990) *Conflict and Peacemaking in Multiethnic Societies*, Lexington: Lexington Books.

Moodie, M. (1996) 'Ratifying the Chemical Weapons Convention: Past Time for Action', *Arms Control Today*, vol. 26 (1), pp. 3–9.

Morgenthau, H. J. (1967) *Politics Among Nations: The Struggle for Power and Peace*, 4th edn, New York: A.A. Knopf.

Morris, J. (1995) 'Force and Democracy: UN/US Intervention in Haiti', *International Peacekeeping*, vol. 2 (3), pp. 391–412.

Morris, N. (1995) Paper on force and humanitarianism, privately distributed.

Moynihan, D. P. (1993) *Pandaemonium: Ethnicity in International Politics*, Oxford: Oxford University Press.

Murphy, A. B. (1994) 'International Law and the Sovereign State: Challenges to the Status Quo', in G. J. Demko and W. B. Wood (eds), *Reordering the World. Geopolitical Perspectives on the 21st Century*, Boulder, CO: Westview, pp. 209–24.

Nasr, S. H. (1993) *A Young Muslim's Guide to the World*, Cambridge: The Islamic Text Society.

Navari, C. (1991) 'Introduction: The State as a Contested Concept in International Relations', in C. Navari (ed.), *The Condition of States. A Study in International Political Theory*, Milton Keynes: Open University Press, pp. 1–18.

Norton-Taylor, R. (1995) *Truth is a Difficult Concept: Inside the Scott Inquiry*, London: Guardian Books/Fourth Estate.

Nye, J. Jr. (1971) *Peace in Parts: Integration and Conflict in Regional Organisation*, Boston: Little Brown.

Nye, J. S. Jr., (1996) 'Conflicts After the Cold War', *The Washington Quarterly*, vol. 19 (1), pp. 5–24.

Pearson, G. S. (1993) 'Prospects for Chemical and Biological Arms Control: the Web of Deterrence', *The Washington Quarterly*, vol. 16 (2), pp. 145–62.

Porter, G. and Brown, J. W. (1991) *Global Environmental Politics*, Boulder, CO: Westview.

Potter, W. C. (1995) 'Before the Deluge? Assessing the Threat of Nuclear Leakage From the Post-Soviet States', *Arms Control Today*, vol. 25 (8), October, pp. 9–16.

Potts, L. (1990) *The World Labour Market: A History of Migration*, London: Zed Books.

Premdas, R. (1991) 'The Internationalization of Ethnic Conflict: Some Theoretical Explorations', in K. M. de Silva and R. J. May (eds), *The Internationalization of Ethnic Strife*, London: Pinter, pp. 10–25.

Princen, M. and Finger, M. (eds) (1994) *Environmental NGOs in World Politics: Linking the Local and the Global*, London: Routledge.

Pugh, M. (1995) 'Peacebuilding as Developmentalism: Concepts from Disaster Research', *Contemporary Security Policy*, vol. 16 (2), pp. 320–46.

Pugh, M. (1996) 'Humanitarianism and Peacekeeping', *Global Society*, vol. 10 (3), pp. 205–24.

Pugh, M. (ed.) (1997) *The UN, Peace and Force*, London: Frank Cass.

Rafferty, K. (1996) 'US Key to Keeping Japan Non-Nuclear', *The Guardian*, 1 March, p. 11.

Reich, R. (1990) 'Who is US?', *Harvard Business Review*, vol. 68 (1), pp. 53–64.

Reiss, M. and Litwak, R. S. (eds) (1994) *Nuclear Proliferation After the Cold War*, Washington DC: Johns Hopkins University Press.

Rivlin, B. (1992) 'Regional Arrangements and the UN System for Collective Security and Conflict Resolution: A New Road Ahead?', *International Relations*, vol. 11 (2), pp. 95–110.

Roberts, A. (1995–96) 'From San Francisco to Sarajevo: The UN and the Use of Force', *Survival*, vol. 37 (4), pp. 7–28.

Roberts, A. and Kingsbury, B. (eds) (1994) *United Nations, Divided World: The UN's Role in International Relations*, 2nd edn, Oxford: Clarendon.

Roberts, G. (1984) *Questioning Development*, London: Returned Volunteer Action.

Rodley, N. (ed.) (1992) *To Loose the Bands of Wickedness: International Intervention in Defence of Human Rights*, London: Brasseys.

Rollo, J. *et al.* (1990) *The New Eastern Europe: Western Responses*, London: RIIA/Pinter.

Ronen, D. (1979) *The Quest for Self-Determination*, New Haven: Yale University Press.

Rosecrance, R. (1991) 'Regionalism and the Post-Cold War Era', *International Journal*, vol. 46, Summer, pp. 373–93.

Rosenau, J. N. (1988) 'The State in an Era of Cascading Politics. Wavering Concept, Widening Competence, Withering Colossus, or Weathering Change?', *Comparative Political Studies*, vol. 21 (1), pp. 13–44.

Rothman, J. (1992) *From Confrontation to Cooperation*, London: Sage.

Rostow, W. (1960) *The Stages of Economic Growth: A Non-Communist Manifesto*, London: Cambridge University Press.

Rowntree Foundation (1995) *Inquiry into Income and Wealth*, York: Joseph Rowntree Foundation.

Roy, O. (1994) *The Failure of Political Islam*, London: I.B. Tauris.

Royal Institute of International Affairs (1939) *Nationalism*, London: Oxford University Press.

Ruggie, J. G. (1997) 'The United Nations and the Collective Use of Force: Wither or Whether?', in M. Pugh (ed.), *The UN, Peace and Force*, London: Frank Cass, pp. 1–20.

Rupesinghe, K. (1990) 'The Disappearing Boundaries Between Internal and External Conflicts', Paper presented to International Peace Research Association Conference, Groningen.

Rupesinghe, K. (ed.) (1995) *Conflict Transformation*, London: Macmillan.

Russett, B. (1967) *International Regions and the International System*, Chicago: Rand McNally.

Ryan, S. (1995) *Ethnic Conflict and International Relations*, Aldershot: Dartmouth.

Sachs, W. (ed.) (1993) *Global Ecology: A New Arena of Political Conflict*, London: Zed Books.

Sakamoto, Y. (ed.) (1995) *Global Transformation: Challenge to the State System*, Tokyo: United Nations University Press.

Sand, P. H. (ed.) (1992) *The Effectiveness of International Environmental Agreements: A Survey of Existing Legal Instruments*, Cambridge: Grotius.

Saurin, J. (1996) 'International Relations, Social Ecology and the Globalisation of Environmental Change', in J. Vogler, and M. F. Imber (eds), *The Environment and International Relations*, London: Routledge, pp. 77–96.

Schumacher, E. F. (1973) *Small is Beautiful: Economics as if People Mattered*, New York: Harper & Row.

Schwartz, H. (1994) *States Versus Markets*, New York: St Martin's Press.

Shaw, M. (1994) *Global Society and International Relations*, Cambridge: Polity Press.

Sheffer, G. (ed.) (1986) *Modern Diasporas in International Politics*, London: Croom Helm.

Sick, T. D. (1992) *Islam and Democracy: Religion, Politics and Power in the Middle East*, Washington DC: United Institute of Peace.

Sidahmed, A. S. and Ehteshami, A. (eds) (1996) *Islamic Fundamentalism*, Boulder, CO: Westview.

Simpson, J. (1995) 'The Birth of an Era? The 1995 NPT Conference and the Politics of Nuclear Disarmament', *Security Dialogue*, vol. 26 (3), pp. 247–56.

Skolnikoff, E. B. (1993) *The Elusive Transformation: Science Technology and the Evolution of International Politics*, New Jersey: Princeton University Press.

Smith, A. (1981) *The Ethnic Revival*, Cambridge: Cambridge University Press.

Smith, A. D. (1991) *National Identity*, Harmondsworth: Penguin.

Smith, M. (1993) 'Beyond the Stable State? Foreign Policy Challenges and Opportunities in the New Europe', in W. Carlsnaes and S. Smith (eds), *European Foreign Policy: The EC and Changing Perspectives in Europe*, London: Sage, pp. 21–44.

Sollenberg, M. and Wallensteen, P. (1995) 'Major Armed Conflicts', in *Stockholm International Peace Research Institute Yearbook, 1994*, Oxford: Oxford University Press, pp. 21–35.

South Commission (1990) *The Challenge to the South*, Oxford: Oxford University Press.

Spear, J. (1994) 'On the Desirability and Feasibility of Arms Transfer Regime Formation', *Contemporary Security Policy*, vol. 15 (3), December, pp. 84–111.

Spear, J. (1996) 'Arms Limitations, Confidence Building Measures, and Internal Conflict', in M. Brown (ed.), *The International Dimensions of Internal Conflict*, Cambridge Mass., MIT Press, pp. 377–410.

Spero, J. (1990) *The Politics of International Economic Relations*, 4th edn, London: Routledge.

Stein, A. A. (1990) *Why Nations Cooperate. Circumstance and Choice in International Relations*, Ithaca and London: Cornell University Press.

Stockholm International Peace Research Institute, *SIPRI Yearbook 1996*, Oxford: Oxford University Press, 1996.

Stockton, N. (1994) 'The Contract Culture', Paper for the Refugee Studies Centre, Elizabeth House, Oxford, 20 Oct.

Stopford, J. and Strange, S. (1991) *Rival States, Rival Firms: The Global Competition for Market Shares*, Cambridge: Cambridge University Press.

Strange, S. (1994) *States and Markets*, 2nd edn, London: Pinter.

Stubbs, R. and Underhill, G. (eds) (1994) *Political Economy and the Changing Global Order*, London: Macmillan.

Stumpf, W. (1995–6) 'South Africa's Nuclear Weapons Program: From Deterrence to Dismantlement', *Arms Control Today*, vol. 25 (10), December/January, pp. 3–8.

Taylor, P. (1993) *International Organization in the Modern World*, London: Pinter.

Teitelbaum, M. S. (1980) 'Right vs. Right: Immigration and Refugee Policy in the United States', *Foreign Affairs*, vol. 59 (1), Fall, pp. 21–59.

Thakur, R. and Thayer, C. (eds) (1995) *A Crisis of Expectations: UN Peacekeeping in the 1990s*, Boulder, CO: Westview.

The Ecologist (1993) *Whose Common Future? Reclaiming the Commons*, London: Earthscan.

The Economist (1991) 'Sisters in the Wood', *A Survey of the IMF and the World Bank*, 12 October.

The Economist (1995a) 'The Return of the Habsburgs', *A Survey of Central Europe*, 18 November.

The Economist (1995b) 'Who's in the Driving Seat?', *A Survey of the World Economy*, 7 October.

Thomas, C. (1992) *The Environment in International Relations*, London: RIIA.

Thomas, C. (1997) 'Poverty, Development and Hunger', in J. Bayliss and S. Smith (eds), *The Globalisation of World Politics*, Oxford: Oxford University Press, forthcoming.

Thomas, C. and Wilkin, P. (eds) (1996) *Globalisation and the South*, London: Macmillan.

Thornberry, P. (1990) *The International Protection of Minorities*, London: Clarendon.

Todaro, M. P. (1989) *Economic Development in the Third World*, New York and London: Longman.

Tolba, M. and El-Kholy, O. A. *et al.* (1992) *The World Environment, 1972–1992: Two Decades of Challenge*, London: UNEP/Chapman & Hall.

UNDP (1994) *Human Development Report, 1994*, Oxford: Oxford University Press.

United Nations (1975) *Yearbook of the United Nations 1972*, vol. 26, New York: United Nations Office of Public Information.

Vallely, P. (1990) *Bad Samaritans: First World Ethics and Third World Debt*, London: Hodder & Stoughton.

van Ham, P. (1994) *Managing Non-Proliferation Regimes in the 1990s: Power, Politics and Policies*, London: Royal Institute for International Affairs.

Vernon, R. (1971), *Sovereignty at Bay*, London: Longman.

Vincent, R. J. (1990) 'Grotius, Human Rights and Interventions', in H. Bull, B. Kingsbury and A. Roberts (eds), *Hugo Grotius and International Relations*, Oxford: Clarendon Press, pp. 241–56.

Vogler, J. (1995) *The Global Commons: A Regime Analysis*, Chichester: Wiley.

Vogler, J. and Imber, M. F. (eds) (1996) *The Environment in International Relations*, London: Routledge.

Waever, O. *et al.* (1993) *Migration, Identity and the New European Security Order*, London: Pinter.

Wallace, W. (1990) *The Transformation of Western Europe*, London: Pinter/RIIA.

Walter, A. (1993) *World Power and World Money*, London: Harvester.

Ward, B. and Dubos, R. (1972) *Only One Earth*, New York: W. W. Norton.

Waters, M. (1995) *Globalization*, London: Routledge.

Welsh, D. (1993) 'Domestic Politics and Ethnic Conflict', *Survival*, vol. 35 (1), pp. 63–80.

Wesley, M. (1995), 'Blue Berets or Blindfolds? Peacekeeping and the Hostage Effect', *International Peacekeeping*, vol. 2 (4), pp. 457–82.

Williams, M. (1994) *International Economic Institutions and the Third World*, London: Harvester Wheatsheaf.

Woollacott, M. (1996) 'How the World Grew to Love the Bomb', *Guardian Weekly*, 11 February, p. 10.

World Bank (1992) *World Development Report 1992: Development and the Environment*, Oxford: Oxford University Press.

World Bank (1995) *Mainstreaming the Environment: The World Bank Group and the Environment since the Rio Earth Summit*, Washington: World Bank.

World Commission on Environment and Development (WCED) (Brundt-land Commission) (1987) *Our Common Future*, Oxford: Oxford University Press.

WTO (1995) *Regionalism and the World Trading System*, London: World Trade Organisation.

Young, O. R. (1989) *International Cooperation: Building Regimes for Natural Resources and the Environment*, Ithaca: Cornell University Press.

Zartman, I. W. (1989) *Ripe for Resolution*, Oxford: Oxford University Press.

Zimmerman, P. (1994) 'Proliferation: Bronze Medal Technology is Enough', *Orbis*, vol. 38 (1), Winter, pp. 67–82.

Zobrist, S. (1995), e-mail message relayed on peacekeeping@gmu.edu, 8 June.

Zolberg, A. (1981) 'International Migrations in Political Perspective', in K. Kritz, C. B. Kealey and S. M. Tomasci (eds), *Global Trends in Migration: Theory and Research on International Population Movements*, New York: The Center for Migration Studies, p. 6.

Zolberg, A., Suhrke, A. and Aguayo, S. (1989) *Escape from Violence*, New York: Oxford University Press.

Zubaida, S. (1989) *Islam, the People and the State*, London: Routledge.

Index